SHELLEY'S LATER POETRY

SHELLEY'S

LATER POETRY

A STUDY OF HIS
PROPHETIC IMAGINATION
by MILTON WILSON

"For we prophesy in part"

Columbia University Press, New York

PUBLISHED IN GREAT BRITAIN, INDIA, AND PAKISTAN
BY THE OXFORD UNIVERSITY PRESS
LONDON, BOMBAY, AND KARACHI
MANUFACTURED IN THE UNITED STATES OF AMERICA
LIBRARY OF CONGRESS CATALOG CARD NUMBER: 59-8675

PREFACE

Using *Prometheus Unbound* as its organizing center, this book describes the materials and traces the unfinished argument of Shelley's poetry in his Italian period. But more is attempted than simply an exposition of meaning. The form of Shelley's argument and the nature of his figures of speech imply a theory of poetry and reveal the way his imagination worked. The book as a whole demonstrates the importance of that theory and tries to justify the activity of a prophetic imagination.

I have received and often taken a good deal of advice in the course of writing these pages. The editorial and critical acumen of Miss Vergene F. Leverenz of the Columbia University Press has saved me many errors and suggested many improvements. I am grateful to Professors Emery Neff and Jerome H. Buckley of Columbia University for their encouragement and criticism at many stages in the book's development, and to my colleague, Dr. George Falle, for reading the whole manuscript and drawing attention to some of my infelicities. But my chief debt is to Dr. A. E. Barker, not only for the detailed commentary with which he surrounded the margins of my pages, but for the benefit of his example as scholar and teacher.

Permission was graciously granted by Harcourt, Brace and Company and by Faber and Faber, Ltd, to quote passages from T. S. Eliot's *Murder in the Cathedral, The Waste Land, Four Quartets,* and *Selected Essays, 1917–1932.* I am also indebted for similar permissions to the Viking Press to quote from Volume Four of *Poets of the English Language,* edited by W. H. Auden and N. H. Pearson; to Rupert Hart-Davis Limited to quote R. S. Thomas's

Song at the Year's Turning; to J. M. Dent & Sons Ltd and New Directions to quote Dylan Thomas's *Ceremony After a Fire Raid;* and to Hutchinson & Co. Ltd. to quote from Ivan Roe's *Shelley: The Last Phase.*

MILTON WILSON

Trinity College
University of Toronto
Toronto, Ontario, Canada
December, 1958

CONTENTS

SHELLEY'S LATER POETRY

PROLOGUE

The Growth of a Poet

The Shelley of critical legend was a changeling, who did not belong to his (or our) world, and made little out of it. He lacked "a firm grasp on actuality," [1] and, when forced to touch it, instead of making the best of the experience he fled back into a world of shadows or abstractions and gave up any attempt to cope with concrete reality. We might say of this Shelley what Wordsworth said of the young Hartley Coleridge in *To H.C.:*

> Thou art a dew-drop, which the morn brings forth,
> Ill fitted to sustain unkindly shocks,
> Or to be trailed along the soiling earth,
> A gem that glitters while it lives,
> And no forewarning gives;
> But at the touch of wrong, without a strife
> Slips in a moment out of life.

Or, if a less sentimental and more vigorous statement of Shelley's role is preferred, we can place him among "the sacred few" of *The Triumph of Life,*

> who could not tame
> Their spirits to the conquerors—but as soon
> As they had touched the world with living flame
>
> Fled back like eagles to their native noon . . . , (128-31)

leaving, presumably, a few relics to be picked up in *Memorabilia* by the more earth-bound Browning:

> For there I picked up on the heather
> And there I put inside my breast
> A moulted feather, an eagle-feather!
> Well, I forget the rest.

If we do "forget the rest," Shelley must share the responsibility, for he liked to fancy himself in this role, and is partly to blame if the "pard-like Spirit beautiful and swift" and the "herd-abandoned deer struck by the hunter's dart" of *Adonais* have obscured other, somewhat different, roles.

For Shelley's experience in "the world which is the world of all of us" was not just so much loss, to be left behind and forgotten as soon as possible. Such a view might appeal to Shelley's Platonism, but, as a disciple of the British empirical school, he knew better. Indeed, even as a Platonist he knew better. The Wordsworth of *Ode: Intimations of Immortality* depicts the child "trailing clouds of glory" at the beginning of his mortal course, and then forgetting "that imperial palace whence he came" under the weight of experience, growth, and imitation. Wordsworth supposed his picture to reflect the Platonic myth of preexistence. But Shelley had only to reread the *Crito* to be aware that Plato shows the ability to remember preexistent reality less as a natural gift than as the product of a careful process of education. Knowledge may be given, but it must also be discovered. Man has to be made what he has been born. Time may not be the ideal teacher, but as a cyclic medium it at least makes recovery as likely as relapse, and in good hands it can be its own worst enemy. This book will try to show Time at work in Shelley's poetry; it will spend most of its energy looking before and after within the poems themselves, watching the coals of Shelley's unextinguished hearth fade to anticlimax and brighten to prophecy. But Time is no less at work outside the poems and groups of poems; it is still the mentor of the man and the poet, as well as of the poem.

It taught Shelley the man a good deal, as is immediately apparent if we compare the brash, brittle letters of the Oxford period, or of the early years of his first marriage, with the rich complexity and precariously held wisdom of some of the later ones. As a young man Shelley had a great deal to learn, and he learned it gradually, by trial and error; not by retreating at the first sign of difficulty, but by trying everything out for himself and profiting from his own experience. To read the biographies or the letters is to realize just how much error was apparently necessary. But by the end we may be prepared to understand what Shelley meant when he said "You can put me down among the nonagenarians," and "I always go on until I am stopped and I am seldom stopped." We may also appreciate better his mood at the end of his life, as it has been brilliantly depicted by Ivan Roe:

He was a deeply unhappy man but not by any means a cheerless one. Contrary to the generality of melancholy poets, he kept his sorrows closely within the bounds of his verse and of his thoughts. The picture of Shelley during the last two months of his life, drawn for us by friends who wrote independently of one another, reveals such a lively companion that, glancing at his brief past, we may feel tempted to sum up his life and character by saying that he lived to make himself unhappy and his friends happy. . . . He was not the half-mad sprite, the fantastic youth drawn with liberal distortion by Hogg, but a tall, stooping man, the youthfulness of whose face was belied by streaks of grey in his hair. He was not the shiftless dreamer of the popular romances that were later to be written about him, but a man who felt himself to be emotionally and materially a failure, a man keeping his family in an uncomfortable house, shouldering a great burden of troubles—his own, his friends' and his relatives'; snatching what time he could to satisfy his appetite for reading, his liking for boating, and his long thwarted desire for solitude.[2]

Shelley was involved, a committed man. His "pursuit of death," such as it was, was life-entangled.

Shelley observed regretfully in a letter of 1818 that "whatever is once known, can never be unknown" (J.IX.296). He was thinking of happy memories at the time, but the observation is applicable to his experience as a whole. His experience remained with him. He became what he contemplated or endured, for whatever he was doing he did with immense energy and gusto. "He lived . . . under great physical tension. His whole life is a fevered record of travelling, reading, writing, grappling with the most distressing problems of practical life."[3] The human misunderstandings and disillusionments of earlier years, and the legal and financial difficulties in which he was involved both for himself and others throughout his life, taught him a tact, patience, and flexibility in his complex relations with Byron and Claire (not to mention Godwin and Hunt) that contrast notably with his conduct of the Irish campaign or of the Elizabeth Hitchener fiasco eight or ten years before. Equally complex and mature was his developing relationship with Mary, a marriage as full of tensions and incompatibilities as of mutual sympathy, and scarred by the death of two children in 1818–19. Claire Clairmont and Emilia Viviani and Jane Williams possessed qualities which Shelley openly admired and which Mary did not possess, and Mary herself seems often to have retired into her shell in a way that she later regretted;[4] but the marriage was made to work, and it is hard to imagine that it could ever have ended as did the earlier one, although it had even more difficulties to make the best of. The peculiarly willful and tough-minded optimism of Shelley's later years was not of the sort that could be easily disillusioned. "Let us believe," he wrote in the autumn of 1819 to Maria Gisborne,

in a kind of optimism in which we are our own gods. It is best that Mr. Gisborne should have returned, it is best that I should have over persuaded you and Henry, it is best that you should all live together, without any more solitary attempts—it is best that this one attempt should have been made, otherwise perhaps the thing which is best might not have occurred; and it is best that we should think all this for the best even if it is not, because Hope, as Coleridge says is a solemn duty which we owe alike to ourselves and to the world—a worship to the spirit of good within which requires before it sends that inspiration forth, which impresses its likeness upon all that it creates, devoted and disinterested homage. (J.X.93)

It would be hard to say where in this passage the mocking parody of Leibnizian optimism ends and Shelley begins in earnest, but begin he certainly does. Even in an *Invocation to Misery* he is willing to suggest with as much seriousness as mockery:

> 'Tis an evil lot and yet
> Let us make the best of it;
> If love can live when pleasure dies,
> We two will love, till in our eyes
> This heart's Hell seem Paradise.

The balance and maturity of the Italian years was won with difficulty and was not always maintained. Shelley was liable to behave foolishly and self-righteously when he was attacked, and the urge to justify himself produced such regrettable things as the letter to Southey in 1820 and the self-portrait in *Adonais*. The Emilia Viviani episode and the appalling household circumstances at Casi Magni no doubt involved incidents that both Shelley and Mary would have liked to forget. But the later Shelley does merit at least some of the personal admiration that his Victorian relatives were so anxious to secure for him, although his peculiar virtues were not so remotely angelic as the Victorians liked to believe.

Perhaps, in emphasizing the fact that Shelley the mature man was made as well as born, I am laboring the obvious. However that may be, to take a further step and see Shelley's poetry as the product of his varied experience and of the continual practice of writing poetry; to see him through trial and error, and by the imitation of models chosen with increasing discrimination, working out his own special poetic instruments from the most unpromising beginnings; this, if we are to judge from the history of Shelley criticism, has been by no means obvious. In one of the most charming and perceptive books on Shelley, Oliver Elton tells us:

He leaves the impression, more than anyone between Blake and Swinburne, that he could not help being a poet. . . .
Once he had begun to sing, it cannot be said that his sheer instinct

for lyric language was greater at the end of his days than it is in the volume containing *Alastor*. He found more and more things to say in song, he invented more and more tunes. But his work of 1822 is not perceptibly more perfect than his work of 1815.[5]

From these statements we might conclude that Shelley the poet developed quite differently from Shelley the man. As an artist he would seem to belong with Schubert and Mendelssohn and Pope, among the precociously mature, at least in controlling his medium.

But Shelley was not a precocious writer. Among the major Romantic poets his juvenilia make him a leading candidate for the least promising of all, his nearest rivals being Byron and Coleridge. They cannot begin to compare with those of Wordsworth, in particular with *An Evening Walk,* which, even as first published, is among the best eighteenth-century poems of its genre. For, although Shelley wrote a great deal of poetry before his marriage, it is surely undeniable that until *Queen Mab* (written when he was twenty) Shelley's poetry is without intrinsic value, or even promise for the future.

The effort that Shelley took to make something out of *Queen Mab* was not in vain. It is obviously not first-rate or even second-rate poetry, but its rhetorical vigor and clarity of statement are delightful and stimulating even today. And by the end of the poem Shelley has learned a good deal about how to write fluent and resonant blank verse:

> Yet, human Spirit! bravely hold thy course;
> Let virtue teach thee firmly to pursue
> The gradual paths of an aspiring change;
> For birth and life and death, and that strange state
> Before the naked soul has found its home,
> All tend to perfect happiness, and urge
> The restless wheels of being on their way,
> Whose flashing spokes, instinct with infinite life,
> Bicker and burn to gain their destined goal. . . . (IX.146–54)

This is the finest passage in *Queen Mab* and does not represent its common level, but, by the sheer activity of trying to write seventeen hundred lines of blank verse (nearly three-quarters of the whole) about something that meant a great deal to him, Shelley has at last shown that he may be capable of becoming a good poet.

To turn from the last section of *Queen Mab,* written in 1812, to the lyrics Shelley wrote from 1813 to 1815 is disconcerting. According to Elton, "his work of 1822 is not perceptively more perfect than his work of 1815." The five lyrics published with *Alastor* in 1816 include, to mention only the best of them, the first of the two Mutability poems, *Stanzas, April 1814* ("Away! the moor is dark beneath the moon"), and *A Summer Evening Churchyard.* They show practically no lyric talent. There are a few mildly effective stanzas, like the last one of *Stanzas, April 1814,* or the last two of *A Summer Evening Churchyard,* but these are no evidence of any remarkable talent for writing lyric poems, such as Elton attributes to Shelley. The lyrics of 1822, however, include *When the Lamp Is Shattered, Lines Written in the Bay of Lerici, A Dirge,* and the poems to Jane Williams—a series of delicate and skillful lyrics. The imagery and the subtle variations of rhythm and caesura in the following famous stanza, from the first of these, were far beyond the range of Shelley's early lyrics:

> Its passions will rock thee,
> As the storms rock the ravens on high;
> Bright reason will mock thee,
> Like the sun from a wintry sky.
> From thy nest every rafter
> Will rot, and thine eagle home
> Leave thee naked to laughter,
> When leaves fall and cold winds come.

But, whatever our reservations about the early lyrics, if we turn to the narrative poem which gives the 1816 volume its title and its value, we do see a Shelley of some consequence. *Alastor* may be a

rather dull and confusing poem which will not bear much reread-
ing, but its versification, as Tennyson claimed, is masterly. The
aging laureate, while he deplored Shelley's poetry in some ways,
thought that "as a writer of blank verse he was perhaps the most
skilful of the moderns."[6] That *Alastor* was in blank verse, however, suggests the reason for its lonely eminence in the 1816 volume.
Shelley had worked hard to learn how to write blank verse, and
his efforts had borne some fruit even in *Queen Mab*. Now, in
another poem of some length (720 lines), he is reworking the same
medium with increased ease, flexibility, and control of paragraph-
ing. One likely reason for the improvement is that Landor, who
was his model in 1812, has been succeeded by Milton and Wordsworth.

The excellence of *Alastor* coexists with the weakness of the lyrics
in the same volume. Shelley needed more practice. He had to learn
how to write good lyrics. The lyric poet par excellence of the
popular imagination had more difficulty learning to write short
lyrics than almost anything else, despite his increasing fondness for
the genre. Even so late a work as *Prometheus Unbound* (1819),
excellent as it is, sags under the weight of the ineptness of many of
its lyrics and is saved mainly by its superb blank verse.

Shelley's first lyric of any consequence is *The Cold Earth Slept
Below,* which was not published with *Alastor,* although written on
November 5, 1815. The poems of 1816 include the impressive *Mont
Blanc,* which, however, is not a lyric and is virtually in blank verse,
despite a liberal sprinkling of rhymes. The *Hymn to Intellectual
Beauty* of the same year is, of course, much more important than
anything of its length and kind that Shelley had done before, and,
if any early work can be said to appear unheralded, it is surely
the *Hymn.* But one swallow does not make a summer, and the
purposeful practice needed to develop Shelley into a lyrist of some
consequence did not occur until *Prometheus Unbound,* which
stands in the same relation to Shelley's ability to write lyrics as
Queen Mab does to his ability to write blank verse. In *Prometheus,*

Shelley is in the process of acquiring lyrical skill, and the failures still outnumber the successes. After *Prometheus,* Shelley's long lyric apprenticeship bore fruit in the many delightful short poems written between 1819 and 1822.

Shelley attempted various styles and verse forms, and each style or form was only learned after a good deal of trial and error. He himself was conscious of new departures and experiments. He warns his publisher:

If I had even intended to publish "Julian and Maddalo" with my name, yet I would not print it with "Prometheus." It would not harmonize. It is an attempt in a different style in which I am not yet sure of myself, a *sermo pedestris* way of treating human nature quite opposed to the idealism of that drama. (J.X.168)

And later in the same year (1820) he wonders whether such variety is a good thing for his poetry:

I do not know if it be wise to affect variety in compositions, or whether the attempt to excel in many ways does not debar from excellence in one particular kind. (J.X.191)

In his last year, according to Trelawny, Shelley made a similar remark: "Considering the labor requisite to excel in composition, I think it would be better to stick to one style." [7]

Because Shelley tried a variety of styles, and because at any one time his stage of development was liable to be different in each, he was able to publish such anomalous mixtures as *Alastor and Other Poems,* or write within a period of nine months two works like *Adonais* and *Swellfoot the Tyrant.* He could also, within a single poem, show masterwork in one medium and apprenticework in another, as in *Prometheus Unbound.*

With few exceptions, the story seems to be the same, whatever style or form we consider. Shelley learned early to write good blank verse, as we have already observed, and he never lost the knack, although, after *Prometheus,* only the hastily written *Hellas* (1821) makes important use of it. Shelley's late development as a lyrist we have also observed, and the practice that was necessary before he could write a perfect lyric like the Song at the end of the fragmentary *Charles the First:*

> A widow bird sat mourning for her love
> Upon a wintry bough;
> The frozen wind crept on above,
> The freezing stream below.
>
> There was no leaf upon the forest bare,
> No flower upon the ground,
> And little motion in the air
> Except the mill-wheel's sound.

In *The Revolt of Islam* Shelley learned with immense labor to write Spenserian stanzas. *The Revolt's* chief claim to our esteem is its effect on *Adonais,* written four years later. The *Ode to the West Wind* and *The Triumph of Life* have their debt to the unsuccessful and fragmentary *Prince Athanase,* in which Shelley tried *terza rima* for the first time, as well as to his study of Petrarch and Dante, the two poets who meant most to him in his later years (although Calderon and Goethe seem to have been strong competitors). In varying degrees, this practical education in the use of his various mediums and styles can be seen in Shelley's theatrical blank verse, his octosyllabic couplets in the sort of descriptive-meditative poem that descends from *Grongar Hill,* and his loose couplets in the conversation poem. Satire he tried twice, in *Peter Bell the Third* and *Swellfoot the Tyrant.* Both show a slight satiric gift, for the most part incompetently handled. Shelley never did learn to write satire. Once, in *The Witch of Atlas,* he conquered a new medium (*ottava rima*) at first touch. The conquest followed, however, an extensive reading of Ariosto, not to mention Byron; and, of course, one of the poem's main charms is its casual lack of concern for technical perfection.

Shelley, then, both the man and the poet, was made as well as born; and the amount of making required was considerable. Moreover, just as the balance and maturity of Shelley the man were precariously held and subject to deplorable lapses, so the skill and precision of Shelley the poet were rarely maintained for many lines at a time. His method seems to have been to write rapidly while the impulse was on him and to revise at leisure. He believed, like most poets or scientists, that his best ideas simply came to him, and that he had to make the best of their inexplicable appearance, which was not controllable by the will. He would have understood Pope's habit of asking for a light so that he could jot down the stray lines of poetry that came to him at odd hours of the night. Shelley knew also that, because such intuitions were transitory, the conscious mind or judgment had to work at this given material in order to create a finished poem. If poetic intuitions could last forever, the judgment would have little work to do (except perhaps to decide between the claims of incompatible intuitions). They did not last, however, and hard work was needed to conceal the fact. "I appeal to the greatest poets of the present day," writes Shelley in *A Defence of Poetry*,

whether it be not an error to assert that the finest passages of poetry are produced by labor and study. The toil and the delay recommended by critics can be justly interpreted to mean no more than a careful observation of the inspired moments and an artificial connection of the spaces between their suggestions by the intertexture of conventional expressions—a necessity only imposed by the limitedness of the poetical faculty itself. . . .   (C.294)

Shelley insists here, of course, less on the importance of judgment than on the primacy of inspiration. But if a writer lacked judgment, Shelley could deplore its absence. In his review of Hogg's *Memoirs of Prince Alexy Haimatoff*, he praises his friend's invention but deplores his failure to revise.

There are passages in the production before us which afford instances of just and rapid intuition belonging only to intelligences that possess this faculty [of "the discernment of shades and distinctions"] in no ordinary degree. As a composition the book is far from faultless. Its abruptness and angularities do not appear to have received the slightest polish or correction. The author has written with fervor, but has disdained to revise at leisure.

Whatever its youthful genius, for Shelley this book cannot expect to deserve the highest praise for its "fervid impatience of sensibilities impetuously disburdening their fullness." It is closer to a beautiful day-dream than to a romance "skilfully interwoven for the purpose of maintaining the interest of the reader and conducting his sympathies by dramatic gradations to the dénouement." Such "negligence," "impatience" and "inexperience" deserve criticism in Shelley's opinion, although, of course, he would not claim that any amount of revision at leisure could do any good without something worth revising.[8]

Shelley's "careful observation of the inspired moments" and his revision at leisure can be traced in his pedestrian prose as well as in his poetry. Good, or potentially good, passages recur in constantly varied forms from one pamphlet or fragment to another. For example, a paragraph on the relation of belief, volition and morality first occurs in *The Necessity of Atheism* (1811). It reappears in modified form in *A Letter to Lord Ellenborough* (1812) and in two different notes to *Queen Mab* (1813), that on "I will beget a son" and that on "There is no God." In its expansion of the original argument, the second of these notes includes in parentheses an interesting new fancy about a graduated barometer of belief. *A Refutation of Deism* (1812–14) gathers up the threads of Shelley's early skeptical and iconoclastic pieces, including the discussion of belief. The parenthetical sentence about a graduated scale is now closely worked into the argument. In *A Treatise on Morals* (1815?) this sentence has become detached from the discussion of belief and volition and is now expanded into an independent paragraph.

Shelley's early prose works take in one another's loose materials to an almost disconcerting extent. The whole corpus from 1811 to 1815 suggests a single work continually being revised and expanded. First thoughts, second thoughts and third thoughts jostle one another, and the difficulties of dating make it impossible to separate them conclusively.

What is true of the early prose is true of the middle prose as well. *On Love,* the Preface to *Alastor, The Coliseum,* and *A Discourse on the Manners of the Ancient Greeks Relative to the Subject of Love* are so closely and so indefinably related in phrase and idea that critical agreement seems impossible. And Shelley's finest essay, *A Defence of Poetry,* has been described by the editor of his prose works as a "patchwork," in which he "has drawn heavily on his own writings, taking over ideas, sentences, and whole paragraphs almost verbatim" (C.276). Yet, despite Shelley's tenacious hold on what he regarded as his "inspired moments," *A Defence* does not read like a heterogeneous grab-bag of quotations. Perhaps Shelley might have defended himself in terms which he applied to Milton:

Milton conceived the Paradise Lost as a whole before he executed it in portions. We have his own authority also for the muse having "dictated" to him the "unpremeditated song." And let this be an answer to those who would allege the fifty-six various readings of the first line of the Orlando Furioso. Compositions so produced are to poetry what mosaic is to painting.   (C.294)

Writers do not necessarily write poetry as they write prose—not even a writer to whom "Lord Bacon was a poet" (C.280). Nor do they always follow their own critical precepts. But students of Shelley's notebooks have made it clear that his poetic practice is in accordance with the aesthetic opinions and the habits of composition which we have been outlining.[9] In the Preface to his edition of fragments and early drafts, Roger Ingpen writes:

He composed rapidly and attained to perfection by intensive correction. He would sometimes write down a phrase with alterations and rejections time after time until it came within a measure of satisfying him. Words are frequently substituted for others and lines interpolated. Sometimes he would write with ink on a page already containing lines written in pencil, and a poem begun on one page is, perhaps, continued on a leaf many pages ahead. A page of manuscript may be so heavily corrected as to yield but a single perfect line. Many such a page, composed at fever heat, with a quill worn to a stub, may seem at first sight to be mere chaos, but with patience the manuscript may at length be made to give up its secrets. . . .

Shelley's notebooks are specially valuable as they enable his method of composition to be studied. . . . He would jot down a single line, or an idea, or the slender outline of a poem, sometimes for the sake of the measure. He would develop the outline into a stanza, changing a word here and there, copying and recopying it until he obtained the desired result.[10]

Thus the evidence of the notebooks (in so far as the meager investigation of recent scholars allows one to generalize) supports Trelawny's contemporary account:

The day I found Shelley in the pine forest he was writing verses on a guitar. I picked up a fragment, but could only make out the first two lines:

"Ariel, to Miranda take
This slave of music."

It was a frightful scrawl; words smeared out with his finger, and one upon the other, over and over in tiers, and all run together in most "admired disorder"; it might have been taken as a sketch of a marsh overgrown with bulrushes, and the blots for wild ducks; such a dashed off daub as self-conceited artists mistake for a manifestation of genius. On my observing this to him, he answered:

"When my brain gets heated with thought, it soon boils, and throws off images and words faster than I can skim them off. In the morning, when cooled down, out of the rude sketch as you justly call it, I shall attempt a drawing." [11]

Sometimes the "drawing" was not made, as is shown by the innumerable fragments published posthumously from the notebooks; sometimes the revision might be as heated and packed with afterthoughts as the first sketch; sometimes the "drawing" was made perfunctorily or only in part, for the continually developing Shelley naturally preferred to try a new poem rather than just improve an old: sometimes he revised or eliminated a good deal, and we have such "a highly wrought work of art" as *Adonais,* or even *Epipsychidion,* for both of which there exist a good many rejected passages and unrevised drafts. One may be surprised to discover that Shelley planned to revise *The Revolt of Islam,* should a new edition have been contemplated by the publisher. Even in the "highly wrought" and revised works, however, modern readers are likely to find passages which the peculiar predilections of Shelley's taste prevented him from eliminating, despite their apparent short-comings. The one line which a heavily scored manuscript page has yielded may not be a "single perfect" one, after all.

One other piece of evidence from Shelley's contemporaries is the extraordinary dialogue between Byron and Shelley which was published eight years after Shelley's death in the *New Monthly and London Magazine,* and which W. E. Peck reprinted in 1927. This dialogue about Shakespeare purports to be the report of an eye-witness. Whether the eyewitness was Thomas Medwin or someone else, and whether the dialogue ever took place or not, seem beyond reasonable conjecture. But the obvious appropriateness to Byron of the remarks attributed to him suggest that, however remote the piece may be from the report of an actual dialogue, it probably represents a characteristic difference of opinion between the two poets as to how poetry gets written and how it should be criticized.[12] Byron, with his hatred of the virtuoso and any sort of "literary" airs and graces, as well as his eighteenth-century view of Shakespeare as a "natural" poet, insists that we must "seek not reason, or consistency, or art, in the wild rhapsodies of this un-cultivated genius."

And thus this will-o'-the-wisp, this meteor of genius, leads us poor mortals, who would fain analyze his nature and detect his "airy pur-poses," a weary and fruitless chase; while the simpler solution of the difficulty would be, that Shakespeare was a man of great genius but no art, and much preferred satisfying his hostess of the Mermaid with a good night's profit, to satisfying the troublesome and inquisitive readers of future ages, which he dreamed not of.[13]

Unabashed by this forthright skepticism, the supposed Shelley goes on to analyze the texture of a famous line from *The Merchant of Venice,* "How sweet the moonlight sleeps upon this bank."

Now, examining this line, we perceive that all the parts are formed in relation to one another, and that it is consequently a whole. *Sleep,* we see, is a reduplication of the pure and gentle sound of *sweet;* and as the beginning of the former symphonizes with the beginning *s* of the latter, so also the *l* in moonlight prepares one for the *l* in *sleep,* and glides gently into it; and in the conclusion, one may perceive that the word *bank* is determined by the preceding words, and that the *b* which it begins with is but a deeper intonation of the two *p*'s which come before it; *sleeps upon this slope,* would have been effeminate; *sleeps upon this rise* would have been harsh and inharmonious.[14]

Byron is raucously incredulous. Shakespeare had nothing of the sort in his mind, and, in any case, "the beauty of the line does not lie in sounds and syllables, . . . but in the beautiful metaphor of the moonlight sleeping." Shelley replies:

Indeed, that also is very beautiful. In every single line, the poet must organize many simultaneous operations, both the meaning of the words and their emphatic arrangement, and then the flow and melting together of their symphony; and the whole must also be united with the current of the rhyme.

Byron. Well, then, I'm glad I'm not a poet! It must be like making out one's expenses for a journey, I think, all this calculation!

Shelley. I don't say that a poet must necessarily be conscious of all this, no more than a lady is conscious of every graceful movement. But I do say that they all depend upon reason, in which they live and move, and have their being; and that he who brings them out into the light of distinct consciousness, besides satisfying an instinctive desire of his own nature, will be more secure and more commanding. . . .[15]

What Shelley has said about a single line, he goes on to say about the structure of a whole play, and analyzes *Hamlet* to make his point. But by the time his analysis is over Byron has fallen asleep.

However convinced Shelley may have been of the "labor requisite to excel in composition," and however exceptional the skill and facility which he managed to acquire, Shelley's poetry remains comparatively uneven, and in many of his finest poems the good and bad are disconcertingly mixed. Moreover, such prolific and crowded inventiveness as is suggested by Trelawny's "frightful scrawl" and the evidence of the notebooks, could be reduced to an

economical drawing only by a process of compression and elimination which is just as likely to produce confused obscurity as lucid
simplicity. Certainly complicated ellipses and half-formed clusters
of images, which come and go at a moment's notice, are often
characteristic of Shelley's style even at its best. To some extent this
obscurity is to be deplored, but the virtues which are partly
responsible for it are not to be deplored, and I see no reason for
not tolerating in Shelley what we are able to tolerate in Donne,
Hopkins, or Auden.

The usual comparison, of course, is not with Donne but with
Keats. Its frequency, however, has been no protection against the
unexamined fallacy. Near the end of Austin Farrer's *A Rebirth of
Images,* the author discusses, in terms of familiar clichés about Keats
and Shelley, just how St. John could not have gone about writing
Revelation:

Conceive St. John—conceive yourself—taking pen in hand and sitting
down to write. How does one start? It is no good saying that such a
work is the product of simple lyrical inspiration, as it might be Shelley
writing about the skylark. You put down what has suggested itself in
direct response to your experience and then you go on from there,
developing and elaborating the images and reflections, as they themselves seem to demand, until the work (let us hope) rounds itself off,
and you stop: then perhaps (but more if you are Keats than if you
are Shelley) you go back over it, pruning, rewriting, rearranging,
until you are content.[16]

I cite this passage not to criticize Mr. Farrer for a minor slip, but
because his assumption is typical. What Shelley's notebooks reveal
about the composition of the *Skylark* is obviously not common
knowledge among readers of poetry, nor are the remarks of Shelley
and Keats about their methods of composition. In reality, it is
Keats who disapproves of revision after the fact, and Shelley who
grants its necessity. According to Woodhouse, Keats

never corrects, unless perhaps a word here or there should occur to
him as preferable to an expression he has already used— He is im-

patient of correcting and says he would rather burn the piece in question and write another or something else— "My judgment, (he says) is as active while I am actually writing as my imagination. In fact all my faculties are strongly excited, and in their full play— And shall I afterwards, when my imagination is idle, and the heat in which I wrote has gone off, sit down coldly to criticise when in Possession of only one faculty, what I have written, when almost inspired." [17]

It is Shelley who tells Medwin that "the source of poetry is native and involuntary, but requires severe labor in its development," [18] who complains of a writer that he "has written with fervor, but has disdained to revise at leisure," and who talks of attempting a drawing when he has "cooled down." [19]

For Keats and Coleridge, judgment and inspiration are both active at the moment of creation, which is characterized by "interpenetration of ... spontaneous impulse and of voluntary purpose"; "judgment ever awake and steady self-possession with enthusiasm profound or vehement." [20] Shelley, basically more skeptical and analytic than they, does not believe in such unity. Even in defending poetry, he does not always forget the time-ridden "limitedness of the poetic faculty." If Wordsworth (who sees the moment of creation as an "overflow of powerful feelings" *preceded* by long and deep thought) offends Coleridge's synthetic comprehensiveness, Shelley (who sees the boiling froth of the imagination skimmed off and *later* solidified into a finished poem) would perhaps offend it even more.

By sad necessity, the Shelleyan moment of creation is incomplete. It displays less than the comprehensive synthesis which Coleridge's definition describes. It looks beyond itself; it demands forethought and afterthought, Prometheus and Epimetheus. And the poems, like the process which gave birth to them, stretch and strain, chafe at their own restrictions and disunity, aspire to a unity and a finality which is beyond them, perhaps beyond Time itself. They are not the products of Coleridge's synthetic imagination, but of an imagination less enclosed in its own circle, more allied to becoming than to being: an imagination which may be most appropriately described as "prophetic."

The Lyrics as Microcosm

Without precise examination of individual poems, any discussion of Shelley's technique would be virtually meaningless. Although in the body of this study we shall be mainly concerned with Shelley's long poems, it is convenient (and complementary) to begin by concentrating on a group of short lyrics. I have chosen some which will not merely illustrate the range, unevenness, and special problems of Shelley's technique when he is writing on a small scale, but will also bring to our attention a number of the themes that I intend to consider in later chapters.

When Passion's Trance Is Overpast, a lyric from 1821, appears only infrequently in anthologies but has been generally praised, and with some reason:

> When passion's trance is overpast,
> If tenderness and truth could last,
> Or live, whilst all wild feelings keep
> Some mortal slumber, dark and deep,
> I should not weep, I should not weep!
>
> It were enough to feel, to see
> Thy soft eyes gazing tenderly,
> And dream the rest—and burn and be
> The secret food of fires unseen,
> Couldst thou but be as thou hast been.
>
> After the slumber of the year
> The woodland violets reappear;
> All things revive in field or grove,
> And sky and sea, but two, which move
> And form all others, life and love.

The first stanza is superb, but it sets both a standard and a theme which the rest of the poem seems unable to sustain. It is concerned with the relation between the passion and the tenderness of love, its strange combination of violence and gentleness. "Passion" is associated with a "trance" and "tenderness" with "truth." The one is ecstatic and exalted, the other sober and clear-eyed. The problem faced in stanza one is their inseparability. The first, by itself, degenerates into lust; but what happens to the second when the first is gone? If only the tenderness could survive after the passion is gone, the speaker would not need to weep its departure. In such a situation, it is implied, the "wild feelings" would merely go underground into "some mortal slumber, dark and deep," to await reawakening.

The first stanza considers the problem in general terms, although the speaker obviously has a personal interest in it. The second is more specific. The loss of passion is not the speaker's but that of someone he loves. She, having lost the passion, has lost the tenderness as well. He, having lost neither, is willing to drive his passion underground into a burning imagination, and to express only his tenderness.

Whatever hope may have been suggested in the previous stanzas is denied in the last, as the poem returns to the more generalized sort of statements with which it began, now given additional distance by the conventional image. That image contrasts the cyclical history of nature with the linear history of man. Human love, like human life, once lost, is lost forever. By his image Shelley completes the meaning of the central figure of the two previous stanzas. In stanza one the passion is supposed to have subsided into "some mortal slumber dark and deep." In stanza two the passion is supposed to have been driven underground where it burns secretly. Whether the passion ever revives is left an open question in each case. The last stanza closes it. The violets slumber underground only to reappear in the spring, but not "life and love."

The argument is neatly developed and felicitously phrased—up to a point. I can see nothing to object to in stanza one except the obscurely made distinction between "last" and "live." Apart from the superb opening of the last stanza, which Shelley could hardly have improved upon, the phrasing of the rest of the poem is merely adequate, and the conclusion is spoiled by a lack of precision: the word "life" is just as applicable to the woodland violets as to the lovers, and the contrast at the center of the stanza is therefore imperfectly communicated. As for the development of the argument, it is skillful and carefully thought out, but the transitions are inadequate. The problem of the first stanza is so broad in its implications that its sudden reduction to a limited situation in stanza two, where only the person loved has lost her passion, and where the underground slumber of passion is only the secret burning of repression, is awkward and unconvincing. And in stanza three, while the theme of passion's submergence is completed, the relation between passion and tenderness, which was central to stanza one and was kept sight of in stanza two, has now disappeared, so that love now seems to be merely the equivalent of passion. The argument has reached an oversimplified conclusion; it has lost rather than absorbed a good deal of the material provided in stanza one.

To complain in this way about the argument of a lyric by Shelley may seem irrelevant. Surely such a poem is supposed to be an overflow of emotion, not a logical argument. But Shelley's lyrics are notably argumentative if we compare them with, say, Wordsworth's Lucy poems or Tennyson's songs from The Princess; they are more inclined to emphasize the presentation of sequences of thought moving to a conclusion than the definition of a personal emotional situation, although such a situation is generally involved in them. In this Shelley is not particularly un-Romantic. There is a good deal of truth in the suggestion of D. J. Greene that structurally one of the most important developments from eighteenth-century to Romantic poetry is from an impressionistic to a logical method of organization.[21] For a representative example of logical structure he chooses Shelley's late lyric Mutability. Now, a poetic argument is not to be judged like a philosophic argument, and it will, of course, persuade the reader for different reasons; but, at the same time, it should not be reduced by the critic to an irrational series of "states of consciousness" just because it occurs in a Romantic poem. "If the *discursive* structure of the typical poem by Keats is analyzed," Greene even suggests, "it will be seen to be, on the whole, neater, more 'logical,' than the typical poem by Pope." [22]

We are perhaps surprised to realize how neatly discursive is the structure of a lyric like *Music When Soft Voices Die:*

> Music, when soft voices die,
> Vibrates in the memory;
> Odors, when sweet violets sicken,
> Live within the sense they quicken.
>
> Rose leaves, when the rose is dead,
> Are heaped for the beloved's bed;
> And so thy thoughts, when thou art gone,
> Love itself shall slumber on.

The poem moves through three carefully balanced analogies to a clear-cut conclusion (disturbed only by a doubt whether "thy" is subjective or objective genitive). This may be what causes T. S. Eliot to attribute to it "a beauty of music and a beauty of content." [23] Similarly, on a much larger scale, in the *Ode to the West Wind,* after three sections describing the effect of the wind on the leaves, the clouds, and the waves, Shelley, in the last two sections, looks forward to its similar effect on himself and, through him, on the process of history.

Quite different in method is *The Tower of Famine,* which explores one complex image and develops it to a last, inclusive statement. This poem, in its surviving form, is probably at an early stage of composition. The final drawing has certainly not been made. Nevertheless, it is in some ways an impressive piece and does illustrate the crowded and half-developed ideas and images which flowed from Shelley's pen and formed the raw material of his poems.

Its theme is a favorite of Shelley's: the corrupted victim. For Shelley the terrible thing about slavery and physical hardship is that the will may allow itself to be corrupted by them. Slavery may make men slaves in reality; cruelty may make them bloody revengers; starvation may make them hungry beasts. The evil done to men becomes the evil done *by* them. This Shelley considered the tragedy of the French Revolution. Evil fetters eat like "poisonous rust into the soul" (C.316).[24]

The Tower of Famine is not about the French Revolution, but about Pisa, sadly depleted after the Napoleonic wars. "A large disagreeable city, almost without inhabitants" (J.IX.309), Shelley called it when he first saw it in May of 1818. According to his wife,

One thing however which disgusted me so much that I could never walk in the streets except in misery was that criminals condemned to labour work publickly in the streets heavily ironed in pairs with a man with a gun to each pair to guard against their escape— These poor wretches look sallow and dreadfully wretched and you could get into no street but you heard the clanking of their chains.[25]

In her note on *The Tower of Famine* (which she dates 1820, when she and Shelley had returned to live in Pisa), Mary identifies the tower as the

prison of Ugolino, which goes by the name of "La Torre della Fame": in the adjoining building the galley slaves are confined. It is situated near the Ponte al Mare on the Arno. (J.IV.405)

Here, now, in the opening lines of the poem, are the desolation, the city, the tower, and the slaves.

> Amid the desolation of a city,
> Which was the cradle and is now the grave
> Of an extinguished people,—so that pity
>
> Weeps o'er the shipwrecks of oblivion's wave,
> There stands the Tower of Famine. It is built
> Upon some prison-homes, whose dwellers rave

> For bread, and gold, and blood; pain, linked to guilt,
> Agitates the light flame of their hours,
> Until its vital oil is spent or spilt.

These slaves are not depicted as noble rebels against the yoke of their oppressors. All they rave about is "bread, and gold, and blood." Their pain is not innocent, it is linked to guilt. Their souls are subdued to the element they live in, as was the soul of Ugolino himself in the Shelley-Medwin translation of Dante's episode: "Famine of grief can get the mastery."

About the tower are the oppressive structures of the merchant-aristocrat and the priest. They have survived wars and shifts of authority and are as much the enemy as are the Bourbons. Unlike the atmospheric pavilions of the sky (which are destroyed and reborn, pulled down and built up, in the cyclical process depicted by Shelley in *The Cloud*), these structures survive the tempest, a dead architecture that will not finally die. Faced by the grim tower, they merely seem to fade and withdraw and leave the city to its barrenness.

> There stands the pile, a tower amid the towers
> And sacred domes; each marble-ribbed roof,
> The brazen-gated temples and the bowers
>
> Of solitary wealth—the tempest-proof
> Pavilions of the dark Italian air—
> Are by its presence dimmed; they stand aloof,
>
> And are withdrawn—so that the world is bare.

The central image of the tower is summed up, and moves to a new climax, in a long concluding simile. The tower becomes a spectral mirror surrounded by a company of fair ladies, the flower of Italian society and art,

> As if a spectre, wrapped in shapeless terror,
> Amid a company of ladies fair
>
> Should glide and glow, till it became a mirror
> Of all their beauty, and their hair and hue,

The life of their sweet eyes, with all its error,
Should be absorbed, till they to marble grew.

In this image of the spectral tower-mirror and the fair ladies who
are reflected in it, Shelley is trying to establish a significant relation
between the basic components of the Italian world he is observing:
its physical and moral degradation, its traditional social structure,
and its beautiful setting of art and nature. With the appearance of
the mirror, the theme of the corrupted victim and the vicious circle
of the despot-slave relation is joined by another favorite of Shelley's:
the soul that reflects, absorbs, and becomes what it contemplates.

That all these components come together with the potential
finality of great poetry, few readers would assert. But they do come
together with an impressive complexity and intensity. The simile
takes up and develops the relation between the tower and the
dimmed, withdrawn pavilions which surround it. For all its desolation the world of the tower stands out and rebukes and drains the
life out of these structures. Whatever life the scene presents belongs
to the tower itself. But it is a death-like life, a phosphorescent glow,
a sinister beauty, shapeless and terrible, a specter which glides into
the midst of a fair company of ladies, absorbs their beauty into its
mirror and, like a new Gorgon's head, turns them to marble. This
spectral mirror absorbs not merely "their hair and hue, / The life
of their sweet eyes . . . ," but their "error." The evil which surrounds the tower becomes its evil as well. And that surrounding
world, drained of its life, withdraws and solidifies. The future lies,
no doubt, with the "shapeless terror," but the poem, as it survives,
is not a hopeful anticipation of rebirth or revolution. It is doubtful
if the terms of Shelley's poem (which sets the "marble-ribbed roof"
and "the brazen-gated temples" against the dissolving and reform-
ing processes of nature) could ever have allowed it to be. At the end,
a dead world stands face to face with an inhuman one.

The Tower of Famine requires for its comprehension some
knowledge of Shelley's habitual objects of thought. I admit to being
impressed, if not satisfied, by the poem. Many readers are likely to

experience a similar reaction to one of Shelley's most famous and controversial lyrics, *When the Lamp Is Shattered*. It may not be a "rude sketch" like the fragment Trelawny picked up in the pine forest, but it is no economical and finished drawing either. Its argument starts off with a series of parallel figures in a manner already familiar to us from *Music When Soft Voices Die:*

> When the lamp is shattered,
> The light in the dust lies dead;
> When the cloud is scattered,
> The rainbow's glory is shed;
> When the lute is broken,
> Sweet tones are remembered not;
> When the lips have spoken,
> Loved accents are soon forgot.

The poem's central story is thus introduced by four figures supposedly analogous to it. The remaining three stanzas attack more directly the story itself.

Before approaching that story, there is, it seems to me, a real problem to be disposed of in the first stanza itself. The four figures are presumably parallel to one another. Let us see what they have in common. The first of them, according to F. A. Pottle, is a version of Shelley's favorite refraction figure [26] (although in negative terms). In that figure, some original material meets an obstacle and is thereby changed into something else:

> Life, like a dome of many-colored glass,
> Stains the white radiance of eternity.

The white radiance passes through the many-colored dome and reaches the eye split into the various colors of the spectrum. So eternity, meeting temporal life, is transformed into the flux of this world. In *When the Lamp Is Shattered* (from Mr. Pottle's point of view) the lamp is supposed to shine on the dust, and the two are supposed to produce "the light in the dust"; but, since now "the lamp is shattered," "the light in the dust lies dead." It is possible,

with some effort, to extend Mr. Pottle's argument to the other
three analogies. The second (rainbow) analogy is obviously a kind
of refraction figure, even though there is no specific mention of the
sun and one of the three components is therefore missing. In the
two images of sound which balance the two images of light, the
reader can no doubt fill in the details which might make them also
refraction figures (lute meets voice and produces "sweet tones";
speech meets lips and produces "loved accents"), but I am not sure
how far he would be justified.

In fact, it might be easier to see the four analogies not as figures of
refraction, with three components, but simply as figures of containment, with two. When the container (lamp) is shattered, the contained (light) lies dead in the dust. Here "in the dust" modifies
"lies," not, as Mr. Pottle insists, "light." One of the difficulties of
regarding these analogies as refraction figures is that whereas in
the first analogy it is the source of supply (lamp) that is shattered,
in the second it is the refracting medium (cloud). No such difficulty arises if we regard them as containment figures. The "shattered" lamp and "scattered" cloud are both containers, whose
destruction is also the destruction of what they contain. The same
may, to a lesser extent, be said of the lute.

But the fourth analogy is a different story. It invites us (as in
part the third does also) to see the analogies not as refraction or
containment figures, but as mutability figures, showing the tran-
sience of human sensation, the limitations of the memory. The first
stanza of *When the Lamp Is Shattered,* from this point of view,
means little more than a reversal of the theme of *Music When Soft
Voices Die.* Music, it now seems, does not keep vibrating in the
memory, the accents of the voice are soon forgotten by Love. Nor
can lutes, clouds, and lamps be expected to last forever.

The best test of these three interpretations ought to come in the
remaining stanzas, when the situation or story to which the
analogies lead is presented. But that story, far from asserting one
of them and denying the others, seems able to compromise with all

three. In fact, refraction dominates stanza two, containment stanza three, and mutability stanza four.

The story to which these analogies lead is about the unstable harmony of human love and the disintegration of its components. Through this disintegration love turns to lust and barren isolation. Stanza two begins by underlining the relevance of stanza one. Just as the loss of the lamp and the lute involves the loss of music and splendor, so do the components of human love affect one another. As restated in the first two lines, the basic figure seems simply one of containment: the light and sound do not survive the container which holds and projects them; as subsequently elaborated, however, in terms of voice, cave, and echo, it is primarily one of refraction. The voice of the spirit breathes into the cave of the heart and produces the echoing song of love. But when the spirit is mute nature fills the vacuum: the wind blows through a ruined cell and produces only sad dirges, or the surges heave until the sea vibrates like a funeral bell. Now only the winds and tides of passion stimulate the heart. It sounds, but it does not sing.

> As music and splendor
> Survive not the lamp and the lute,
> The heart's echoes render
> No song when the spirit is mute:—
> No song but sad dirges,
> Like the wind through a ruined cell,
> Or the mournful surges
> That ring the dead seaman's knell.

After hearts have mingled it is the spirit (Love capitalized) which fails first. The passion of the heart remains, but it is now literally passion, something for the lover to suffer and endure, not possess.

> When hearts have once mingled,
> Love first leaves the well-built nest;
> The weak one is singled
> To endure what it once possessed.

Why, asks the poet, must the spirit of Love enter such a fragile dwelling as the human heart, which is too weak to hold it? This

inadequate dwelling is first the cradle of Love, then its home, and
finally its bier.

> O Love! who bewailest
> The frailty of all things here,
> Why choose you the frailest
> For your cradle, your home, and your bier?

In the great final stanza we are in the midst of the futile passions
of the heart, that frail nest which had once seemed substantial. The
address to the spirit of Love, relatively impersonal (you) in stanza
three, is now more personal (thee); indeed the Love addressed
seems now to include the lover (as the "weak one" of stanza three
seemed to be both the containing heart and a single suffering lover),
who supposes against reason that his love can be enclosed in the
stormy and mutable human heart.

> Its passions will rock thee,
> As the storms rock the ravens on high;
> Bright reason will mock thee,
> Like the sun from a wintry sky.

Finally the passions themselves fail. The heart falls apart. The nest
rots (the irony of "well-built nest" in stanza three is now apparent,
and "eagle home" reinforces it). Nothing remains but nakedness,
scorn, desolation, and winter. The heavy spondaic feet of the last
line bring the whole terrible process to its dead end.

> From thy nest every rafter
> Will rot, and thine eagle home
> Leave thee naked to laughter,
> When leaves fall and cold winds come.

So the dust is no worthy substance to reflect the light of the lamp.
Or the lamp is no worthy container to hold the light of Love. The
harmony is at best temporary, and "hollow sounds" succeed the
"sweet tones" when once the mutable lute is broken. The attempt
to enclose eternity in time, to enclose the unchanging spirit in the
changing heart, fails. The heart cannot hold the spirit and is itself

destroyed in the attempt. Basically this poem is a Platonic denial of the possibility of incarnation.[27]

It deserves its fame;[28] the scornful comments of some critics seem ill-advised, based on inattentive reading and inadequate premises.[29] But, whatever its virtues, it suffers from grammatical looseness (see "first" in stanza two and "its" in stanza three), elliptical compression, an uneasy combination of the personal and the impersonal, and a somewhat incoherent multiplicity of figurative images. One difficulty, for example, is that whereas the analogies of the first stanza suggest, in the main, that the heart shatters or decays and thus disperses the spirit (unable to exist in this world without some human agent), the story claims that the spirit starts the process of decay by leaving home, which turns (ultimately) into a bier. In one case the heart dies and the spirit flees: in the other the spirit flees and the heart dies. It takes little thought to discover a *modus vivendi* for these antitheses, but Shelley shows no signs of having taken such thought. He has explored his material up to a point. We can be impressed by his journey so far, without feeling that he has gone far enough.

The most finished of Shelley's short lyrics is the *Hymn of Pan,* written, along with its companion piece the *Hymn of Apollo,* for the opening scene of Mary Shelley's verse play *Midas.* In this scene old Tmolus judges a singing contest between Apollo with his lyre and Pan with his pipe. Midas enters in the midst of preparations for the contest and, invited by Tmolus to remain and listen, tells the reader, in an aside, of his preference for "my guardian God, old horned Pan."[30] But, when Apollo and Pan have sung, Tmolus promptly awards the palm to Apollo, commending the wisdom, beauty, and divine power of his music. The infuriated Midas interrupts and expresses his own decided preference for Pan's song. He says, in the words given him by Mary Shelley,

> Immortal Pan, to my poor, mortal ears
> Your sprightly song in melody outweighs
> His drowsy tune; he put me fast asleep. . . .

Whereupon Apollo turns on Midas and gives him asses' ears as a symbol of his "blunted sense." [31]

Pan's hymn is addressed not merely to the judge, Tmolus, but also to Apollo, his rival. In fact, it is something of a reply to the other hymn.

> I am the eye with which the Universe
> Beholds itself, and knows itself divine,
> All harmony of instrument or verse,
> All prophecy, all medicine are mine,
> All light of Art or Nature,

sings Apollo. It is a sweeping claim, and old Tmolus is duly impressed. But Apollo does not shine in lonely, unapproachable eminence. He has to compete with Pan, and, although a hill-god like Tmolus may prefer him, a deluded mortal like Midas may prefer Pan. In reading the *Hymn of Pan,* we must recognize in the background some such dialectic between the bright spiritual light of Apollo and the lush, sweet world of forests and fauns and dewy caves and moist river-lawns and shadowy mountains which surrounds the pipings of Pan. And the rapid, darting movement of the *Hymn of Pan* gains if we hear it against the equally light but nevertheless firm and solemn movement of the *Hymn of Apollo.* We need to relate the pipe and the lyre.

No poem of Shelley's shows a subtler control of rhythmic variation than the *Hymn of Pan.* Indeed, no poem I know surpasses it in the handling of that most difficult of all rhythms for an English poet, the anapestic. The loss of final "e" in late Middle English administered a sedative to English verse which, with occasional lapses, has been gradually taking effect ever since. By the time of Keats, rhythm can hardly be said to move at all; the saturation point of spondees has been reached. The modern reader reads Chaucer badly, not because he finds it hard to reverse the Great Vowel Shift, but because he finds it hard to imagine quick verse. Nineteenth-century poets, like Poe and Byron and Tom Moore, sometimes tried to lighten their rhythms by pouring their lines into ready-made anapestic patterns, and their failure spoiled the anapest for later poets. Even the sprung verse and free verse of Hopkins and Whitman did only a little to repair the damage which had been accumulating for centuries. Among the few nineteenth-century poets who successfully counteracted the spondaic tendency belong Coleridge, Byron (in *Don Juan*), Shelley, and Browning.

The metrical principle behind the *Hymn of Pan* is the alternation of anapestic and iambic feet. Or, to be more precise, iambic feet do not normally occur in succession, although anapests often do. Such a pattern noticeably lightens the usual rhythm of English verse, but does not confine it in a strait jacket, as persistent anapests generally seem to do. A line in the *Hymn of Pan* usually contains three feet, but some expansion is liable to occur near the end of a stanza. Run-on lines and decisive caesuras are infrequent.

In such a rhythmic world, a succession of iambic feet or even an initial trochee is a call to attention. One could drop a dozen spondees into a page of the *Idylls of the King* and hardly disturb the surface; a spondee or two in the *Hymn of Pan* or *When the Lamp Is Shattered* could be a major event. We have already observed one unforgettable example from the end of the latter: "When leaves fall and cold winds come." The most significant examples from the *Hymn of Pan* also occur at the end. In the first stanza Shelley is mainly concerned to establish his norm, and he diverges from it with great restraint. He keeps his iambic feet well spaced and brings them together only for a simple effect in the short second line; if accents are juxtaposed, it is only in passing, perhaps to emphasize the attention of old Tmolus or of the noiseless waves.

> From the forests and highlands
>   We come, we come;
> From the river-girt islands
>   Where loud waves are dumb,
>   Listening my sweet pipings;
> The wind in the reeds and the rushes,
>   The bees on the bells of thyme,

> The birds on the myrtle bushes,
>   The cicale above in the lime,
> And the lizards below in the grass,
> Were as silent as ever old Tmolus was
>   Listening my sweet pipings.

The big effects are saved for the last few lines of the poem.

Before looking at the versification beyond the first stanza, we need to consider the plot of Pan's song, what sort of story or argument it presents. Roughly speaking, the poem is a dramatic monologue, an *apologia pro vita sua,* an account of his past success as a musician, aimed (unsuccessfully, as Pan realizes in the course of his performance) at arousing the sympathy of his present listeners. The places he has visited, the audiences he has charmed, the extent of his repertoire, all these are sketched in some profusion. Traditionally a forest and mountain god, he has extended his range to include a lowland world of "river-girt islands" and "moist river-lawns." The inhabitants of this region are as responsive to his songs as old Tmolus (a hill-god) has been in the past. In the second stanza Pan paints a vivid picture of his control over nature and its denizens. "Liquid Peneus" flows faster, and the shadows of night lengthen faster (the listening Apollo could hardly approve!), under the influence of his pipings. The demi-gods of the earth, water, and forest listen to him in "silent love":

> Liquid Peneus was flowing,
>   And all dark Tempe lay
> In Pelion's shadow, outgrowing
>   The light of the dying day
>   Speeded by my sweet pipings.
> The Sileni, and Sylvans, and Fauns
>   And the nymphs of the woods and the waves
> To the edge of the moist river-lawns,
>   And the brink of the dewy caves,
> And all that did then attend and follow
> Were silent with love, as you now, Apollo!
>   With envy of my sweet pipings.

In stanza three Pan appeals to his unresponsive listeners by tracing the progress of his art to its climax in the lyric of disappointment and suffering, which, for Pan, are the fate of men and gods alike.

> I sang of the dancing stars,
>   I sang of the daedal earth—
> And of heaven—and the giant wars—
>   And Love, and death, and birth,
>   And then I changed my pipings
> Singing how down the vale of Menalus,
>   I pursued a maiden and clasped a reed,
> Gods and men, we are all deluded thus!
>   It breaks in our bosom and then we bleed!
> All wept, as I think both ye now would
> If envy or age had not frozen your blood,
>   At the sorrow of my sweet pipings.

But his present audience fails to respond. Both Apollo and Tmolus hear Pan's outcry with dry eyes. The silence of Apollo is the silence of envy not love (as Pan has already claimed at the end of stanza two), and the silence of old Tmolus is now revealed as the insensitivity of old age. So the poem ends with Pan singing his sweetest songs that tell of saddest thought to an audience which he regards as too prejudiced or insensitive to respond. The Apollo of the *Hymn of Apollo* would be, of course, incapable of envying the *Hymn of Pan,* but he would be equally incapable of appreciating it. The lyre of Apollo is only the mutable instrument of an otherworldly wisdom; the pipe of Pan is the very substance of human disappointment and transformation.

The force of the climactic (and anticlimactic) third stanza is intensified by the skill of Shelley's versification. We recall that in stanza one a number of effective variations from the norm (such as successive iambic feet, the spondee, the emphatic caesura) were held back for later use. Stanza two is also comparatively restrained, although lines two to four show significant irregularities. Most significant is the versification of line eleven, where Pan addresses Apollo directly: "Were silent with love, as you now Apollo!" The direct address and the new emphasis on the present are pointed up by the caesura and the conjunction of accents in "you now."

The restraint of stanzas one and two is rewarded in stanza three, particularly after the structural shift in line five. In the early part of the stanza Pan outlines the range of his art. It includes poetry of nature (praising the vitality and intricacy of creation); poetry of supernature (about "heaven," whatever that may involve in this context—perhaps Shelley means hymns and dithyrambs); mythological narrative (about the wars of the Titans and the Olympians); and philosophical poetry (about the recurrent fundamentals of human existence, whose cyclical repetition is underlined by a striking change to a line of three successive iambic feet: "And Love, and Death, and Birth"). Normally the next line would bring the first part of the stanza to an end with a version of the refrain. But Pan's fifth and last genre is a new departure into the lyric of personal suffering. Shelley has the brilliant idea of making Pan's sudden change seem more radical by ending the first part in line four and turning the refrain line into the first line of the new part. And whereas stanzas one and two broke up clearly into two parts of one sentence each, this second part of stanza three is chopped up into a number of separate sentences. The continuity of the earlier stanzas is lost.

In the lines

> Gods and men, we are all deluded thus!
> It breaks in our bosom and then we bleed,

the *Hymn of Pan* reaches its moment of greatest impact. I can think of no lyric in which such a moment is achieved with more economy and coordination of means. A technical critic can only inadequately point to the initial strong accent (here created simply by omitting the weak accent which normally precedes it), the caesura after "men," the reduction of anapests to one in the line, and the expansion from trimeter to pentameter; the following line shows the same iambic concentration combined with a powerful alliteration.

Shelley still has some surprises to offer. Line ten begins with a spondee followed by a caesura, and the line as a whole is rigid with accents stronger than the reader anticipates.

> All wept, as I think both ye now would
> If envy or age had not frozen your blood,
> At the sorrow of my sweet pipings.

But in the last two lines the anapestic rhythm reasserts itself and takes control. The poem ends with a burst of speed and a return to normal, which submerge the "sorrow" beneath the "sweet pipings."

We need not look for such sorrow and liveliness, such a dramatic rise and fall of tension, in an Apollonian hymn. Nor would Apollo move from scene to scene, audience to audience, genre to genre. Apollo follows a prearranged cyclical pattern, like the sun-god he is, although he regrets the necessity of even that concession to time, preferring to remain at noon forever, rather than descend "into the clouds of the Atlantic even." Nor would Apollo ever fall upon the thorns of life and make sweet songs out of his own pain and delusion. He may describe his own activity, to be sure, but with a confident impersonality.

> Whatever lamps on Earth or Heaven may shine
> Are portions of one power, which is mine.
>
> I stand at noon upon the peak of heaven,
>   Then with unwilling steps I wander down
> Into the clouds of the Atlantic even—
>   For grief that I depart they weep & frown;
> What look is more delightful than the smile
> With which I soothe them from the western isle?
>
> I am the eye with which the Universe
>   Beholds itself and knows itself divine.
> All harmony of instrument or verse,

> All prophecy, all medicine is mine;
> All light of art or nature;—to my song
> Victory and praise, in its own right, belong.

There could be no split between this singer and his audience, or, if there were, he would not be aware of it. He knows that his song deserves the victory "in its own right."

The argument in the lyrics we have been examining is characterized by a sort of dialectic without synthesis. Passion and tenderness, spirit and heart, Pan and Apollo, meet but do not cooperate. The very slight, but very charming, lyric, *The Keen Stars Were Twinkling,* seems to attempt something of a synthesis.

> The keen stars were twinkling,
> And the fair moon was rising among them,
>   Dear Jane.
> The guitar was tinkling,
> But the notes were not sweet till you sung them
>   Again.
>
> As the moon's soft splendor
> O'er the faint cold starlight of heaven
>   Is thrown,
> So your voice most tender
> To the strings without soul had then given
>   Its own.
>
> The stars will awaken,
> Though the moon sleep a full hour later
>   To-night;
> No leaf will be shaken
> Whilst the dews of your melody scatter
>   Delight.
>
> Though the sound overpowers,
> Sing again, with your dear voice revealing
>   A tone
> Of some world far from ours,
> Where music and moonlight and feeling
>   Are one.

Two pairs and the inner relations of each dominate the first two stanzas: one is stars and moon, the other guitar and voice. In the first stanza, stars and moon are juxtaposed, but no significant relation is yet established, such as we already observe between guitar and voice. The second stanza establishes a parallel relation. The moon's splendor covers "the faint cold starlight," as the tender voice gives its soul to the soulless tinkling of the guitar. The harmonious duet of stars and moon is repeated in that of guitar and voice. In each pair, one is cold, sparkling, and soulless, and the other is soft, radiant, and soulful.

Such schematic simplicity is lost in the second half of the poem. The moon rises late, and the melody sounds by starlight in a leafy stillness. The tinkling guitar has faded into the background, and the poet is entranced only by the voice of the soul. That voice reveals the oneness of music and moonlight and feeling, but such oneness is no hardly achieved union of opposites, like the "still unravished bride" of Keats. Moreover, it is revealed only as existing in a "world far from ours." At the end of the poem, the soul does not enter the soulless and harmonize with it, it overpowers us with a revelation of a world whose oneness is both simple and far away. "Sing again," says the poet in the last stanza, returning to the word which concluded the first. Before, however, the voice had repeated and completed the music of the guitar; now it is just repeating itself.

To stress the metaphysical framework of such a poem, whose chief claim to our affection is its capricious but subtly moulded rhythm, is no doubt to break a butterfly upon a wheel. But it is worth observing that Shelley's world is a world neither of synthesis nor of paradox. The conflicting parts do not fuse. When he mixes two notes together, he gets neither a third term nor a star, but simply an unstable mixture. Whatever oneness is asserted seems both unearned and outside.

What I have been saying might be repeated with the substitution of "aesthetic" for "metaphysical." As Fogle remarks in another

connection, Shelley's poetry is mechanical rather than organic.[32]
His poems are not whole poems, because oneness must necessarily
be outside them. Shelley the critic does not always admit that "the
mind in creation is as a fading coal" or stress "the limitedness of
the poetic faculty" (C.294). A poet under fire must defend poetry.
But what the critic may hesitate to admit, his poems may admit or
demonstate. They are compromises, looking before and after, not
aesthetic wholes. His poems may mean: I doubt if they can be said
to be. Perhaps, indeed, they have better things to do than assert
their aesthetic wholeness. They are potential poetry; the acorns that
contain all oaks prophetically, "pregnant with the lightning that
has yet found no conductor" (C.291).

I

LYRICAL DRAMA

When Shelley called *Prometheus Unbound* a "lyrical drama," he may well have been doing no more than drawing attention to its many outbursts of song, its solos, duets, and choruses. From Shelley's point of view, what was lyrical about *Prometheus Unbound* (or *Hellas,* to which he applied the same term) was perhaps the fact that much of it could be sung or imagined as sung, and what was dramatic the fact that the story was presented as if for the stage, without direct narration, description, or comment, except in the form of brief stage directions. At any rate, if he did restrict his consideration of the term to lyrical and dramatic media rather than lyrical and dramatic forms or subjects, he would have found no obvious paradox in such a subtitle. After all, the Greeks had mixed their drama and song without finding themselves on the horns of a dilemma, and Shelley himself had frequently seen a more thorough mixture in the Italian opera.

But it is perhaps unfair to limit the range of Shelley's reference; it is certainly unfair to limit our own. For our use of the terms "drama" and "lyric" ordinarily does involve some distinctions of form and subject. Certainly this is true when we use the adjectives "dramatic" and "lyrical" to define the quality of something. *Tamburlaine* and *The Deserted Village* are often called "lyrical," but not in the limited, technical sense we have been considering. Similarly, the word "dramatic" is often used quite intelligibly where the question of stage performance does not arise at all. Lyrics (at least, as the tradition descends to us from the second half of the nineteenth century) are generally assumed to be personal, sincere, spontaneous, emotional, intense, brief, simple, unified, and relatively static. Dramas have action, variety of situation and character (including striking developments or reversals and conflicts within characters or between characters), impersonality, and artifice. Things happen in the drama, and they do not necessarily happen in the soul of the author. Very little happens in a lyric; a mood or state of soul is expressed, just as the author himself feels it. Such is a *reductio,* not quite *ad absurdum,* of our casual assumptions about lyric and drama.

If we restrict ourselves to the formal side of these popular distinctions, it appears that lyrics are static and dramas are dynamic. Dramas keep moving from one place to another; lyrics turn round and round, examining the same spot. Characters and situations are modified or changed in the one, revealed or intensified in the other. The one *can* be long, the other *must* be short. (Poe's view of poetry was lyrical, and therefore he denied the possibility of a long poem.) Presumably pure lyric or pure drama is formally impossible ("How can we know the dancer from the dance?"), but as a pair of dialectical opposites, or convenient poles of reference, lyric and drama are useful terms, provided that they do not swallow up everything else, and provided that we drop them as soon as they have served their purpose. Their purpose here is to suggest, first, that *Prometheus Unbound* can be called "lyrical" not merely because it is songful, but because it has assimilated about as much formal lyricism as a work of its size can, and, second, that it belongs to a genre which has a number of representatives in the literature of the world, a genre for which the title "lyrical drama" is as appropriate as any.

If we first examine some of the structural features which critics have observed in *Prometheus Unbound* and which they regard as undramatic, we can then decide to what extent they are attributable to an aim which is lyrical rather than dramatic. There is, we are sometimes told, no real conflict at the climax of the play, when

Jupiter is overthrown. His downfall, which follows almost inevitably from Prometheus' behavior in Act One, is flat and automatic. Indeed, the hero, Prometheus himself, shows no inner conflict, nor does he modify or change himself during the course of
the play. He is saved by an act of will in the course of his first
speech, where the happy outcome of the play is assured. How, we
are asked, can you have a drama which, in so far as it is dramatic,
has ended by line fifty-three? The rest of the play is a long anticlimax with nothing in doubt, no tension, no resolution, no real
action—in effect, no play.

This criticism, basically quite sound, can be reduced to one apparently damaging fact: *Prometheus Unbound* is static; its only
dramatic act occurs in Prometheus' opening speech. The drama,
per se, is over before it has begun. The rest of the play, if not an
anticlimax, is, at least, something of a foregone conclusion. But if
we see *Prometheus Unbound* not as aiming at, and failing to reach,
the dramatic structure of an *Oedipus Tyrannus* or a *King Lear,* but
as belonging to a different and more specialized genre, then to
complain about these things will seem more irrelevant than damaging.

Dr. Johnson would have found no difficulty in defining the form
of *Prometheus Unbound,* although it is unlikely that he would have
approved. It has a middle, but no beginning, and, indeed, no recognizable end either. The end is continuously waiting off-stage; its
entrance is heralded by an act and a half of peroration (perhaps
the most persistent series of full closes outside of Beethoven), but,
in fact, the play seems to come to a stop, rather than to a dramatic
end. A pure lyric, one supposes, would be all middle; it could have
no real beginning and no end; it would just start and stop arbi-
trarily, like certain of Swinburne's lyrics, in which a shuffling about
or elimination of some stanzas would damage the form of the
work very little. In music the greatest examples of the relatively
pure lyric on a large scale are to be found in certain slow move-
ments by Beethoven (for example, the *larghetto* of the *Violin Con-*

certo), whose static nature makes it impossible to end them, and which, as Tovey has observed, have to be broken into abruptly to prevent them from going on forever.[1] Demogorgon has to stop the exultation at the end of *Prometheus Unbound;* without his descent from the machine, it is hard to see by what device the revels could have been cut off.

The problems of writing a drama so saturated with lyricism are many. How is the author to prevent his unbalanced, oversized, so-called drama from simply collapsing in an amorphous heap? Fortunately for the critic, although *Prometheus Unbound* is an extreme case, the problem is by no means unique. Other writers, in attempting something similar, shed a good deal of light on Shelley's achievement.

The most obvious place to look for analogies is in Greek drama, and, more particularly, the work which Shelley uses as a starting point: Aeschylus' *Prometheus Bound,* which, like Shelley's sequel, has often been regarded as conspicuously undramatic. When the play opens, Prometheus is being bound to the Caucasian mountains, and he is soon presented as the defiant opponent of the vindictive Zeus. When the play ends, the two are still in the same relationship. The middle of the play simply deepens, elaborates, and intensifies our awareness of the positions of Prometheus and Zeus. For example, the prudent advice of Oceanus inspires Prometheus to state his opposition to Zeus more strongly and in greater detail than before; the narrative of Io allows us to see more clearly than before just what sort of enemy Prometheus is up against. In the scene with Hermes, Prometheus' defiance reaches its climax, and Zeus imposes new torments at the end of the play. Also, scene by scene, in addition to the causes of his plight, we learn more and more of the grounds for his hopes: his secret and the deliverance which lies in the future. We may, therefore, agree with Kitto that

the solitary hero is everything; not what he does, but what he feels and is. Of action, between the prologue and the catastrophe, there is none. Prometheus' narratives, though they may give the illusion of action, were not designed for this. It is a drama of revelation, not action; of increasing tension in a situation which does not move.[2]

In other words, *Prometheus Bound* is a lyrical drama of the sort we have been trying to define.

Prometheus Bound is, of course, an extreme case of a tendency that is present in Greek drama as a whole. By restricting itself to a short period of crisis, Greek drama puts the gradual transformation of a Macbeth or the regeneration of a Lear outside its range of possibility. Even so, the moral education of Neoptolemus in *Philoctetes* shows how far Sophocles could go in a dynamic conception of character. And even when characters do not change or develop, they often make new and significant decisions or reveal further facets of their character under the pressure of new situations, as do Philoctetes, Ajax, Oedipus (in the *Tyrannus*) or Eteocles (in the *Septem*).

The play of Sophocles to which the term "lyrical drama" would be most appropriate is *Oedipus at Colonus*. Oedipus knows what he wants from the beginning and has reached the end of his journey. Upon arriving in the grove of the Eumenides, he announces: "nevermore will I depart from my rest in this land."[3] S. M. Adams summarizes the situation at the end of the prologue as follows:

So, as the prologos ends, we know, in general terms, what Apollo's oracle decreed; and we know what Oedipus has in mind. Chastened in spirit, made by his sufferings into a kind of "holy man," he is determined to follow the oracle of the god whose oracles he once sought to circumvent: *he means to make this oracle come true.* He must not leave his "station" in this land. He has been divinely guided to it; he must be on guard against any and all attempts to make him leave it; and Caution, based on knowledge, shall be his watchword.[4]

This old Oedipus is as clear-eyed and knowing as the young one was blind and ignorant. He accomplishes with complete awareness and willingness the end designed for him and is not to be swayed from his purpose. At the end of the play he reaps the reward for his steadfastness. He does not discover his purpose as the play progresses, nor does he grow in wisdom and virtue, although he does increase in vigor and authority under the stimulus of opposition. By resisting successfully the opposition offered by the Chorus, Creon, and Polynices, he merely reveals to us in practice the character which he has already become.

It is noticeable in the two plays we have examined that what follows the presentation of the opening position is in the main a series of temptations which consolidate the central figure in his resolve. Something of an archetype for this sort of dramatic structure would be the account of Christ's temptation in the wilderness in the gospels of Matthew and Luke. As in *Oedipus at Colonus*, the temptations are preceded by a prologue in which the central character takes up a stance or assumes his basic role. Christ is baptized and comes to full manhood and Godhead. In what follows Satan attempts to dislodge Him from this position by a series of temptations.

This episode might loosely be termed dramatic. It involves the conflict of two wills, Christ's and Satan's. One obviously undramatic feature, however, is that we are never given any cause to doubt the outcome; there is no depiction of a spiritual struggle within Christ, and He is not observed to change or develop by means of the conflict. The series of temptations, increasing in significance and preceded by the baptism, simply reveals to us more clearly what He is. When Milton makes the episode the basis of *Paradise Regained,* his Christ remains fundamentally a lyrical character, but Milton does create at least the illusion of drama in two different ways. First, he underplays the maturity of Jesus, about whom in Book One there is something remarkably boyish and tentative, after as well as before the baptism. Second, the dramatic development which he cannot give to Christ he transfers to Satan's awareness of Christ. Satan struggles against the unwelcome recognition, which finally is unavoidable, of the identity and historical role of his opponent.

Much more relevant to our discussion, however, is *Samson*

Agonistes. Since the two Greek dramas which seem to have influenced Milton most in *Samson* are *Prometheus Bound* and *Oedipus at Colonus,* we might well expect *Samson* to be in some degree a lyrical drama. But whereas Milton did not directly dramatize Christ, he does dramatize Samson, and we are likely to be struck by the extent to which Milton has not allowed the form of Greek tragedy to preclude drama of character. *Samson* approaches the genre of the lyrical drama but remains well outside it.

As in *Prometheus Bound, Oedipus at Colonus,* and *Paradise Regained,* the central scenes of *Samson Agonistes* are a series of temptations, out of which Samson emerges, fully revealed and prepared for what lies ahead of him. But Samson is not merely revealed, he is radically changed, and the Samson of the end of the play differs widely from the Samson of the beginning, although only a few hours have passed. This is to some extent made possible by the special situation in which Samson finds himself. It is a Philistine holiday, he is released from work, and at last he can collect himself and sort out the

> restless thoughts, that like a deadly swarm
> Of Hornets arm'd, no sooner found alone,
> But rush upon me thronging, and present
> Times past, what once I was, and what am now.

He is enabled to sort them out and advance beyond them by means of his encounters with Manoa, Dalila, and Harapha, which, although they do not always advance Samson straightforward on all fronts at once, do show him gradually conquering his pride, his disobedience, and his despair.

But Milton does not abandon the lyrical drama altogether. For Samson's first soliloquy does contain, explicitly or implicitly, literally or figuratively, what Samson is ultimately to discover. "Whom have I to complain of but myself?" he asks, and soon goes on to state, "I must not quarrel with the will / Of highest dispensation." Even his loss of despair and his new confidence in the possibility of again becoming an instrument of God are suggested, although not literally, by Samson's address to his guide: "A little onward lend thy guiding hand," and by his reaction to the spring air:

> but here I feel amends,
> The breath of Heaven fresh-blowing, pure and sweet,
> With day-spring born.

Among Shakespeare's plays, some interesting resemblances to the lyrical drama are found in *Henry IV,* whether we consider the two parts as independent or continuous. In *Part One* the plot, in so far as it concerns Prince Hal's character, is fundamentally static. It is a morality play without a moral struggle, as Tillyard recognizes.[5] Prince Hal's soliloquy at the end of his first scene with Falstaff has something of the function of Prometheus' at the beginning of *Prometheus Unbound.*[6] It tells us that Hal is already saved. The act of will has already been made, and the regeneration which ultimately follows will, despite superficial appearances, simply be the revelation of a *fait accompli.* At no time is there any serious doubt in Hal's mind about what he ought to do and about the fact that he will do it. Hal's chivalry at Shrewsbury and, for that matter, his rejection of Falstaff in *Part Two* are almost as preordained and undramatic as the downfall of Jupiter.

Shakespeare experiments with the lyrical drama most interestingly in *The Tempest,* whose structure and theme are both relevant to *Prometheus Unbound.* The dramatic center of the plot is Prospero's conversion, his discovery that "virtue" is preferable to "vengeance." Like Prometheus, Prospero has been exiled by an ally who betrayed his trust, and he has had many years to meditate revenge. When the play begins, the opportunity which he must make the best of has arrived. He tries to show his enemies the error of their ways, he repairs some of the original damage by the betrothal of Ferdinand and Miranda, and then he forgives the "three men of sin," two of whom have shown no signs of repentance at all, although they have been illuminated in more than one way.

But when did Prospero decide on virtue rather than vengeance? Throughout the play he is obviously working under an emotional strain, which breaks out when his will is crossed. The projected usurpation by Caliban, Stephano, and Trinculo touches a very sore spot indeed, and, when suddenly reminded of it, he needs to retire and calm his "beating mind." But in none of Prospero's outbursts does he suggest that he is still planning to execute bloody revenge on his opponents. When he tells Ariel that he plans to forgive them (the statement is made in response to Ariel's non-human sympathy), we are not shown any internal crisis which is now being resolved. In fact, we must assume that Prospero has made his decision long ago, certainly before the play begins. Whatever tempest there may have been in Prospero's mind is over when we first meet him. The scars remain, and memory may touch them, but Prospero's moral drama is over. *The Tempest* treats it in retrospect and in its consequences—lyrically more than dramatically.

It would be possible to examine a number of other works which have something in common with the genre of the lyrical drama, such as *Murder in the Cathedral, Faust,*[7] and even the Book of Job (the symposium section of which is dramatic in surface technique but lyrical in structure and characterization), but it is better to return from *The Tempest* to *Prometheus Unbound*. We have observed in different contexts one of the structural methods appropriate to a lyrical drama in which the dramatic action, in so far as it concerns the moral identity of the central figure, is over at or near the beginning of the play. Although the main character does take up his final position early in the play, we can observe him consolidating that position under the attacks of a series of tempters. By this means we can be shown all the difficulties that his position involves and come to grips with the total meaning of the decision that has already been made. According to Mrs. Shelley, "Shelley believed that mankind had only to will that there should be no evil, and there would be none" (J.II.269). The temptations by Mercury and the Furies show how much is involved in that "only" and what obstacles stand in the way of Prometheus' act of will.

But the temptation by the Furies is over before the end of Act

One, and there are four acts to Shelley's drama. The structure we have been describing, a decision followed by a series of temptations which increase in both intensity and significance, is that of only Act One. The rest of the play does, of course, stem from Prometheus' initial decision and can be said, like Act One, to explore the significance of that decision, but it does so in a different way.

For there are two main ways in which such a lyrical structure can be sustained. They overlap to some extent but can be discussed separately. One way concentrates as closely as possible on the act itself and what is involved in the committing of it. The second moves beyond the act itself and depicts the consequences that follow from it. In *The Tempest,* although Prospero is tempted, his temptations are not a significant part of the action. The play depicts the consequences of Prospero's moral regeneration, although that regeneration is not revealed to us unequivocally until Act Five. Other works to which I would attribute something of this structure are Hardy's *The Mayor of Casterbridge* and *Tess of the D'Urbervilles, Tamburlaine Part One,* and *Henry V.*

Both in Hardy and in Shelley we need to be aware of the connection between the significant act and the series of consequences. In *Prometheus Unbound* the consequences of Prometheus' act of will start to operate only in Act Three. Act Two is concerned with establishing the link between cause and effect. Shelley, as a student of Hume, knew how mysterious and perhaps inexplicable was the nature of causality,[8] and, although he would not have accepted the Christian doctrine of grace, he knew that some sort of power was needed to make the will effective. "Between the conception and the creation . . . falls the Shadow." Asia's journey to the cave of Demogorgon is Shelley's attempt to make something of this darkness visible, despite the fact that "the deep truth is imageless" (II.iv. 116).

The consequences depicted in Acts Three and Four are somewhat heterogeneous. This is mainly because Shelley has to wind up the story of Prometheus as well as usher in the millennium. Jupiter falls; Prometheus is released by Hercules and reunited to Asia; then Prometheus and Asia retire to the grove at Colonus and he continues his activities as a culture hero, devising scientific and artistic gifts for mankind. Mankind itself, however, is depicted enjoying the millennium that would be possible for it if men were to duplicate the act of Prometheus. The millennium is followed (or continued, should one say,) by the Promethean age, the ecstatic celebrations of which are only interrupted by the reappearance of Demogorgon, who brings the play to a stop.

From this outline of *Prometheus Unbound* as a lyrical drama in which an act of decision is first consolidated and then produces far-reaching consequences, the main points of attack for the structural critic should be apparent. But my account of *Prometheus Unbound* will not be concerned simply with the elements that compose its lyrico-dramatic structure. *Prometheus Unbound* stands at the entrance to Shelley's later poetry. It shows us the components of that poetry and, by their unstable relation to one another, indicates the direction in which Shelley is moving. To a modern reader (fortunately gifted with hindsight) the poem's arc is an earnest of the completed shape of things to come.

Such a statement assumes a recognizable process of change in Shelley's Italian poetry. It does not, however, assume an exactly parallel development in Shelley's prose or in his day-to-day opinions. These may be used, with caution, to substantiate the existence of some component in his poetic universe, but not to discover its place in that universe or in a particular poem. In fact, Shelley's view of poetry assumes some discontinuity between poetic beliefs and prose beliefs, and he is quite capable of treating the same matter with skepticism in his prose and credulity in his poetry.[9]

According to D. L. Clark, who is mainly concerned with the prose, "Shelley's mind grew; but it grew in breadth and in depth, and not by radical change from one position to another."[10] But critics have generally argued for something more than the mere expansion from a constant center. Those who do assume a significant change have, depending on their degree of perception or area of interest, described it as proceeding from materialism to idealism, from Godwin to Plato, from Necessity to the One, from atheism to Christianity, from Milton to Dante, or in some other more or less plausible direction. My terms will be radicalism and Platonism.

But the terms themselves are a good deal less important than the meaning that an examination of Shelley's poetry can give them. Most of that examination is still ahead, and no more than a few pointers are appropriate now. The radical world is, roughly speaking, the world of the *philosophes* (adulterated, to some extent, by a Christian emphasis on the will). It is empirical in its epistemology and centers upon the egoism-altruism opposition in its ethics. Its historical goal is the Earthly Paradise, its means the regeneration of the will. The Platonic world is (again roughly speaking and with an awareness of the misunderstanding, vulgarizing, and even biblicizing of Plato involved [11]) Plato's world of discontinuity and rivalry between the One and the Many and between the Form and the Image (without too much Christian and Renaissance blurring of the opposition). It is otherworldly in its epistemology and negative in its view of evil. Its (nonhistorical) goal is the City of God or "the burning fountain," its means Death and the ultimate Apocalypse.

But poetic worlds are made up of physical even more than metaphysical materials. The radical or the Platonic world has its images, its figures, its key words. The vision of any artist has its characteristic focus, its kind of selectivity; and an account of a poet's direction in a poem or group of poems must point out the topography of the journey and the peculiar limits of the poet's eyesight. The chapter on "Shelley's Italian Imagery" is intended as a preliminary investigation of this area, which will only later be absorbed into the mainstream of my argument.

In a sense, my whole argument is the argument of *Prometheus Unbound,* writ large and extended beyond the last act. Indeed, the same might be said of the structure of Shelley's whole poetic life from 1818 to the end. For that reason I have chosen *Prometheus*

Unbound as the center from which to approach the other poems of this final, Italian period. If, in what follows, *Prometheus* should sometimes appear to be left behind for an unconscionably long time, it is hoped that this "breach" may ultimately be seen as an "expansion," when the wanderings of the argument have at last seen fit to "hearken home."

II

THE REGENERATION OF PROMETHEUS

Although Mrs. Shelley cannot be regarded as an ideal interpreter of her husband's works (her special favorite seems to have been *Rosalind and Helen*), she is surely right in her note on *Prometheus Unbound* in attributing to the Shelley of that poem a belief in the ability of the human will to expel evil. Her statement "mankind had only to will that there should be no evil, and there would be none" (J.II.269), does, of course, in its naïve and casual use of "only," suffer if we compare it with Demogorgon's statement of what is involved in such willing:

> To suffer woes which hope thinks infinite;
> To forgive wrongs darker than death or night;
> To defy Power, which seems omnipotent;
> To love, and bear; to hope till Hope creates
> From its own wreck the thing it contemplates. (IV.570–74)

Nevertheless, fundamentally Mrs. Shelley is right about Shelley's belief, for, despite his awareness of the almost superhuman difficulties to be met and his increasing pessimism about the likelihood of mankind's actually meeting them, he did believe that man was capable of successfully willing "that there should be no evil," and he disapproved strongly of those who dismissed the problem of evil by calling it "inevitable," although he recognized that evil was overpowering enough to excuse such a belief. For Shelley the "world's wrong" was "not destiny but man's own wilful ill."[1] He was in a position similar (with some important differences stemming from the doctrine of grace) to that of the Christian who insists on the validity of the injunction "be thou perfect" but at the same time admits that "there is no health in us"; who sees man both as depraved and as made in the image of God. Shelley insisted on the possibility of the regeneration of the human will and at the same time recognized the almost insurmountable obstacles in the way of such regeneration. This view is something of a paradox, but it is neither naïvely optimistic nor naïvely pessimistic. Shelley is stating a situation but not solving a problem. In the chorus "Worlds on worlds" in *Hellas,* Shelley envisions a "progressive state" of what he calls in his notes "more or less exalted existence, according to the degree of perfection which every distinct intelligence may have attained." But he continues his note by insisting:

> Let it not be supposed that I mean to dogmatize upon a subject, concerning which all men are equally ignorant, or that I think the Gordian knot of the origin of evil can be disentangled by that or any similar assertions.   (C.333)

Asia and Demogorgon reach a similarly undogmatic conclusion in Act Two of *Prometheus Unbound.* Despite the schematic and somewhat melodramatic nature of the myths or plots in which Shelley developed his religious and moral concepts, he remains, to a considerable extent, tentative and even skeptical in his thinking about ultimate problems, the problem of immortality as well as the problem of evil.

But, although the Gordian knot might have to remain tied, Shelley did assume (parting company, apparently, with both Godwin and Plato [2]) that the key to the problem lay in the will rather than the intellect. "It is our will / That thus enchains us to permitted ill," says Julian in *Julian and Maddalo,*

> "We might be otherwise; we might be all
> We dream of happy, high, majestical.
> Where is the love, beauty and truth we seek,
> But in our mind? and if we were not weak,
> Should we be less in deed than in desire?"   (170–76)

As Cythna said a year or so before, in canto eight of *The Revolt of Islam*:

> High temples fade like vapour— Man alone
> Remains, whose will has power when all beside is gone.   (xvi)

Whereupon Maddalo interrupts his friend contemptuously and tries to puncture his argument:

> "Ay, if we were not weak—and we aspire
> How vainly to be strong!" said Maddalo;
> "You talk Utopia." "It remains to know,"
> I then rejoined, "and those who try may find
> How strong the chains are which our spirit bind;
> Brittle perchance as straw. We are assured
> Much may be conquered, much may be endured
> Of what degrades and crushes us. We know
> That we have power over ourselves to do
> And suffer—what we know not till we try;
> But something nobler than to live and die."   (177–87)

Maddalo admits that theoretically Julian may be able to present a good case. Practically, however, such aspiring Utopianism is no more than a vain and destructive illusion. The exemplum which follows (the visit to the cell of the idealistic madman, and his morbid narrative) is intended to clarify the argument between the two friends and perhaps decide in favor of one of them. But it is an ambiguous and badly told tale, and the moral is never explicitly drawn. There is no doubt, however, that the stand taken by Julian in the argument with Maddalo would have been accepted by the Shelley of *Prometheus Unbound,* the first act of which he wrote during the same period as the debate between the two friends. "O'er all things but thyself I gave thee power, / And my own will," said Prometheus to Jupiter in the curse which is recalled in Act One; and at the end of Act Three the Spirit of the Hour, after describing the millennium, tells us that man's guilt and pain "were, for his will made or suffered them" (III.iv.199).

I have already assumed that Prometheus wills during the first speech of the play the decision which regenerates him. But the question "when does Prometheus make the decision on which the whole play rests?" is important enough to require further scrutiny. The crucial passage in Prometheus' opening speech occurs between lines 47 and 59. Before these lines Shelley has been establishing the relation of the two main characters (Prometheus and Jupiter), the scenic background of the action, and the torments which Prometheus (and mankind as well) suffers at the hands of Jupiter. Beginning at line 47, however, Prometheus starts to look forward to the downfall of Jupiter and anticipate the pleasures of revenge which that downfall will give him. Suddenly he pulls himself short and repudiates what has just been passing through his mind. The moment of conversion occurs in line 53 and is then elaborated on:

> The crawling glaciers pierce me with the spears
> Of their moon-freezing crystals; the bright chains
> Eat with their burning cold into my bones.
> Heaven's winged hound, polluting from thy lips
> His beak in poison not his own, tears up
> My heart; and shapeless sights come wandering by,
> The ghastly people of the realm of dream,
> Mocking me; and the Earthquake-fiends are charged
> To wrench the rivets from my quivering wounds
> When the rocks split and close again behind;
> While from their loud abysses howling throng
> The genii of the storm, urging the rage
> Of whirlwind, and afflict me with keen hail.
> And yet to me welcome is day and night,
> Whether one breaks the hoar-frost of the morn,
> Or starry, dim, and slow, the other climbs
> The leaden-coloured east; for then they lead
> The wingless, crawling hours, one among whom—
> As some dark Priest hales the reluctant victim—
> Shall drag thee, cruel King, to kiss the blood
> From these pale feet, which then might trample thee
> If they disdained not such a prostrate slave.
> Disdain! Ah, no! I pity thee. What ruin
> Will hunt thee undefended through the wide Heaven!

How will thy soul, cloven to its depth with terror,
Gape like a hell within! I speak in grief,
Not exultation, for I hate no more,
As then ere misery made me wise. The curse
Once breathed on thee I would recall. (I.31–59)

Such moments of conversion are not plausible to most modern readers, and critics of Shakespeare and Milton are fond of explaining them away so as to satisfy their taste for continuity and growth. Carlos Baker, one of the best of Shelley's recent critics, sees in line 53 a recovery by Prometheus after a momentary lapse, rather than the crucial moment of conversion:

The very suddenness of the recantation, as if he had momentarily forgotten himself into the past and given way once more to a pride intellectually but not emotionally abjured, serves to emphasize the comparative recency of conversion.[3]

Baker's contention (for which the evidence is the "suddenness" of the change and perhaps the "then" of line 58) means that the regeneration of Prometheus has occurred before the play begins, and that all the opening speech gives us is just an echo of it after a brief lapse. I find this unlikely. The moment of regeneration has, of course, been imminent for some time. Misery has made Prometheus wise and has undermined the possibility of hate. Hate, nevertheless, still survives at the beginning of the play. The time is just after midnight on the crucial day, which must surely be the day not merely of Jupiter's fall but of Prometheus' regeneration as well. Baker seems to have been put off by the modern distaste for momentary falls and recoveries, and therefore distributes the regeneration between two impulses: a final one now, and a temporary or partial one (perhaps more than one) before the play begins. As J. V. Cunningham remarks in a discussion of Shakespeare:

The restriction of the process to a point of time and a single scene contributes to the feeling of implausibility. Our natural tendency, as can be seen in the novel, is to consider the process of choice as distributed through a number of scenes and as in large measure unconscious. We

tend to find the condensed incredible and the diffused plausible. . . .
[But the Middle Ages and Renaissance] believed firmly in sin and repentance, each of which takes place in a point of time. . . . Man's destiny
hung on each decisive act. . . . It is clear, then, that the restriction of
the process of choice in Elizabethan drama to a single scene is not the
result merely of foreshortening and condensation for dramatic purposes,
but is a result of the Elizabethan view of the moral life.[4]

When, in Canto Five of the *Inferno,* Francesca tells the story of
her fatal act of will, she does not describe the gradual process by
which one may accept the fact of love. The scene is set; the two read
of Lancelot; although they blush several times when their eyes
meet, they are without any suspicion. "Ma solo un punto fu quel
che di vinse." That one moment is decisive.

This view does not, of course, die out with the seventeenth century: indeed it is given a new lease on life by the Evangelical move-
ments of the eighteenth and nineteenth centuries, and still exists
in the consciously traditional poetry of today:

> The awful daring of a moment's surrender
> Which an age of prudence can never retract
> By this, and this only, we have existed.[5]

But it is perhaps just to say that from Milton to Browning and
Henry James the idea of instantaneous conversions and momentary
decisions gains much of its special interest from the tension between
it and the idea of growth or continuity. In *The Rime of the Ancient
Mariner,* for example, there is no problem about the Mariner's initial act of sin—not if we, like the Elizabethans discussed by Cunningham, accept the possibility of a willful act of evil, inexplicable
simply in terms of its antecedents, like Lord Jim's decision to
jump overboard or Wordsworth's sudden fit of despair in *Resolution and Independence.* But his recovery is another matter. Coleridge
manages to make it seem both instantaneous and gradual. The act
of blessing the water snakes is a decisive one and has immediate
results, although it is "unaware" and even accidental—just as un-
conditioned, therefore, as the shooting of the albatross itself. But

the penance is such a long-drawn-out and unfinished process, and the actual repentance of the Mariner remains so shadowy and un-expressed, that we lose the sense of any final turning point in the Mariner's moral life. In *Prometheus Unbound,* although Prometheus' conversion is instantaneous, we are not allowed to forget that three thousand years of torment lie behind him, that seemingly endless misery ("pain, pain ever, forever") has made him wise, and that the millennium [6] is not likely to appear unheralded.[7]

In a sense the conversion is not sudden at all. The arbitrary act has long been prepared for. The French Revolution was, for Shelley, the classic example of how disastrous an apparently admirable change could be, if the will had not been morally prepared for it. A revolution (as Shelley points out in the Preface to *The Revolt of Islam*) in which slaves become "liberal minded, forbearing, and independent," is not to be achieved automatically by the removal of external fetters:

This is the consequence of the habits of a state of society to be produced by resolute perseverance and indefatigable hope, and long-suffering and long-believing courage, and the systematic efforts of generations of men of intellect and virtue. Such is the lesson which experience teaches now.

(C.316)

The fact that Shelley believes both in instantaneous conversion and in gradual preparation for the millennium need not convict him of gross inconsistency or confusion—not, certainly, without some pretty illustrious companions in guilt. Thinkers a good deal more rigorous than Shelley have believed that moral acts exist out of time in splendid isolation, and, at the same time, have recognized that they exist also in time, in the gradual unfolding of the pattern of history.

More important than when the regeneration of Prometheus occurs is what it consists of. Apart from the obvious fact that he rejects hate, or, more positively, substitutes pity for a desire to be revenged, we learn little from Prometheus' opening speech and have to wait for the temptation scenes before the significance of his decision is elaborated. This matter will, therefore, be discussed in

connection with the latter part of Act One. But before the temptation scenes Shelley does give us some knowledge of an act or process
which is more relevant than any other to Prometheus' regeneration,
but which cannot be presented directly in the play, namely, his
degeneration.

Immediately after the opening soliloquy Shelley faces a familiar
dramatic problem, which his particular plot has made more pressing
than usual. Some plays (*King Lear* and *Macbeth* are the most
striking examples) begin almost literally from scratch. An initial
situation is presented and we move on from there. We are not
meant to speculate on the childhood of Goneril and Regan or the
courtship of the Macbeths. On the other hand, the action of Ibsen's
plays often consists of the gradual revelation of the past, as in
such a *tour de force* as *The Wild Duck*. In Shelley's play the details
of the past are not of great or immediate importance, and we are not
told about most of them until Act Two. But one thing from the
past is of crucial importance: the character of the unregenerate
Prometheus; and this, because of the structure of *Prometheus Unbound*, cannot be easily depicted. A momentary exhibition of cruel
revengefulness in Prometheus' first speech is not enough. If the
opening of the play presents a change of character and revolves about
the contrast between then and now, some method must be found to
show us Prometheus before the moment of conversion as well as
after. Then we can put the new Prometheus beside the old.

Shelley solves this problem by one of the most brilliant inven-
tions in the play: the recall of the curse. Immediately after the
moment of regeneration, Prometheus becomes anxious to recall
the curse he had once directed at Jupiter.

> The curse
> Once breathed on thee I would recall.   (I.58–59)

During the rest of his opening speech he addresses the Mountains,
Springs, Sun, and Whirlwinds and asks them to repeat the curse
which they all heard. He wishes to hear it word for word so that he

may repudiate it utterly. Nature, however, cannot muster the courage to speak the curse, which strikes it "mute with wonder" or silent with fear, although (as the Whirlwinds put it) "silence is a hell to us" (I.90, 106).

Disappointed in this attempt, Prometheus complains to his mother, the Earth. Here again, however, words fail. The "inorganic" (I.135) voice of the Earth does not communicate verbally with Prometheus, although the sympathy between them enables him to understand the sense of her speeches (at first, very vaguely, but later more precisely). Indeed, she dares not "speak like life,"

> lest Heaven's fell king
> Should hear, and link me to some wheel of pain
> More torturing than the one whereon I roll.   (I.140–42)

She speaks the language of the dead, which cannot be understood by the immortals. Although he cannot hear her words, Prometheus tells us that

> Obscurely through my brain, like shadows dim,
> Sweep awful thoughts, rapid and thick.   (I.146–47)

The situation has seemed obscure to many readers, perhaps with some reason. I am assuming that the Earth continues to speak in an inorganic voice like "the inarticulate people of the dead" (I.183) (which we can understand verbally but Prometheus can not) throughout her scene with him. She communicates with him sympathetically, not verbally, and he gradually becomes more and more attuned to what she is saying. In the earlier stages of their dialogue she is disappointed that he cannot escape the limitations of immortality and understand the language of mortality; and it is possible that Prometheus' increased understanding reflects a new decision on Earth's part to "speak like life." [8] But, if so, neither Shelley nor the Earth has bothered to inform us or Prometheus; and, as the situation is understandable (and perhaps more apt) without assuming the change of voice, I see no point in assuming it.

At any rate, the Earth, like the Mountains, Springs, Sun, and

Whirlwinds, cannot or will not give Prometheus what he wants. In answer to the question "How cursed I him?" (I.137), he wants the Earth to speak the exact words: "Mine own words, I pray, deny me not" (I.190). Shelley is here making use of primitive belief in the effective power of words to produce the thing which they invoke. As Prometheus says at the end of his opening speech,

> If then my words had power,
> Though I am changed so that aught evil wish
> Is dead within; although no memory be
> Of what is hate, let them not lose it now!
> What was that curse? for ye all heard me speak.   (I.69–73)

In order to repudiate the curse, he wishes to repudiate the words themselves. This primitive conception (which he probably derived from a number of passages in *Prometheus Bound*) is used by Shelley for a dramatic purpose. It allows him, by eliminating those who will not put it into words, to work up gradually to the actual statement of the curse; and it provides a convincing reason for having the entire curse spoken word for word. Shelley wants to have it spoken so that he can show us the old Prometheus here and now: the Aeschylean conception of the efficacy of words [9] allows him to do it convincingly.

For, although the Earth insists on speaking in an inorganic tongue, she has a plan which will satisfy Prometheus without harming herself. She will allow Prometheus to call up a shade from the underworld and ask it to repeat the curse which is imprinted on the memory of everything that exists. The shade will not, of course, understand the language it is speaking, but a purely verbal repetition is all that Prometheus requires. In one of Shelley's most famous passages the Earth depicts this underworld and its inhabitants, "The shadows of all forms that think and live":

> There thou art, and dost hang, a writhing shade,
> 'Mid whirlwind-peopled mountains; all the gods
> Are there, and all the powers of nameless worlds,
> Vast, sceptred phantoms; heroes, men, and beasts;

And Demogorgon, a tremendous gloom;
And he, the supreme Tyrant, on his throne
Of burning gold. Son, one of these shall utter
The curse which all remember. Call at will
Thine own ghost, or the ghost of Jupiter,
Hades or Typhon, or what mightier Gods
From all-prolific Evil, since thy ruin,
Have sprung, and trampled on my prostrate sons.
Ask, and they must reply: so the revenge
Of the Supreme may sweep through vacant shades,
As rainy wind through the abandoned gate
Of a fallen palace.   (I.191–218)

Prometheus makes a choice which intensifies the climax of this episode: he calls up the shade of Jupiter, who appears, compelled to repeat words whose import he cannot understand, but which apply directly to himself. He asks, in a language which Prometheus understands,

Why have the secret powers of this strange world
Driven me, a frail and empty phantom, hither
On direst storms? What unaccustomed sounds
Are hovering on my lips, unlike the voice
With which our pallid race hold ghastly talk
In darkness?   (I.240–45)

And Prometheus demands:

Speak the words which I would hear,
Although no thought inform thy empty voice.   (I.248–49)

But the Phantasm of Jupiter is more than a Voice, he is an Image as well. The Magus Zoroaster had the opportunity of meeting his own image in the garden. Prometheus has the opportunity of calling up any image from the world "underneath the grave." He does not, however, call up his own, but that of Jupiter. What this Phantasm says is of primary importance, but, to a lesser extent, so is what the "Tremendous Image" (I.246) looks like. As the Phantasm prepares to utter the curse, Prometheus describes it in terms that may suggest something of what we have heard of Jupiter (including Panthea's words of a few moments before):

> I see the curse on gestures proud and cold,
> And looks of firm defiance, and calm hate,
> And such despair as mocks itself with smiles,
> Written as on a scroll: yet speak! Oh, speak!   (I.258–61)

But they are even more appropriate to the speaker of the curse which immediately follows:

> Fiend, I defy thee! with a calm, fixed mind,
> All that thou canst inflict I bid thee do;
> Foul tyrant both of Gods and humankind,
> One only being shalt thou not subdue.   (I.262–65)

What appearance could suit these words better than "looks of firm defiance and calm hate"? And what of the despair which "mocks itself with smiles"; is this a desperate cynicism attributed to Jupiter, or Prometheus' mixture of hope and despair thirty centuries before? Indeed, the only word in Prometheus' description that might, at first sight, seem inapplicable to Prometheus himself is "cold," until we remember that the old Prometheus is distinguished from the new by his lack of pity for his enemies—in other words, by his coldness. Baker is correct, I think, in suggesting that the Phantasm of Jupiter goes so far as to imitate Prometheus' "original gestures." [10] Prometheus, like Zoroaster, has "met his own image"—but an image of what he was, not is.

It would be a mistake to exaggerate this point. The phantasm that Prometheus meets, whatever its talent for mimicry, remains the Phantasm of Jupiter; were it otherwise, some of the significance of the incident would be lost. The fact that Prometheus merges with Jupiter for a moment in such a way as to make the cruelty, pride, firmness, and hate of the one seem parallel to the cruelty, pride, firmness, and hate of the other underlines a complex relationship which Shelley is going to touch again in the following scene, but which ought to be discussed in some detail now.

In the *Essay on Christianity* (written some time before *Prometheus Unbound*) Shelley takes a notably severe view of man's responsibility for the external ills which oppress him.

> In proportion as mankind becomes wise, yes, in exact proportion to that wisdom should be the extinction of the unequal system under which they now subsist. Government is in fact the mere badge of their depravity.[11]   (C.211)

As early as *Queen Mab* Shelley had written (in an unrepresentative passage), "Man . . . fabricates / The sword which stabs his peace" (III.199–200), and we have observed that in *Prometheus Unbound* personal reform precedes institutional reform, as, many years before, Shelley had insisted that it must in Ireland. Shelley certainly did not neglect to observe that both the good which we seek and the evil which we shun are creations or choices of man's mind.

> He who taught man to vanquish whatsoever
>   Can be between the cradle and the grave
> Crowned him the King of Life. Oh, vain endeavour!
>   If on his own high will, a willing slave,
> He has enthroned the oppression and the oppressor.[12]

But, despite the examples which I have cited, Shelley was disinclined to emphasize man the fabricator of evil at the expense of man the victim of it. "To be evil is miserable," Shelley might have said (adapting Milton), "doing or suffering." [13] His view of evil often expresses itself in terms of the distinction or relation between active and passive. The guilt and pain the elimination of which the Spirit of the Hour announces in Act Three existed because man's will "made or suffered them." In *Julian and Maddalo* there is some relation between "wilful ill" and "permitted ill" (211, 171), and the Madman asks:

> What Power delights to torture us? I know
> That to myself I do not wholly owe
> What now I suffer, though in part I may.   (320–22)

Far from overplaying evil committed at the expense of evil permitted, Shelley's sense of "injured merit" and his sympathy with the victims of oppression made him particularly fond of contemplating undeserved suffering. Stricken deer and virtuous martyrs are all too common in his poetry, victims persecuted (like himself) by tyrants or mobs. Prometheus, when he sees the vision of the crucified Jesus, cries out:

> I see, I see
> The wise, the mild, the lofty, and the just,
> Whom thy slaves hate for being like to thee,
> Some hunted by foul lies from their heart's home, . . .
> Some linked to corpses in unwholesome cells;
> Some—hear I not the multitude laugh loud?—
> Impaled in lingering fire. . . .   (I.604-7, 610-12)

And Prometheus himself is, among other things, an innocent victim of persecution.

It is artistically dangerous for any artist to be persecuted. His reactions, which we can excuse or justify or sympathize with as he is a man, we may deplore as he is an artist. Even a Dante or a Milton is not always able to make anything edible out of such unpalatable grist. The temptation to self-pity or self-righteousness is continually present. Shelley, while much less successful in meeting this difficulty than they, can, nevertheless, rise above the mere depiction of sensational figures of persecuted virtue. For Prometheus is a great deal more than an innocent victim. When Shelley is at his best, the interplay between doing and suffering evil is not just a melodramatic contrast of light and darkness, with tyrants and victims facing one another over an impassable psychological gulf. The relation between them is more tragic than that. Persecutor and persecuted are not opposed and irreconcilable species, who divide the world between them. As the French Revolution had taught Shelley, tyrant and victim are quite capable of changing places.[14]

For Shelley, man exists in a reciprocal world of evil, giving and receiving, a vicious circle in which those to whom evil is done respond by doing the same. As he says in reviewing Mary Shelley's *Frankenstein, or The Modern Prometheus,*

Treat a person ill and he will become wicked. Requite affection with scorn; let one being be selected for whatever cause as the refuse of his kind—divide him, a social being, from society, and you impose on him the irresistible obligations—malevolence and selfishness. It is thus that too often in society those who are best qualified to be its benefactors and its ornaments are branded by some accident with scorn, and changed by neglect and solitude of heart into a scourge and a curse.   (C.307-8)

Those who are treated as slaves become slaves (or prospective tyrants), and those who assume arbitrary power are corrupted by it and become tyrants (or prospective slaves). Oppressed and oppressor are united in mutual evil.

> Men must reap the things they sow,
> Force from force must ever flow,
> Or worse; but 'tis a bitter woe
> That love or reason cannot change
> The despot's rage, the slave's revenge.[15]

From a similar point of view Shelley, in the fragmentary *A Satire on Satire,* disputes the familiar assumption that satire is a means "to make men wise and just," and insists on the contrary that

> Suffering makes suffering, ill must follow ill.
> Rough words beget sad thoughts, [   ] and, beside,
> Men take a sullen and a stupid pride
> In being all they hate in others' shame,
> By a perverse antipathy of fame.

Such interrelations, again in the words of the review of *Frankenstein,* "are the children, as it were, of Necessity and Human Nature" (C.307).[16]

Shelley presents us with his most pessimistic statement of this situation in the person of Beatrice in *The Cenci.* Beatrice, despite her considerable merits, is unable to break out of the circle and therefore becomes what she is forced to suffer, as both her act of revenge and perhaps her lie are intended to show. It is the fact of her revenge that makes Beatrice a tragic character, according to Shelley's Preface; and her tragedy seems to have been for Shelley the basic ethical tragedy of human nature. Behind this conception lies the Sermon on the Mount, the *Oresteia,* and no doubt Godwin as well.

But Beatrice's tragedy need not be regarded as inevitable, although at certain moments "Necessity and Human Nature" seem to have made it so. As Shelley argues in the hopeful conclusion of *A Philosophical View of Reform:*

Men, having been injured, desire to injure in return. This is falsely called a universal law of human nature; it is a law from which many are exempt, and all in proportion to their virtue and cultivation. (C.261)

Men can and must escape from the circle of reciprocal evil, like the martyrs of passive resistance in *The Mask of Anarchy,* who

> With folded arms and steady eyes,
> And little fear, and less surprise,
> Look upon them as they slay,
> Till their rage has died away.   (341–44)

Prometheus does escape at the beginning of *Prometheus Unbound,* and this is the basis of the regeneration of his will. He may be praised as Shelley praises the Spaniards: [17]

> Glory, glory, glory,
> To those who have greatly suffered and done!
> Never name in story
> Was greater than that which ye shall have won.
> Conquerors have conquered their foes alone,
> Whose revenge, pride, and power, they have overthrown.
> Ride ye, more victorious, over your own.

A theologian would no doubt like to consider the human surrender to evil in more ultimate or "original" terms. It is all very well to see man as needing to extricate himself from an inextricable tangle of mutual evil. But which came first, the deed or the response? Is man originally the victim or the fabricator? The problem is particularly acute for the theologian because it involves the recurrent controversy whether the source of man's corruptions lies in society or in himself.

Shelley, who seems uninterested in the Creation, seems equally uninterested in anything as original as the Fall itself, except perhaps in canto one of *The Revolt of Islam.* That particular Gordian knot, he tells us in the Notes to *Hellas,* our state of knowledge makes us unable to cut. The critic, at this point, can only speculate on the mists which for Shelley surrounded the problem and end up on the very superficial level which he (perhaps rightly) preferred. The critic can point out that in the unregenerate will external and internal evil are so intermingled that it is hard to say whether bad government is simply the badge of man's depravity or whether man's depravity is simply the consequence of his bad institutions. In the present both are obviously responsible. Neither can be considered in isolation, and perhaps, in so far as Shelley is concerned with recoveries not falls, it matters very little which came first, the chicken or the egg, if either. Even by the theologian man may be regarded as a social animal before the Fall, and therefore as falling privately and publicly at the same time.[18] From such a point of view man who forms society and society which conditions man fall together, and neither is to be seen as causing the other's fall. Most Christian thinkers, however, prefer to give Pelagius a wide berth by emphasizing the more salutary and exemplary conception of the Fall as private first and institutional second.

Shelley's preference is to see man as a responsible victim. It is obvious that, although Prometheus has to reform the evil in his own will, we are invited to see him originally as a victim of evil, unlike Jupiter, who, as Panthea remarks, looks "Like one who does, not suffers wrong" (I.239). Although Shelley believes that without private reform institutional reform can at best be only partial and uncertain, when he considers the formation of evil rather than its elimination, he begins with the external instead of the internal.

Man moves from suffering evil to doing it, rather than vice versa. (If we went back far enough, we would, no doubt, have to find an unmoved mover of evil, but Shelley does not go back that far.)

At first sight, this seems like an abdication of human responsibility for evil. But Shelley does not allow the original cause to obscure the ultimate effect. Man has been acted on by evil; but man has also responded in kind. This second fact cannot be excused by the first. By returning evil for evil, man has corrupted himself. For this moral failure he is responsible, and he can conquer evil only by first conquering the evil response in himself. Such is the victory of Prometheus.

But the Prometheus legend gave Shelley an opportunity to make man's responsibility more complex and subtle than this; for Prometheus himself is responsible for giving Jupiter power in the first place. He has made the mistake of using his knowledge to clothe Jupiter "with the dominion of wide heaven" (II.iv.46). Like man as described in the *Ode to Liberty*, "He has enthroned the oppression and the oppressor." In a very real sense he may be said to have created the God Jupiter and made him "an awful image of calm power" (I.296). As Prometheus says later to Mercury, "I gave all / He has" (I.381-82). Before his moral error, he committed an intellectual one. Like his debased counterpart, Frankenstein, he has created the monster which becomes his enemy. Like the "moonstruck sophist" described by Cythna in canto eight of *The Revolt of Islam,* he has

> stood,
> Watching the shade from his own soul upthrown
> Fill Heaven and darken Earth.   (vi)

III

THE TEMPTATIONS OF PROMETHEUS

Prometheus is regenerated when he abjures hate for pity, and revenge for forgiveness. We might expect, therefore, the temptations to center on this fact, and to aim at stimulating Prometheus to a new access of hate and revengefulness. In the long run, this is no doubt the conclusion to which they are moving: the Furies, when they leave, recognize that it is the pity of Prometheus that has finally defeated them. But the main body of the temptation scene seems to be concerned with other temptations than hate and revenge, such as self-contempt and despair. This is partly because Jupiter has a special end in view: to wrest from Prometheus his secret knowledge of Jupiter's downfall. The Furies are immediately concerned, therefore, with breaking Prometheus' resistance; and in order to do this they try to undermine his hope and self-respect. But we discover that the sins from which Prometheus has recovered are related to those toward which the Furies are tempting him; and Cythna's sermon in canto eight of *The Revolt of Islam* confirms our discovery. She attributes man's insistence on punishment to "the dark idolatry of self" (xxii) and describes hate as

> that shapeless fiendly thing
> Of many names, all evil, some divine,
> Whom self-contempt arms with a mortal sting.   (xxi)

Shelley was interested in tracing the numerous complicated varieties of self-love and self-contempt and their development; and he observed a significant relation between them and hate or revenge, and between all of these and despair. The Furies do not attack Prometheus by directly stimulating his hate, but by leading him toward contempt and despair for humanity or himself.

The proposal of Mercury, which opens the temptation scene, is perhaps more interesting for the way Mercury behaves in presenting it than for its effect on Prometheus. Mercury is the half-unwilling messenger of evil, bringing temptation from Jupiter to Prometheus. He does evil without willing it; he suffers evil without being the victim of it. As a messenger who unsuccessfully tries to make another's will his own, he is a hypocrite. Whether the justice he is carrying out be true or false, the substitute's position is a difficult one, as Mercury's semi-namesake Angelo found out. "Thy will be done," or "Our peace in his will"—it is not easy for Mercury or anyone else to say it with conviction. But Mercury, as the emissary not of a supposed good but of a recognized evil, knows all the difficulty and falseness of his role, regrets them, and is unwilling to do anything about them. Like Bulstrode in *Middlemarch,* he is a hypocrite self-revealed. All that Mercury, like Prometheus, can do is pity, but his pity is unproductive because he cannot will.

> To thee unwillingly, most unwillingly
> I come, by the great Father's will driven down.   (I.353-54)
>
> Alas! I pity thee, and hate myself
> That I can do no more: aye from thy sight
> Returning, for a season, heaven seems hell. . . . (I.356-58)
>
> Oh, that we might be spared: I to inflict
> And thou to suffer!   (I.410-11)

When Prometheus, tiring of useless talk, demands that he call up the Furies, Mercury can only say, remorsefully but certainly, "I must obey his words and thine" (I.435). Mercury is caught between Prometheus and Jupiter and cannot give his wholehearted allegiance to either. He is incapable of moral choice, a sort of Romantic version of a Hollow Man. But this play is really not for Hollow Men (such is no doubt one of its limitations), and we never learn how Mercury responds to the downfall of Jupiter.

The first temptation by which Mercury tries to persuade Prometheus to relinquish his secret is, like Becket's in *Murder in the Cathedral,* a sensual one:

> *Mercury.*   If thou might'st dwell among the Gods the while,
> Lapped in voluptuous joy?
> *Prometheus.*   I would not quit
> This bleak ravine, these unrepentant pains.
> *Mercury.*   Alas! I wonder at, yet pity thee.
> *Prometheus.* Pity the self-despising slaves of Heaven,
> Not me. . . .   (I.425–30)

In other words, "pity your own self-contempt." As for the temptation itself, it is hardly worth trying. "I remember / Not worth forgetting," [1] says Becket of his lost pleasures, and Prometheus, too, is quite unconcerned by Mercury's offer. He does take the opportunity, however, of restating his rejection of revenge, not merely on the oppressor, but on his deluded flatterers like Mercury.

> Let others flatter Crime, where it sits throned
> In brief Omnipotence: secure are they:
> For Justice, when triumphant, will weep down
> Pity, not punishment, on her own wrongs,
> Too much avenged by those who err.   (I.401–5)

If Mercury's offer has caused Prometheus no qualms, the same cannot be said for the temptations of the Furies. First of all, the very contemplation of such loathsome evil seems contaminating to him. That the individual may become what he suffers was a familiar idea to Shelley, as we have already observed; here Prometheus is afraid of becoming what he has merely to contemplate. Such a fear follows easily not only from Platonic educational theory, but also from eighteenth-century empiricism, in whose extreme form man is simply the sum of his perceptions. In Shelley's fragment *Prince Athanase,* we learn that Zonoras, sitting in his olive bower at Oenoe,

> With soul-sustaining songs, and sweet debates
> Of antient lore, there fed his lonely being:—
> "The mind becomes that which it contemplates,"—
>
> And thus Zonoras, by forever seeing
> Their bright creations, grew like wisest men.   (II.13-17)

In Act Four of *Prometheus Unbound,* the Moon drinks "Beauty, majesty and might" (482) from the Earth who embraces her, just

> As a lover or a chameleon
> Grows like what it looks upon,
> As a violet's gentle eye
> Gazes on the azure sky
> Until its hue grows like what it beholds. . . .   (IV.483-87)

But the idea need not be applied to such favorable material. Although, according to Demogorgon, Hope may create the thing it contemplates, so may a great many less attractive passions, such as fear or loathing. "Horrible forms," cries Prometheus,

> What and who are ye? Never yet there came
> Phantasms so foul through monster-teeming Hell
> From the all-miscreative brain of Jove;
> Whilst I behold such execrable shapes,
> Methinks I grow like what I contemplate,
> And laugh and stare in loathsome sympathy.[2]   (I.445-51)

These first furies,

> the ministers of pain and fear,
> And disappointment, and mistrust, and hate,
> And clinging crime,   (I.452-54)

are succeeded by further legions which seem even more loathsome to Prometheus. The Furies rejoice to hear him describe their "loathed selves," and he asks the terrible question, soon to be explored in *The Cenci:* "Can aught exult in its deformity?" The Second Fury explains. Only by the evil they commit and the agony of their victims does their shapelessness achieve form:

The beauty of delight makes lovers glad,
Gazing on one another: so are we.
As from the rose which the pale priestess kneels
To gather for her festal crown of flowers
The aerial crimson falls, flushing her cheek,
So from our victim's destined agony
The shade which is our form invests us round,
Else we are shapeless as our mother Night.   (I.465-72)

These Furies, contemplating the evil in themselves, in one another, and in their victims, an evil both done and suffered, are the perfect instruments of the temptation which Prometheus is now facing: the temptation to contemplate the evil which, by the act of perceiving, is inside as well as outside him, and which grows with contemplation. Indeed, their picture of evil dwelling beside and through the soul it yet can never obscure, is one of Shelley's most devastating pictures of what the "accident" of evil could mean for him:

Thou think'st we will live thro' thee, one by one,
Like animal life, and tho' we can obscure not
The soul which burns within, that we will dwell
Beside it, like a vain loud multitude
Vexing the self-content of wisest men:
That we will be dread thought beneath thy brain,
And foul desire round thine astonished heart,
And blood within thy labyrinthine veins
Crawling like agony?   (I.483-91)

When Clutton-Brock remarked: "Shelley . . . did not understand wickedness at all. Therefore he was not fit to write a play about it," [3] he must have forgotten passages such as this. That perfectly placed adjective "astonished" would itself be enough to demonstrate the inadequacy of such a judgment.

These opening pages in the scene between Prometheus and the Furies are a concentrated statement of something that in one form or another had continually been a matter of concern to Shelley: the relation between self-contemplation, self-love, self-contempt, and, finally, the love of evil.

He had been concerned with egoism as a personal (as well as theoretical) problem since his Oxford days. Shelley's early letters, with their disconcerting mixture of the naïve and the penetrating, show him engaged in a battle, probably both sham and real, with what he calls "self" (frequently underlined). "But adieu to egotism," he writes, somewhat prematurely, while still at Oxford,

I am sick to death at the name of *self*. Oh your theory cost me much reflection, I have not ceased to think of it since your letter came. . . . Is it not, however, founded on that *hateful* principle? Is it *self* which you propose to raise to a state of superiority by your system of infinite perfectibility in love? (J.VIII.32)

But, although he condemns selfishness, he is likely to be faced with it, in himself, as well as in his friends. "What a strange being I am; how inconsistent, in spite of all my boasted hatred of self" (J.VIII.82). He calls Hogg's attempt to seduce Harriet "self-centered, self-devoted, self-interested" (J.VIII.184). Notopoulos points out

Shelley's interest in a problem which Aristotle raises in *Ethics IX*, chapter 8: whether a man should love himself most or someone else. Shelley became so interested in the problem that he translated in mid-May 1811 this chapter of the *Ethics*. To describe the opposite of Aristotle's φίλαυτος he coined with the alpha privative prefix the noun ἀφιλαυτία for the concept of disinterested love.[4]

Among Notopoulos's examples of Shelley's use of the term is the following remark in an early letter to Hogg: "Solitude is most horrible, in despite of the ἀφιλαυτία which, perhaps, vanity has a great share in." Shelley continues with an even stronger remark, often quoted in connection with *Alastor:* "I cannot endure the horror, the evil, which comes to the *self* in solitude" (J.VIII.81–82). In 1819 the aversion is still with him. *"Self,* that burr that will stick to one," he writes to Leigh Hunt. "I can't get it off yet" (J.X.69).

Much of this discussion can serve as commentary on the remark in the Preface to *Alastor:* "The poet's self-centred seclusion was avenged by the furies of an irresistible passion pursuing him to a speedy ruin" (C.314). Indeed, in the light of this remark it has been possible to interpret the poem as mainly the story of a destructive narcissism. Certainly, it is not hard to derive such an interpretation from the Poet's behavior. But, since, apart from certain very limited criticisms in the Preface, Shelley nowhere suggests the culpability of the Poet nor presents him in unmistakable terms as a victim of self-love, it has not won general acceptance. Perhaps the most interesting support of Shelley's criticism in the Preface comes from a number of mirror images in the poem. Unfortunately, these images, while striking and significant, are also casual; they stem certainly from Shelley's concern with self-love, but they are not worked into the poem in anything but a superficial way. None of them, for example, occurs before the Poet has his vision; his mental state, therefore, is not established in terms of such an image. There is a superb one after the vision has disappeared, when he gazes "on the empty scene as vacantly / As ocean's moon looks on the moon in heaven" (201-2), although even here the image is reversed and the reflection gazes on the original; but the two most emphatic occur only after he has embarked on the sea of death. After the rough voyage in the Caucasian whirlpool, a breath of wind carries his craft into more gentle regions:

> Where the embowering trees recede, and leave
> A little space of green expanse, the cove
> Is closed by meeting banks, whose yellow flowers
> For ever gaze on their own drooping eyes,
> Reflected in the crystal calm. (404-8)

Here the mirror, self-love, and Narcissus are clearly brought together, and we may agree with Hoffman that the decayed and exhausted frame of the Poet (who wishes to deck himself with the flowers) is meant to suggest Ovid's Narcissus, worn out with self-love.[5] But the image remains casual: Shelley does not weave it closely into the poem. The same may be said of the picture sixty lines later of the Poet gazing at his reflection in a well. Here what is being emphasized is the delusion of personal immortality rather than that of self-love, although no doubt the two are seen as related. The significance of the mirror images, then, is merely that Shelley, aware of the difficulty of escaping from egoism and also aware of its close relation to love, could not help at moments associating a few such images with the Poet's quest. But they remain decorative not functional, and certainly none of them is as explicit as the observation in the later *Prince Athanase:*

> How many a one, though none be near to love,
> Loves then the shade of his own soul, half seen
> In any mirror. . . .   (II.117–19)

The self-love which at certain moments Shelley saw in the Poet of *Alastor* is shown in *The Cenci* with far greater penetration and complexity in a group of deluded individuals whose destruction, with one exception, merits no such elegiac music as Shelley provided at the end of *Alastor*. Cenci, Orsino, Giacomo, and even Beatrice herself, are the victims of self-contemplation, of the centripetal pressures of the ingrown soul, and their problems are the best possible commentary on the temptation with which the Furies begin their attack on Prometheus.

We have observed Shelley's concern with self-love not merely in *Alastor* but in letters as well, where he speaks of "seeking anything rather than a continued communion with *self*" (J.VIII.82). In the early letters to Hogg and to Elizabeth Hitchener, Shelley does a good deal of self-analysis, some of it acute; he doubts his sincerity, his consistency, his feelings of love. He seems also to doubt the value of this self-examination. In a letter to Elizabeth Hitchener a particularly revealing passage occurs. He quotes a sentence from his correspondent: "Reason sanctions an aberration from reason," and goes on to say,

I admit it, or rather on some subjects I conceive it to command a dereliction of itself. —What I mean by this is an habitual analysis of our own thoughts; it is this habit, acquired by length of solitary labour, never

then to be shaken off which induces gloom, which deprives the being
thus affected of any anticipation or retrospection of happiness, and leaves
him eagerly in pursuit of virtue, yet (apparent paradox!) pursuing it
without the weakest stimulus. —It is this then against which I wish to
caution you, this is the tree [of] which it is dangerous to eat, but which
I have fed upon to satiety. . . . How racking it is to the soul, when
enquiring into its own operations, to find that perfect virtue is very
far from attainable, to find reason tainted by feeling, to see the mind
when analyzed exhibit a picture of irreconcileable inconsistencies, even
when perhaps a moment before, it imagined that it had grasped the
fleeting phantom of virtue. (J.VIII.106–7)

One might regard this as some sort of definition of original sin
("This is the tree [of] which it is dangerous to eat"), although
"sin" rather than "error" would perhaps distort Shelley's emphasis
here. The passage also suggests the process by which self-contemplation turns into self-contempt.

We can see something of this process in Count Cenci, whose
self-love has developed into the militant form of self-contempt
which is the end of the ingrown soul. The Count is a self-
contemplating, self-justifying Renaissance monster, whose crimes
reach their climax in an act of incest with his daughter Beatrice.
But the whole family has to some degree Cenci's ingrown soul, not
merely the son Giacomo, but Beatrice herself. And Orsino, her
ally in murdering Cenci, is a weakly Machiavellian priest, a sort
of pale reflection of Cenci, whose character merely lacks the
strength to make his self-contempt final.

A more detailed account of the psychological state which Shelley
is examining in *The Cenci* should perhaps begin with Orsino's
description of a major flaw in the Cenci family: the tendency to
probe the inner workings of the mind and to accept what is found
there.

> It fortunately serves my close designs
> That 'tis a trick of this same family
> To analyse their own and other minds.
> Such self-anatomy shall teach the will

> Dangerous secrets: for it tempts our powers,
> Knowing what must be thought, and may be done,
> Into the depth of darkest purposes:
> So Cenci fell into the pit.   (II.ii.107–14)

Here is Orsino's explanation of Cenci's downfall. Cenci knows the workings of his own and other minds too well. He recognizes the inevitability of evil not merely as a religious dogma but as a discovery of his own psychological analysis. Such a secret is dangerous; it is the tree of which it is "dangerous to eat"; it is the knowledge that virtue is a "phantom." Cenci's next step is crucial. "What must be thought," "may be done." What the mind cannot avoid considering, the evil which it cannot escape from, lies ready to be acted. His powers are tempted and he falls into the pit. The inevitable in thought becomes the desirable in action. The knowledge of inevitable evil leads Cenci to the bottom of the pit. In a sense what he does is accept the doctrine of original sin as a doctrine of self-justification. He invokes the doctrine ironically before his dinner guests:

> But I do hope that you, my noble friends,
> When you have shared the entertainment here,
>
> .   .   .   .
>
> Will think me flesh and blood as well as you;
> Sinful indeed, for Adam made all so,
> But tender-hearted, meek and pitiful.   (I.iii.7–8, 11–13)

He has invoked it more directly to Camillo:

> All men delight in sensual luxury,
> All men enjoy revenge; and most exult
> Over the tortures they can never feel;
> Flattering their secret peace with others' pain.

And then he adds: "But I delight in nothing else" (I.i.77–81). Cenci's analysis of his "own and other minds" has ended in the love of evil.

In the Preface Shelley points out the coexistence in *The Cenci*, and in the society which it depicts, of religious conviction and "a cool and determined perseverance in enormous guilt" (C.323). For Shelley the terms of that religious conviction in Renaissance and Catholic Italy serve not as "a rule for moral conduct" (C.324) but as a framework by which the individual can explain himself and his world and which can be adapted to "the temper of the mind which it inhabits" (C.324). Theology is a sort of neutral language in which anything can be set forth conveniently. Certainly Cenci is an intensely religious man ("rigidly devout" suggests the Preface), in the sense that his thinking is intensely preoccupied with the dogma of his religion. The deaths of Rocco and Cristofano, for example, are seen as the answer to his prayers. He responds to Lucretia's claim that in a dream a voice warned her of the death and damnation ahead of him, with a delightfully irresponsible statement of his creed:

> Why—such things are:
> No doubt divine revealings may be made.
> 'Tis plain I have been favoured from above,
> For when I cursed my sons they died—Ay—so—
> As to the right or wrong, that's talk—repentance—
> Repentance is an easy moment's work,
> And more depends on God than me.   (IV.1.37–43)

Grace certainly overpowers the human will in Cenci's creed. "An easy moment's work" turns the responsibility over to God. But when Lucretia admits that her claim is a lie, he is outraged in the severest religious terms:

> Vile palterer with the sacred truth of God,
> Be thy soul choked with that blaspheming lie!   (IV.1.73–74)

Like Tamburlaine or Hamlet he sees himself as an instrument to scourge mankind for its sins, including the inevitable sin it has inherited from the unremembered world of Adam: [6]

> I do not feel as if I were a man,
> But like a fiend appointed to chastise
> The offences of some unremembered world.   (IV.1.160–62)

And like most such scourges he has his moment of hubris when he is no longer an instrument of some power but its rival. "He does his will, I mine!" (IV.i.139) cries Cenci, in the culminating blasphemy of the play.

In these passages Cenci emerges as what some moderns would see as a Christian *manqué:* like Baudelaire he at least is "man enough for damnation," [7] and for him sexual operation is certainly a moral act. In him we can see what Shelley means by saying in the Preface:

Religion pervades intensely the whole frame of society, and is according to the temper of the mind which it inhabits, a passion, a persuasion, an excuse, a refuge; never a check. Cenci himself built a chapel in the court of his palace, and dedicated it to St. Thomas the Apostle, and established masses for the peace of his soul.   (C.324)

And, in particular, we have seen how for Cenci the conviction of universal and inevitable depravity, which his interest in analytical psychology as well as in theology inspires, has become an excuse, a persuasion, and, above all, a passion.

Orsino is inspired to give his account of the analytical "trick" of the Cenci family by his conversation with Giacomo, Cenci's son, in which he plays on this tendency in order to further his plot to murder the Count. Giacomo has already thought of murder but has refused to recognize his own desires. Orsino realizes what is going on in Giacomo's mind and forces him to turn his troubled gaze inward, believing that once Giacomo sees clearly "what must be thought," he will accept it and consider acting upon it. "Fear not to speak your thought" (II.ii.74), says Orsino, and Giacomo responds:

> Ask me not what I think; the unwilling brain
> Feigns often what it would not; and we trust
> Imagination with such phantasies
> As the tongue dares not fashion into words;
> Which have no words, their horror makes them dim
> To the mind's eye. My heart denies itself
> To think what you demand.   (II.ii.82–88)

Orsino then goes on to describe his role as the unfolder of the hidden self:

> But a friend's bosom
> Is as the inmost cave of our own mind
> Where we sit shut from the wide gaze of day,
> And from the all-communicating air.
> You look what I suspected: (II.ii.88–92)

All Giacomo can do is beg relief from this merciless probing:

> Spare me now!
> I am as one lost in a midnight wood,
> Who dares not ask some harmless passenger
> The path across the wilderness, lest he,
> As my thoughts are, should be—a murderer.
>
> . . . .
>
> Pardon me, that I say farewell—farewell!
> I would that to my own suspected self
> I could address a word so full of peace. (II.ii.92–96, 101–3)

Giacomo is discovering that he is a murderer in mind, and, the idea having become familiar and then attractive, he becomes an accomplice in the act. But Giacomo lacks the courage to maintain his conviction when the crime has been discovered, and he turns against Orsino for having tempted him. When Orsino tries to defend himself ("You cannot say / I urged you to the deed"), Giacomo recalls his tempter's method:

> O, had I never
> Found in thy smooth and ready countenance
> The mirror of my darkest thoughts; hadst thou
> Never with hints and questions made me look
> Upon the monster of my thought, until
> It grew familiar to desire— (V.i.18–24)

Beatrice, far more than Giacomo and more like her father, has a piercing, analytical, illusion-destroying gaze, as Orsino has found— and as the wretched Marzio is to find in the trial scene: "Let her not look on me! / I am a miserable guilty wretch" (V.ii.90–91). This gaze makes Orsino decidedly uncomfortable, as he plays Giacomo to Beatrice's Orsino:

> Yet I fear
> Her subtle mind, her awe-inspiring gaze,
> Whose beams anatomize me nerve by nerve
> And lay me bare, and make me blush to see
> My hidden thoughts.   (I.ii.83–87)

It is this family characteristic that Cenci decides to make use of in order to degrade her. She may become, as Orsino recognizes, "subdued even to the hue / Of that which thou permittest" (III.i.176–77). By his act of incest Cenci will force Beatrice to turn her stern gaze inward, to recognize the contamination within her and to realize that she is what she contemplates. Cenci tries to make the unwilling Beatrice follow his own development.

> She shall become (for what she most abhors
> Shall have a fascination to entrap
> Her loathing will) to her own conscious self
> As she appears to others.   (IV.i.85–88)

His act, then, is not caused by the desire to experience the forbidden pleasures of incest. What Cenci seeks is a superior pleasure: the "greater point" is, as he explains in a soliloquy, "to poison and corrupt her soul" (IV.i.44–45). The mirror image, which was casually used to represent self-love in *Alastor,* is used with greater clarity of purpose in *The Cenci.* We have already heard Giacomo speak of "the mirror of my darkest thoughts"; in the following passage Cenci uses it to elaborate the substance of his plot against Beatrice. He imagines the child which may come of his incestuous union with her and prays:

> May it be
> A hideous likeness of herself; that, as
> From a distorting mirror, she may see
> Her image mixed with what she most abhors,
> Smiling upon her from her nursing breast.   (IV.i.145–49)

The child, then, will be the objective image of a "soul within her soul" but that soul will not be, as in *On Love,* "a mirror whose surface only reflects the forms of purity and brightness" (C.170), but a formless horror at the bottom of the soul, a deep truth which like Demogorgon's is "imageless." As Beatrice tells Lucretia, she

> can feign no image in my mind
> Of that which has transformed me: I, whose thought
> Is like a ghost shrouded and folded up
> In its own formless horror.   (III.i.108-11)

Shelley's account of Beatrice, however, has something of the shifting uncertainty that can be observed in *Alastor,* an uncertainty which he defends in the Preface to *The Cenci* on dramatic grounds. He has left it ambiguous whether Cenci's plot was successful or not. A good deal of evidence can be educed to prove that Beatrice was subdued to that which she permitted. Most readers, I think, have found much that is unsympathetic in the Beatrice of the last two acts. She has become (to use a word Cenci applies to himself) "hardened" (I.i.94). Particularly disconcerting are her callous disregard of Marzio and Olympio and her self-righteous lying. The later Beatrice has also taken over some of the characteristics of her father. She too sees herself as the scourge of that God who "made / Our speedy act the angel of his wrath" (V.iii.113-14), although there is a significant difference between her self-portrait as a chastising angel and his as a revenging fiend. Just as Cenci before his crime tells us

> My blood is running up and down my veins;
> A fearful pleasure makes it prick and tingle, (IV.ii.163-64)

so Beatrice before hers tells us,

>   My breath
> Comes, methinks, lighter, and the jellied blood
> Runs freely through my veins.   (IV.iii.42-44)

And both are able to sleep soundly in the midst of their deeds. Cenci is able to belie his conscience "with an hour of rest, / Which will be deep and calm, I feel" (IV.ɪɪ.181–82). And Beatrice, off to counterfeit sleep after the murder, announces:

> I scarcely need to counterfeit it now:
> The spirit which doth reign within these limbs
> Seems strangely undisturbed. I could even sleep
> Fearless and calm: all ill is surely past.

Her trial scene has reminded Bates of Vittoria Corrombona's in *The White Devil*,[8] and Vittoria was no innocent victim of persecution. More important, since, beyond a single remark of Medwin,[9] there is no evidence that Shelley ever read Webster, are the reminiscences of Lady Macbeth, which Baker emphasizes justly.[10] Beatrice eggs on the murderers, as Lady Macbeth does her husband, in a pair of scenes in which the echoes of word and idea leave no doubt what is in the back of Shelley's mind. When the murderers hear noises and think someone is coming, she calls them "conscience-stricken cravens" with "baby hearts" and explains the noises as the iron gate "swinging to the wind" (IV.ɪɪ.39–41). Later, when they return from Cenci's room, the deed still undone, there are further suggestions of *Macbeth*:

> *Beatrice.*   I ask if all is over?
> *Olimpio.*   We dare not kill an old and sleeping man;
> His thin gray hair, his stern and reverent brow,
>
> . . . .
>
> And the calm innocent sleep in which he lay,
> Quelled me. Indeed, indeed, I cannot do it.
> *Marzio.*   But I was bolder;
>
> . . . .
>
>   And now my knife
> Touched the loose wrinkled throat, when the old man
> Stirred in his sleep, and said, "God! hear, O, hear,
> A father's curse! What, art thou not our Father?"
> And then he laughed. I knew it was the ghost
> Of my dead father speaking through his lips,

And could not kill him.
Beatrice.   Miserable slaves!
Where, if ye dare not kill a sleeping man,
Found ye the boldness to return to me
With such a deed undone? Base palterers!
Cowards and traitors!   (IV.iii.8–10, 12–14, 16–26)

Beatrice then snatches a dagger from one of them and prepares to
do the deed herself, being restrained only by the renewed resolution
of Olympio.

Outside of the play itself, another sign of the degradation of
Beatrice is Shelley's account of her in the Preface, where, just as in
the Preface to *Alastor,* he considers the moral and psychological
state of his main character. Although "gentle and amiable," she was
"violently thwarted from her nature by the necessity of circumstance and opinion" (C.322). Her overt crime was revenge. But

the fit return to make to the most enormous injuries is kindness and for-
bearance, and a resolution to convert the injurer from his dark passions
by peace and love. Revenge, retaliation, atonement, are pernicious mistakes. If Beatrice had thought in this manner she would have been wiser
and better; but she would never have been a tragic character.   (C.333)

At the same time, Shelley insists that although Beatrice thought
that Cenci's act contaminated her, such a belief was an illusion.
"No person can be truly dishonoured by the act of another" (C.323).
Beatrice was the victim of *"what she considered* a perpetual contamination of *body and mind"* (C.322; italics mine). There is, in
other words, something illusory about Beatrice's sense of guilt. Her
tendency toward psychological analysis, the "trick" of the Cenci
family, seems to have played her false, and, although Cenci himself
may have failed to contaminate her, his act causes her to contaminate herself. She murders Cenci and by her "pernicious mistake" (Shelley's translation of *hamartia*) becomes a tragic character.

Nevertheless, as Shelley notes, the spectator of the drama (with his own trick of "restless and anatomizing casuistry") will not be entirely convinced of her guilt.

It is in the restless and anatomizing casuistry with which men seek the justification of Beatrice, yet feel that she has done what needs justification; it is in the superstitious horror with which they contemplate alike her wrongs and their revenge, that the dramatic character of what she did and suffered consists.   (C.323)

And, whereas the darker side of Beatrice resembles Lady Macbeth, the brighter side at moments in the last act reminds us of Desdemona.[11] It is hard to imagine Lady Macbeth and Desdemona in the same heroine, but Shelley's unconscious reminiscences of Shakespeare force us to do so. Beatrice sings a pathetic swan song and like Desdemona goes to her death in an atmosphere of domestic courtesies.

But in many ways the most interesting and best drawn character in *The Cenci* is the priest Orsino—half-hearted both for good and evil, trying to further "some such mingled plot of good and ill / As others weave," willing to make use of evil and "flatter the dark spirit," but also interested in salving his mild conscience by doing "as little mischief as I can" (V.ii.80–81; II.ii.159, 119). He has one passionate love speech (a soliloquy), but, on the whole, his love of Beatrice, of money, and of intrigue are alike casual, and he manages to slip out of the consequences of his murder plot, as his more whole-hearted colleagues cannot or will not.

Orsino, though not a Cenci, has the same moral weakness as the Cenci, the self-analysis which leads him to make the best of his shortcomings, whose deformities gradually become familiar and even attractive to him. After telling us of the trick of the Cenci family, Orsino describes its working in himself, with Beatrice as its agent:

> It fortunately serves my close designs
> That 'tis a trick of this same family
> To analyse their own and other minds.

· · · ·

> So Cenci fell into the pit; even I,
> Since Beatrice unveiled me to myself,
> And made me shrink from what I cannot shun,
> Show a poor figure to my own esteem,
> To which I grow half reconciled. I'll do
> As little mischief as I can; that thought
> Shall fee the accuser conscience.   (II.ii.107–9, 114–20)

To be sure, Beatrice's gaze gives him the occasional qualm, and he remains half reconciled rather than hardened; but, nevertheless, he manages the intrigue with some skill and succeeds in surviving the ultimate failure of his plans. He lives in a world of nets, threads, and devices which, however, lack much substance and are eventually "snapped." Orsino thinks of himself as a hard-headed realist and, when Giacomo tries to blame his ruin on Orsino's prompting, the priest responds with priestly realism:

> 'Tis thus
> Men cast the blame of their unprosperous acts
> Upon the abettors of their own resolve;
> On anything but their weak, guilty selves.   (V.i.24–27)

But the same Orsino is soon to ask, "Have I not the power to fly / My own reproaches?" (V.i.97–98). He is a Machiavellian without conviction, only half reconciled to the world of egoism which he sees so clearly, weaving his mingled threads of good and ill, offering an occasional sop to the accuser conscience and even at moments recoiling from the evil within. The characterization of Orsino is Shelley's greatest achievement in the play, and his final soliloquy sums up this achievement brilliantly:

> I thought to act a solemn comedy
> Upon the painted scene of this new world,
> And to attain my own peculiar ends
> By some such plot of mingled good and ill
> As others weave; but there arose a Power
> Which grasped and snapped the threads of my device
> And turned it to a net of ruin.

                                      . . . 'Tis easy then
For a new name and for a country new,
And a new life, fashioned on old desires,
To change the honours of abandoned Rome.
And these must be the masks of that within,
Which must remain unaltered. Oh, I fear
That what is past will never let me rest!
Why, when none else is conscious, but myself,
Of my misdeeds, should my own heart's contempt
Trouble me? Have I not the power to fly
My own reproaches? Shall I be the slave
Of—what? A word? which those of this false world
Employ against each other, not themselves;
As men wear daggers not for self-offence.
But if I am mistaken, where shall I
Find the disguise to hide me from myself,
As now I skulk from every other eye?   (V.i.77-83, 88-104)

Shelley took care, in writing his Preface, to distance himself from
the play; and he claimed that in presenting these objective, historical
figures he "sought to avoid the error of making them actuated by
my own conceptions of right or wrong" (C.323). But by this he
can hardly mean more than that none of the characters is actuated
by his own moral ideal; Shelley wants no reader to imagine that he
is recommending the conduct of any of the characters in his drama.
The reader must not suppose that the author is condoning either
incest or revenge. His later remark to Trelawny on the remoteness
of *The Cenci* from his own passions is likewise an extreme and
somewhat misleading disclaimer. Shelley's precaution was, of course,
useless, but it is obviously still a precaution, not a sign that in *The
Cenci* Shelley has escaped from the preoccupations of his other
work. *The Cenci* is a strangely disquieting vision of evil, in which
the characters peer into themselves and greet the depths which they
discover with various degrees of horror, fascination, and acceptance.
    The play can be regarded both as a defense of the idea of natural
depravity and as an attack on it, or at least on our tendency to
justify our shortcomings by making them seem inevitable and

universal. To be convinced of our natural depravity may be simply a particularly emphatic form of self-love (as it is, to be sure, in the Byronic hero as well as in Count Cenci). This, at any rate, is one of the things which Cythna seems to be saying in her sermon in canto eight of *The Revolt of Islam* (note also her distinction between self-love or self-contempt, and self-knowledge). She tells the sailors:

> Reproach not thine own soul, but know thyself,
> Nor hate another's crime, nor loathe thine own,
> It is the dark idolatry of self,
> Which, when our thoughts and actions once are gone,
> Demands that man should weep, and bleed, and groan;
> Oh, vacant expiation!   (xxii)

It has never, I think, been recognized how seriously Shelley is concerned with the dangers of self-contempt. Self-contempt is the sting which arms hate, he tells us in *The Revolt,* and in *Prometheus Unbound* the Furies are particularly delighted with "the self-contempt implanted / In young spirits sense-enchanted" (I.510–11). And later in the poem, when Asia lists the woes of human existence before the throne of Demogorgon, the list reaches its climax with

> Abandoned hope, and love that turns to hate;
> And self-contempt bitterer to drink than blood. (II.iv.24–25)

Shelley combines a knowledge of human potentiality for evil with an equally strong awareness of the dangers of such knowledge. It must never lead to "such a self-mistrust as has no name" (III.iv.152). Perhaps, as Elizabeth Hitchener suggested: "Reason sanctions an aberration from reason." There must be some way of recognizing evil and remaining capable of confident action. Otherwise, the more evil is recognized, the worse it is liable to become, as the soul becomes more and more ingrown. For Cythna it is possible to "know thyself" and yet "reproach not thine own soul." In Shelley the injunction "know thyself" is always unequivocally good. It refers to fruitful, out-going, self-knowledge. But his work shows clearly how well he knew the thinness of the line that separates "the dark idolatry of self" from self-knowledge. And, strikingly enough, it is self-knowledge that Shelley invokes as the end for which *The Cenci* is designed.

The highest moral purpose aimed at in the highest species of the drama is the teaching the human heart, through its sympathies and antipathies, the knowledge of itself; in proportion to the possession of which knowledge, every human being is wise, just, sincere, tolerant or kind. (C.323)

But a paradox or two lie hidden in this statement if we read it in the light of the play. For Cenci analyzed his own and other minds, and through his knowledge did not become just, tolerant, or kind, but "fell into the pit"; and Orsino, fearful of what he sees within, exits crying, "Where shall I / Find the disguise to hide me from myself . . . ?" Beatrice seems to have found her disguise and stands trial, fiercely proclaiming her innocence, but Shelley, however he may admire her, does not find her innocent.

Act One of *Prometheus Unbound*, like *The Cenci*, attacks the two things which were central in Shelley's view of "man's own wilful ill": revenge and the various kinds of self-love. Throughout the act Shelley is concerned with the folly of revenge, but, in the Furies themselves and in Prometheus' initial response to them,

> Methinks I grow like what I contemplate
> And laugh and stare in loathsome sympathy,

we can see Shelley's continuing fascination with the problem he was to consider with so much elaboration six months later in *The Cenci*. At the same time, Prometheus' horrified self-contemplation does not paralyze or corrupt his will, as it does Orsino's or Cenci's.

> Yet am I king over myself, and rule
> The torturing, and conflicting throngs within. (I.492-93)

With these words he withstands this temptation. The millennial consequences of such a victory are described in Act Three by the Spirit of the Hour:

I wandering went
Among the haunts and dwellings of mankind,
And first was disappointed not to see
Such mighty change, as I had felt within
Expressed in outward things; but soon I looked,
And behold, thrones were kingless, and men walked
One with the other even as spirits do,
None fawned, none trampled; hate, disdain, or fear,
Self-love or self-contempt, on human brows
No more inscribed, as o'er the gate of hell,
"All hope abandon ye who enter here."   (III.iv.126–36)

The main temptation which the Furies offer is this "abandoned hope" which an intense awareness of insuperable human ills can sustain. They offer it in a form to which a culture hero like the mythical Prometheus would be particularly susceptible, and in which the modern Prometheus of the physical sciences has sometimes had to face it. (The title of Mrs. Shelley's famous horror story was, we may remember, *Frankenstein, or the Modern Prometheus*.) The road to hell is paved with good intentions. Good itself may produce evil. "Evil minds / Change good to their own nature" (I.380–81). Perhaps all that Prometheus can do for man will only make man's fate worse. Should Prometheus become convinced of the futility of his efforts, he will fall into despair and give up resisting Jupiter. Such, at any rate, is the Furies' next angle of attack.

In order to make their root idea as vivid as possible, the Furies present Prometheus with two main examples: the development of Christianity and the aftermath of the French Revolution. These are presented by means of a pair of scenes, which the Furies reveal behind a veil. The first scene depicts "a youth / With patient looks nailed to a crucifix" (I.584–85), on whom the Chorus of Furies comments:

One came forth of gentle worth,
Smiling on the sanguine earth;
His words outlived him, like swift poison
    Withering up truth, peace, and pity.

> Look! where round the wide horizon
>   Many a million-peopled city
> Vomits smoke in the bright air.
> Hark that outcry of despair!
> 'Tis his mild and gentle ghost
>   Wailing for the faith he kindled.   I.546-55)

There are two complementary sides to what Prometheus is seeing: first, the horror of the Crucifixion itself, and, second, the horror of the wars and persecutions which that Crucifixion ultimately led to. Both are described graphically, and each contributes to the other. The greater the bloodshed in the name of Christ, the more in vain and therefore more horrible does the Crucifixion seem; and the more the suffering of Christ to save mankind is emphasized, the more horrible seem the unintended consequences. "Oh horrible!" cries Prometheus, "Thy name I will not speak— / It hath become a curse" (I.603-4). Unfortunately, Shelley's Crucifixion scene (which, for me, is more painful than moving), with its "sick throes," "pale fingers" playing with "gore," and "the anguish of that lighted stare" (I.601, 602, 597), displays the strained sentiment and the sheer physical pain of many fifteenth- and sixteenth-century Italian paintings of the Crucifixion, and I have no doubt that this passage is the not too palatable fruit of Shelley's first exposure to Italian art.[12]

The second scene depicts the relapse of newly awakened nations into discord and servitude: "there was strife, deceit and fear," Prometheus reluctantly tells Panthea;

> Tyrants rushed in and did divide the spoil.
> This was the shadow of the truth I saw.   (I.653-55)

For Shelley the most vivid example of a real good producing a real evil was the French Revolution and its consequences: the Terror, the Napoleonic wars, and the counterrevolution, with the restoration of the Bourbons. The Furies direct Prometheus' horrified gaze to this example:

See a disenchanted nation
Springs like day from desolation;
To truth its state is dedicate,
And Freedom leads it forth, her mate;
A legioned band of linked brothers,
Whom Love calls children—

                        'Tis another's.
See how kindred murder kin!
'Tis the vintage-time for Death and Sin;
Blood, like new wine, bubbles within;
    Till Despair smothers
The struggling world, which slaves and tyrants win.   (I.567–77)

As Shelley observed in the Preface to *The Revolt of Islam,* men who have been hungry and enslaved, when they are suddenly released, do not overnight become "liberal minded, forbearing, and independent," but greedy and revengeful; and their revenge does not stop with killing their enemies. The sacred "Names" of Truth, Liberty, and Love (like Liberty, Equality, and Fraternity) may be borne aloft, but these are not the effective mottoes of a suddenly "disenchanted nation" springing from "desolation." For, as a warning spirit sings in a later passage, which K. N. Cameron has discussed brilliantly,[13] "Desolation is a delicate [i.e. insidious] thing" (I.772), and, despite the dreams of idealistic revolutionaries, a very unlikely prelude to love. The best and gentlest,

  . . . soothed to false repose by the fanning plumes above,
And the music-stirring motion of its soft and busy feet,
Dream visions of aërial joy, and call the monster, Love,
And wake, and find the shadow Pain, as he whom now we greet.
                                (I.776–79)

Just after the veil has been torn, and even before anything has been said about the scenes themselves, the Furies are already applying their moral to Prometheus' own situation:

Dost thou boast the clear knowledge thou waken'dst for man?
Then was kindled within him a thirst which outran

> Those perishing waters; a thirst of fierce fever,
> Hope, love, doubt, desire, which consume him for ever.   (I.542–45)

And as Prometheus turns his gaze on the Crucifixion scene, a Fury
drives the moral home more bluntly:

> Behold an emblem: those who do endure
> Deep wrongs for man, and scorn, and chains, but heap
> Thousandfold torment on themselves and him.   (I.594–96)

But the Furies have a final turn of the screw to come. The earlier
vision of evil to which they subjected Prometheus showed the
human mind and heart receiving and even welcoming evil—unable
by their very nature to prevent "dread thought" and "foul desire"
penetrating within "like animal life." Even the new hordes who
appeared were leaving not merely shipwreck and famine and
slaughter but the more subtle ills of the "self-contempt / Implanted
in young spirits sense-enchanted," and the cruelty aroused in a
fearful dreamer. But the ills which they went on to present as the
consequence of Christianity and the French Revolution were mainly
the bloodshed and slavery of great historical catastrophes or political
oppressions. Prometheus sees

> mighty realms
> Float by my feet, like sea-uprooted isles,
> Whose sons are kneaded down in common blood
> By the red light of their own burning homes.   (I.612–15)

Now, however, the Furies move beyond the evil which is immediately obvious to the senses and return to the sort of subtle
internal horror with which they began:

> In each human heart terror survives
> The ravin it has gorged: the loftiest fear
> All that they would disdain to think were true:
> Hypocrisy and custom make their minds
> The fanes of many a worship, now outworn.
> They dare not devise good for man's estate,
> And yet they know not that they do not dare.

The good want power, but to weep barren tears.
The powerful goodness want: worse need for them.
The wise want love; and those who love want wisdom;
And all best things are thus confused to ill.   (I.618–28)

In the first place, the very fact of fearing something means
admitting the thing that is feared. And this is true not merely of the
fear of oppression or death, but of the fear of ourselves. We may
disdain to believe that we are capable of cruelty, revenge, hatred,
and lust, but the very fear of these things is a measure of the grip
they have on us. By fearing something we, to some extent, confirm
it within ourselves. Man creates what he endures, contemplates, and
fears.

In the second place, even those ills we have outgrown remain
with us, embodied in our institutions and habitual assumptions.
Hypocrisy and the dead weight of custom are able to overcome
our moral advances. Shelley makes it quite clear elsewhere that the
wisdom of an age can often be superior to its religious, political,
and social institutions. Even if man fails to regenerate himself like
Prometheus, some reform is still feasible, because man's institutions
are behind even his present limited capabilities. In the Preface to
Prometheus Unbound Shelley looks forward to redressing this
balance, and sees it already in progress.

The cloud of mind is discharging its collected lightning, and the equi-
librium between institutions and opinions is now restoring or is about
to be restored.   (C.328)

This idea of the lost balance caused by the perpetuation of institutions which are no longer relevant or which have grown beyond
their function recurs in a famous passage from *A Defence of
Poetry*:

We have more moral, political, and historical wisdom than we know
how to reduce into practice; we have more scientific and economic knowledge than can be accommodated to the just distribution of the produce
which it multiplies. . . . There is no want of knowledge respecting
what is wisest and best in morals, government, and political economy,

or at least, what is wiser and better than what men now practice and endure. But we let *"I dare not* wait upon *I would,* like the poor cat i' the adage."[14]   (C.293)

We may find such an idea either cheering or depressing. It is cheering to recognize that some measure of progress is possible to us without remaking ourselves fundamentally, like a Prometheus, but it is depressing to realize that man is not only unregenerate, but also seems unable to make use of the partial advances in wisdom which he *has* been able to achieve. Man lags in the rear not merely of what he could be, but of what he is: "And yet they know not that they do not dare." In this way men are worse off even than "the poor cat i' the adage."

Finally, this sense of disintegration between and within man's capabilities and achievements leads to a lamentable vision of human impotence. Wisdom, power, goodness, and love are all needed if man is to achieve the ends which Prometheus desires for him. But each of these seems to inhibit the others; at any rate, they rarely exist together, so that (and here the spokesman Fury sums up the significance of this temptation) the good which a man possesses is frustrated by the good which he lacks, and is thereby itself turned to evil.

> The good want power, but to weep barren tears.
> The powerful goodness want; worse need for them.
> The wise want love; and those who love want wisdom;
> And all best things are thus confused to ill.

There is a Shelleyan fragment (*Love, Hope, Desire and Fear*), which suggests the state of mind which the Furies are trying to induce in Prometheus:

> Such hope, as is the sick despair of good,
> Such fear as is the certainty of ill,
> Such doubt, as is pale Expectation's food
> Turned while she tastes to poison, when the will
> Is powerless. . . .

But, although the Furies' words torture Prometheus, with clear insight he recognizes that the fact that these things *do* torture him is one measure of his moral life.

> Thy words are like a cloud of winged snakes;
> And yet I pity those they torture not. (I.632–33)

This "pity" of those who are not tortured by the human predicament reaches back to Prometheus' initial act of pity for Jupiter, the act which signalized his conversion. Its recurrence now is the seal of defeat for the Furies, as their spokesman realizes. "Thou pitiest them?" he asks; "I speak no more!" (I.634). Then he and his companions vanish. The temptations are over, a failure. The tyrant has been "subtle" (I.638), as Prometheus recognizes, but

> This is defeat, fierce king, not victory.
> The sights with which thou torturest gird my soul
> With new endurance, till the hour arrives
> When they shall be no types of things which are. (I.642–45)

Two of the details with which Shelley enriches the conclusion of this episode deserve comment. First, it is a verbal slip of the spokesman Fury that inspires Prometheus to the comment which brings on the abrupt termination of the episode. "They know not what they do" (I.631) is the Fury's comment on the strong and rich whose intentions are good, but who are simply unaware of the feelings of others. Prometheus seizes on this unconscious quotation from Jesus and responds to the Fury with the pity involved in the missing part of the quotation. Secondly, while Prometheus shows no sign of succumbing to despair when the Furies are present, he falters for a moment after they leave—although only to recover himself immediately. Like that favorite of Shelley's youth, the Wandering Jew, he laments his immortality and envies the refuge of the grave.

> Alas! pain, pain ever, for ever! [15]
> I close my tearless eyes, but see more clear
> Thy works within my woe-illumined mind,

> Thou subtle tyrant! Peace is in the grave.
> The grave hides all things beautiful and good:
> I am a God and cannot find it there,
> Nor would I seek it.   (I.635-41)

Perhaps the most remarkable thing about this great temptation scene—great in conception, if not always in execution—is that the Furies tempt Prometheus with the truth. Everything they show or tell him is true, and Prometheus knows it. But the consequence for him is not self-contempt or despair. This terrible knowledge serves simply to strengthen his belief in a new truth which will supplant the old.

In order to comfort Prometheus after his terrible ordeal, the Earth calls up a series of spirits, the first four of whom present hopeful omens for the future, signs of human wisdom and virtue. But the sequence of songs is unexpectedly (though typically) continued by two pessimistic spirits who depict the terrible aftermath of a revolution and the thwarting of love by "desolation." A final chorus, however, returns to hope and prophesies the victory of Prometheus over "Ruin," despite the apparent inseparability of "Love" and "Ruin" in the present. And in one of the most appealing (if grammatically confused) stanzas of the first act they invest the victory of Prometheus with the atmosphere of spring:

> In the atmosphere we breathe,
> As buds grow red, when snow-storms flee,
>   From spring gathering up beneath,
> Whose mild winds shake the elder brake,
> And the wandering herdsmen know
> That the white-thorn soon will blow:
> Wisdom, Justice, Love, and Peace,
> When they struggle to increase,
>   Are to us as soft winds be
>   To shepherd boys, the prophecy
>   Which begins and ends in thee.   (I.790-800)

What follows is as unexpected as most of the details in Act One. Prometheus does not respond to the hopeful spirits with a new surge of energy. Instead, after a momentary vision of Asia, his lost bride, he relapses almost into apathy, into something like Carlyle's Centre of Indifference or Keats's Cave of Quietude.

> All things are still. Alas! how heavily
> This quiet morning weighs upon my heart;
> Though I should dream I could even sleep with grief,
> If slumber were denied not. I would fain
> Be what it is my destiny to be,
> The saviour and the strength of suffering man,
> Or sink into the original gulf of things.
> There is no agony, and no solace left;
> Earth can console, Heaven can torment no more.   (I.812–20)

Prometheus has reached the dead moment between cause and effect, between the regeneration of his will and the release which follows from it. In the interim we turn to Asia and her journey to the cave of Demogorgon, where the power is stored up which can make Prometheus' regeneration effective. As the act concludes, Panthea recalls Asia in "that far Indian vale" and determines to visit her.

IV

SHELLEY'S ITALIAN IMAGERY

Before we accompany Panthea to the Caucasian vale and visit the cave of Demogorgon, other aspects of *Prometheus Unbound* and of Shelley's work as a whole deserve our attention. Instead of the dramatic and ethical values of the play, I turn to its poetic texture and to some of the qualities of style which make it recognizably Shelleyan. However, what begins as a digression will seem less parenthetical as our study of *Prometheus Unbound* and Shelley's Italian poetry develops. These stylistic qualities are various ways of perceiving and coordinating the images which make up the poet's apparent world; and what Shelley does to the images of his world (his special focus and organization) affects or is affected by his ethics, his religion, and his view of history.

In Act Two of *Prometheus Unbound,* after Asia and Panthea have passed into the forest accompanied by the richly elaborated lyrics of two semichoruses of spirits, a pair of Fauns, denizens of the place, discuss the spirits whose voices they have heard. The First Faun is ignorant and curious, and listens attentively to the complex scientific explanations of his companion before questioning him further:

> If such live thus, have others other lives,
> Under pink blossoms or within the bells
> Of meadow flowers or folded violets deep,
> Or on their dying odors, when they die,
> Or in the sunlight of the sphered dew? (II.iii.83–87)

But the more experienced Second Faun has explained enough.

Ay, many more which we may well divine.
But should we stay to speak, noontide would come,
And thwart Silenus find his goats undrawn,
And grudge to sing those wise and lovely songs
Of Fate, and Chance, and God, and Chaos old,
And Love and the chained Titan's woeful doom,
And how he shall be loosed, and make the earth
One brotherhood; delightful strains which cheer
Our solitary twilights, and which charm
To silence the unenvying nightingales.   (II.iii.88–97)

Most of the scene of which this speech is the conclusion has been richly and even heavily sensuous, and the First Faun's question retains some of this quality. But the Second Faun's answer is remarkably chaste and unelaborate, a model of sustained simplicity and repose. It is not, however, a model of concrete imagery. The language is relatively abstract and, even when Shelley invokes objects of sight and hearing, he does so without much particularity, like Milton in *L'Allegro* and *Il Penseroso* or in his description of Paradise, and like Wordsworth in the Lucy poems.

Poetry as unparticularized as this seems to repel a good many modern readers, perhaps because they assume that poetry is precise or accurate only within a special, limited range of subject matter. Certainly if the poetry of ideas on a fairly high level of abstraction is to be excluded, Shelley's reputation will suffer. Stephen Spender remarks at the end of his pamphlet on Shelley that

. . . he forged a language which was highly capable of expressing eloquently and beautifully abstract thought and intellectual ideas. In different circumstances, Shelley might have been held to have invented in England something corresponding to the *"dolce stil nuovo"* of the group of Italian poets immediately preceding Dante. It is possible that a more constructively critical study of his work than has yet been given us, might still illuminate for modern poets a path out of their intellectual obscurity, and show how the most complex ideas can be expressed with lucid ease.[1]

Shelley's skill in such expression can be illustrated in passages more complex (if not necessarily more beautiful) than the Second Faun's speech. In *The Triumph of Life,* as he sees the figure of Napoleon depart, Shelley says,

> 　　　　　　　　　　　　I felt my cheek
> Alter, to see the shadow pass away,
> Whose grasp had left the giant world so weak
>
> That every pigmy kicked it as it lay;
> And much I grieved to think how power and will
> In opposition rule our mortal day,
>
> And why God made irreconcilable
> Good and the means of good; and for despair
> I half disdained mine eyes' desire to fill
>
> With the spent vision of the times that were
> And scarce have ceased to be.　　　　　(224-34)

The image which opens this quotation is brilliant and strikingly concrete, but no more impressive, I think, than the abstract statement of grief over the human predicament into which it leads. And in the following passage from *Epipsychidion* the garden, the well, and the light are less images than abstract counters in an argument which illustrates Shelley's skill in the poetic statement of ideas:

> If you divide suffering and dross, you may
> Diminish till it is consumed away;
> If you divide pleasure and love and thought,
> Each part exceeds the whole; and we know not
> How much, while any yet remains unshared,
> Of pleasure may be gained, of sorrow spared.
> This truth is that deep well, whence sages draw
> The unenvied light of hope; the eternal law
> By which those live, to whom this world of life
> Is as a garden ravaged, and whose strife
> Tills for the promise of a later birth
> The wilderness of this Elysian earth.　　　　　(178-89)

If such poetry is rejected as "abstract," we may find ourselves rejecting Pope, Shakespeare, Chaucer, and even the supposedly concrete Keats. Shakespeare's Sonnet 129 ("The expense of spirit in a waste of shame") is not likely to be criticized for its abstractness even by those who reject Shelley. Yet, despite the conceits, it is almost imageless. And, although the "concreteness" of Keats is not to be despised, one of the things which makes the revised version of *Hyperion* so exciting is Keats's new skill in handling a language which sometimes lacks the sensuous immediacy of the Odes and *The Eve of St. Agnes*. Fortunately, the use of "concrete" and "abstract" as automatic terms of praise and blame is no longer as common as it was, except perhaps in manuals of freshman English.[2]

However, it is probably true that those who accuse Shelley of being too abstract and of fleeing from "actuality" are thinking less of his success in dealing with abstractions than of his failure to be sufficiently concrete in passages which demand concreteness. Here are three brief passages (all from Act Two, scene 1, of *Prometheus Unbound*) in which Shelley is certainly intending to be concrete:

> As you speak, your words
> Fill, pause by pause, my own forgotten sleep
> With shapes. Methought among the lawns together
> We wandered, underneath the young gray dawn,
> And multitudes of dense white fleecy clouds
> Were wandering in thick flocks along the mountains,
> Shepherded by the slow, unwilling wind;
> And the white dew on the new-bladed grass,
> Just piercing the dark earth, hung silently. (141–49)

> What shape is that between us? Its rude hair
> Roughens the wind that lifts it, its regard
> Is wild and quick, yet 'tis a thing of air,
> For through its gray robe gleams the golden dew
> Whose stars the noon has quenched not. (127–31)

> The point of one white star is quivering still
> Deep in the orange light of widening morn
> Beyond the purple mountains; through a chasm
> Of wind-divided mist the darker lake
> Reflects it; now it wanes; it gleams again
> As the waves fade, and as the burning threads
> Of woven cloud unravel in pale air. (17–23)

For comparison I set beside them some lines of Keats which also aim at concreteness. (Many familiar passages would suit my purpose, but I choose two less familiar ones.) The first describes Endymion's retreat:

> Some mouldered steps lead into this cool cell,
> Far as the slabbed margin of a well,
> Whose patient level peeps its crystal eye
> Right upward, through the bushes, to the sky.
> Oft have I brought thee flowers, on their stalks set
> Like vestal primroses, but dark velvet
> Edges them round, and they have golden pits:
> 'Twas there I got them, from the gaps and slits
> In a mossy stone, that sometimes was my seat,
> When all above was faint with mid-day heat.   (I.869–78)

The second is Keats's vision of America in *Lines to Fanny:*

> Where shall I learn to get my peace again?
> To banish thoughts of that most hateful land,
> Dungeoner of my friends, that wicked strand
> Where they were wreck'd and live a wrecked life;
> That monstrous region, whose dull rivers pour,
> Ever from their sordid urns unto the shore,
> Unown'd of any weedy-haired gods;
> Whose winds, all zephyrless, hold scourging rods,
> Iced in the great lakes, to afflict mankind;
> Whose rank-grown forests, frosted, black, and blind,
> Would fright a Dryad; whose harsh herbaged meads
> Make lean and lank the starv'd ox while he feeds;
> There bad flowers have no scent, birds no sweet song,
> And great unerring Nature once seems wrong.

All five passages are excellent poetry, it seems to me: but the images of the two groups resemble one another in little besides excellence. Shelley's images are obviously more tenuous and fragile; Keats's thicker and more palpable. It would be easy to move on from these distinctions to the common assumption that Keats's images are a good deal more concrete than Shelley's. However, the distinctions have less to do with relative concreteness, than with the sort of objects about which the poet is being concrete. In trying to correct certain illusions about "the importance of sense-perception" in Shelley's poetry, R. H. Fogle speculates

that the widespread misconception of its characteristics has arisen partly from the thinness and tenuity of the material with which he works, his clouds, mists, dews, water scenes, etc.; so that his critics have confused his subject matter with his ability to handle it.[3]

The connotations of the word "concrete" itself may have contributed to such a misconception. We assume too easily that the heavy, firm, thick, static, opaque, and earthy are more concrete and as a result more real than the transparent, fluid, sparkling, dissolving, and evanescent. An imagery of water, dew, clouds, mists, skies, shores, and distant mountains is assumed, therefore, to lack a grip on actuality, whatever the strength and precision shown by the poet in using it. Our gardens must have real toads in them, rather than real dew. I sympathize with the preference for the static and opaque over the evanescent and transparent, and to some extent I share such a prejudice. But a too exclusive taste for the former will certainly blind any reader to the peculiar excellences of Shelley's imagery.

This imagery seems to have flowered in Italy. The seeds were certainly present in the earlier poetry, but it is difficult not to agree with John Lehmann that

his contact with the actual Mediterranean world, when he left England on his last journey in 1818, and breathed for the first time the air of Italy and saw the remains of classical civilization before him in their exuberant natural setting under the southern sun, so quickened his genius that the poems he began to write were not simply better than what he had written before, but transformed.[4]

The first poems of any importance that Shelley wrote in Italy (*Julian and Maddalo* and *Lines Written among the Euganean Hills*) are saturated with the Italian atmosphere. And of *Prometheus Unbound* Shelley himself says in the Preface:

This Poem was chiefly written upon the mountainous ruins of the Baths of Caracalla, among the flowery glades and thickets of odoriferous blossoming trees, which are extended in ever winding labyrinths upon its immense platforms and dizzy arches suspended in the air. The bright blue sky of Rome, and the effect of the vigorous awakening spring in that divinest climate, and the new life with which it drenches the spirits even to intoxication, were the inspiration of this drama.   (C.327)

It is interesting to set the letters Shelley wrote to Peacock in 1818 and 1819 beside the poems of the same years—and, indeed, those of later years as well. At times we see him translating (consciously or unconsciously) his prose descriptions into poetic imagery; or perhaps all we are observing is just the same experience flowing into both. Here is Shelley describing an excursion from Naples to Baiae:

We set off an hour after sunrise one radiant morning in a little boat, there was not a cloud in the sky nor a wave upon the sea, which was so translucent that you could see the hollow caverns clothed with the glaucous sea-moss, and the leaves and branches of those delicate weeds that pave the unequal bottom of the water. . . .   (J.X.16)

There can be no doubt that this journey is one of the causes of Panthea's description of her underwater sleep:

> erewhile I slept
> Under the glaucous caverns of old Ocean
> Within dim bowers of green and purple moss.   (II.i.43–45)

Other by-products of the same experience are contained in the Second Faun's description of "the pale faint water-flowers that pave the oozy bottom of clear lakes and pools"; in "the sea-blooms and the oozy woods which wear the sapless foliage of the ocean" from *Ode to the West Wind;* and in two passages from poems whose titles explicitly connect them with Naples:

> I see the Deep's untrampled floor
> With green and purple sea-weeds strown;
>
> .   .   .   .

the Baian ocean
Welters with air-like motion,
Within, above, around its bowers of starry green,
Moving the sea-flowers in those purple caves,
Even as the ever stormless atmosphere
Floats o'er the Elysian realm.[5]

Shelley was in Naples only once (from November 29, 1818, to February 28, 1819), but obviously his experiences there were never forgotten. The undersea flowers occur, therefore, not merely in work written during or immediately after his stay, but also in a poem written about eight months later and in another written a year and a half later. Shelley was continually digesting, using and re-using his experiences, old and new. Both as man and poet, he was changed by his mature experience far more than most, and it is interesting to speculate on what extraordinary development might have been in store for him had he been able, like Byron, to visit Greece or the Near East.

Another experience, which remained in his mind for some time before finding its place in poetry, was his visit to the English cemetery in Rome.

The English burying-place is a green slope near the walls, under the pyramidal tomb of Cestius, and is, I think, the most beautiful and solemn cemetery I ever beheld. To see the sun shining on its bright grass, fresh, when we first visited it, with the autumnal dews, and hear the whispering of the wind among the leaves of the trees which have over-grown the tomb of Cestius, and the soil which is stirring in the sun warm earth, and to mark the tombs, mostly of women and young people who were buried there, one might, if one were to die, desire the sleep they seem to sleep. (J.X.14)

It is hardly necessary to quote the relevant stanzas (XLIX, L) of *Adonais,* written two and a half years later, two years after he had seen Rome for the last time.

What is true of such particular experiences as the boat trip to Baiae and the visit to the English cemetery in Rome is also true of more generalized experiences, which cannot necessarily be centered on a particular incident. The letters to Peacock are full of Shelley's delight in and amazement at the Italian sea and sky and "the enchanting atmosphere which envelops these tranquil seas and majestic mountains in its radiance" (J.X.8).[6] Here are a few representative passages:

The colours of the water and the air breathe over all things here the radiance of their own beauty.   (J.X.16)

What colours there were in the sky, what radiance in the evening star; and how the moon was encompassed by a light unknown to our regions!
(J.X.17)

In a letter to Hunt he speaks of

the green earth and transparent sea and the mighty ruins of ancient time, and the aërial mountains, and the warm and radiant atmosphere which is interfused through all things.   (J.X.10)

Shelley was fascinated by the Italian atmosphere not merely when the sky was clear but when it was cloudy or hazy as well (particularly near the mountains). At first, he seemed surprised to discover that the sky ever had stormclouds, but his fascination did not diminish.

The atmosphere here, unlike that of the rest of Italy, is diversified with clouds, which grow in the middle of the day, and sometimes bring thunder and lightning, and hail about the size of a pigeon's egg, and decrease toward evening, leaving only those finely woven webs of vapour which we see in English skies, and flocks of fleecy and slow-moving clouds, which all vanish before sunset; and the nights are for ever serene. . . .[7]   (J.IX.313–14)

It was a cloudy morning, and we had no conception of the scene that awaited us. Suddenly the low clouds were struck by the clear north wind, and like curtains of the finest gauze, removed one by one, were drawn down from before the mountains, whose heaven cleaving pinnacles and black crags overhanging one another, stood at length defined in the light of day.   (J.X.4)

These passages should be set beside the three quotations which I
made earlier from Act Two, scene 1, of *Prometheus Unbound*: and
to those quotations might be added Asia's description of the moun-
tain-top entrance to the cave of Demogorgon, with its "wide plain
of billowy mist" (III.iii.19), blown by "the curdling winds"

> and islanding
> The peak whereon we stand, midway, around,
> Encinctured by the dark and blooming forests,
> Dim twilight-lawns, and stream-illumined caves,
> And wind-enchanted shapes of wandering mist;
> And far on high the keen sky-cleaving mountains
> From icy spires of sunlike radiance fling
> The dawn. . . .   (II.iii.23–30)

But perhaps the most striking of Shelley's evocations of the Italian
atmosphere in *Prometheus Unbound* is purely figurative, when
Panthea describes how the love of Prometheus seemed to flow over
her,

> an atmosphere
> Which wrapped me in its all-dissolving power,
> As the warm ether of the morning sun
> Wraps ere it drinks some cloud of wandering dew.
> I saw not, heard not, moved not, only felt
> His presence flow and mingle through my blood
> Till it became his life, and his grew mine,
> And I was thus absorbed, until it passed,
> And like the vapours when the sun sinks down,
> Gathering again in drops upon the pines,
> And tremulous as they, in the deep night
> My being was condensed.   (II.i.75–86)

There is no more brilliantly conceived and precisely executed piece
of metaphysical wit in Donne himself—unless one assumes that
water vapor is per se a less precise image than, say, "stiff, twin com-
passes."

This Italian atmosphere, which is one of the most delightful features of Shelley's later poetry, is not simply vaporous and dissolving. It has brilliance and clarity and sparkle, and at times something of the hardness of a precious stone. It is translucent and crystalline, and this fact qualifies the fluidity which might otherwise be dangerous to it. At its best Shelley's Italian atmosphere achieves a perfect balance between the softness and dissolving outlines of mist and the sharpness and sparkle of "elemental diamond." Perhaps the passage in which this balance is most perfectly achieved is the description of the Aegean isle in *Epipsychidion;* which I shall therefore quote and discuss at some length:

> It is an isle under Ionian skies,
> Beautiful as a wreck of Paradise,
> And, for the harbours are not safe and good,
> The land would have remained a solitude
> But for some pastoral people native there,
> Who from the Elysian, clear, and golden air
> Draw the last spirit of the age of gold,
> Simple and spirited, innocent and bold.
> The blue Aegean girds this chosen home
> With ever-changing sound and light and foam
> Kissing the sifted sands and caverns hoar;
> And all the winds wandering along the shore
> Undulate with the undulating tide;
> There are thick woods where sylvan forms abide,
> And many a fountain, rivulet and pond,
> As clear as elemental diamond,
> Or serene morning air; and far beyond,
> The mossy tracks made by the goats and deer
> (Which the rough shepherd treads but once a year)
> Pierce into glades, caverns, and bowers, and halls
> Built round with ivy, which the waterfalls
> Illumining, with sound that never fails
> Accompany the noonday nightingales;
> And all the place is peopled with sweet airs;
> The light clear element which the isle wears
> Is heavy with the scent of lemon-flowers,

Which floats like mist laden with unseen showers,
And falls upon the eyelids like faint sleep.

. . . .

It is an isle 'twixt Heaven, Air, Earth, and Sea,
Cradled and hung in clear tranquillity;
Bright as that wandering Eden, Lucifer,
Washed by the soft blue Oceans of young air.

(422–49, 457–60)

There are no clouds in this passage; their place is taken by the
foam of the ocean, the undulation of the tide, the sifting of the
sand, the sounds of waterfalls and nightingales, and the scent of
lemon flowers, which is the only "mist" on this Ionian isle. But
Shelley is continually modifying these images of evanescence and
process by others which suggest sharpness and clarity and hardness: "clear and golden air," "as clear as elemental diamond," "the
light clear element," "clear tranquillity." The word "clear" recurs
like a *leitmotif* in the passage; while certain other adjectives or
verbs also contribute to a sense of solidity or sharpness in the midst
of fluidity: there are *"thick* woods," the *"rough* shepherd," and the
tracks which *"pierce"* into the glades and caverns which are *"built*
round with ivy." Similarly, the diction combines simplicity and
smoothness with a number of unobtrusive touches of wit, which
prevent the smoothness from becoming too soft. This wit (here and
elsewhere in Shelley) is generally the result of unexpected adjectives or participles, as in "Undulate with the undulating tide," "Accompany the noonday nightingales," "Cradled and hung in clear
tranquillity"; or, most brilliantly, but still unobtrusively, and without any sense of *discordia concors,* "Washed by the soft blue oceans
of young air."

The passage also contains, far more than is usual in Shelley, a
good many spondaic feet, with a consequent crowding together of
two or three heavy accents to balance the rapidity of movement
which generally characterizes Shelley's versification. The last line

quoted will serve as a double illustration of this point, but a good
many others might be chosen. Here are two short descriptive passages from a later section of the poem which will serve to illustrate
again in a short compass most of the things I have been emphasizing:

> and the owls flit
> Round the evening tower, and the young stars glance
> Between the quick bats in their twilight dance;
> The spotted deer bask in the fresh moonlight
> Before our gate, and the slow silent night
> Is measured by the pants of their calm sleep.   (530–535)

> We too will rise, and sit, and walk together
> Under the roof of blue Ionian weather,
> And wander in the meadows, or ascend
> The mossy mountains, where the blue heavens bend
> With lightest winds, to touch their paramour;
> Or linger, where the pebble-paven shore,
> Under the quick faint kisses of the sea
> Trembles and sparkles as with ecstasy. . . .   (541–48)

Another important influence on Shelley's description of the Ionian
isle is the pastoral convention, which, for Shelley, was exemplified
not merely by the classical eclogues or pastoral elegies, but in
English by *A Midsummer Night's Dream, The Winter's Tale, The
Tempest, The Faithful Shepherdess, The Sad Shepherd,* and most
of the early poems of Milton. This convention, whatever sensuous
suggestions it may allow, demands that the images be judiciously
generalized, or, at least, achieve a balance between numbering the
streaks of the tulip and sketching a remote panorama. For this
reason, the descriptive style of *Epipsychidion,* while sensuous
enough, avoids the notable concreteness of my earlier quotations
from *Prometheus Unbound.* At those moments when the pastoral
background is particularly emphasized (as in ll.424-29 and ll.483-
90), Shelley displays a quiet freshness and a transparent simplicity
which Wordsworth might have envied. Elsewhere he uses this
style most successfully in the Second Faun's speech and in a good

deal of *The Witch of Atlas*. The pastoralism of *Adonais* is quite another matter.

The simplicity and reserve of the pastoral convention and the "light clear element" are checks which prevent the fluidity of Shelley's imagery in *Epipsychidion* from degenerating into a complicated and undifferentiated flux. But there is a further aspect of Shelley's Italian imagery which provides a more consistent and far-reaching framework of stability within which Shelley's interest in process and transformation can achieve its greatest impact. Everyone observes the effect of movement, of disintegration and reformation in *Ode to the West Wind*. Not all readers, however, visualize the scene clearly enough to see beyond the procession of clouds, leaves, and waves to the framework within which the transformation takes place.[8] In the second section of the poem, the "loose clouds" are "Shook from the tangled boughs of Heaven and Ocean" and the night forms

> the dome of a vast sepulchre,
> Vaulted with all thy congregated might

> Of vapours, from whose solid atmosphere
> Black rain, and fire, and hail will burst.

The "commotion" of the storm exists within a firm, and even inflexible, framework. The "steep" sky is "vaulted," a "dome" of "congregated" vapors, from whose "solid" atmosphere the "black rain" is bursting. In the third section this image of the heavens is reversed. The "sea blooms and the oozy woods" which grow under the waves "tremble and despoil themselves" under the influence of the West Wind, and the waves themselves are separated by great troughs; but Shelley also sees "old palaces and towers quivering within the wave's intenser day" from under the "crystalline streams" of the Mediterranean; and even the waves are described with a certain architectural immobility, when "the Atlantic's level powers cleave themselves in chasms." Similarly, in that masterpiece of transformation and natural process *The Cloud*, what is being assembled, destroyed, and reassembled is an architectural structure, and both the cloud and the sky are described as the solid parts of a building—less solid as a tent in stanza four, and more solid as an arch with columns in stanza five and as a pavilion with a dome in stanza six. There is something paradoxical in a poem which describes the transformations of water vapor in terms of such rigid forms. The peculiarity of the imagery is duplicated by the versification, which combines rapidity of movement with inflexibility of meter.

These two famous poems illustrate strikingly the architectural and geometric side of Shelley's imagery, which either forms a framework within which process can take place, or, at other times, mingles with the process itself. As Fogle remarks,

he habitually pictures objects or phenomena almost inaccessible to the senses of the average man, and he emphasizes the evanescence and etheriality of these objects; but if we look we shall usually find that he has strengthened and solidified his descriptions by reinforcing them with a thin but strong thread of steel, that his misty veils, his cloud-capped towers are firm of outline and composed of visible, even tangible, elements.[9]

Fogle goes on to illustrate "this union of the solid and the etherial" [10] in a number of passages, particularly in the striking description of the Moon and the Earth in Act Four of *Prometheus Unbound*, with its "solid clouds," "white light scattered in strings," "emerald light of leaf-entangled beams," odors, music and light which "seem kneaded into one aerial mass" and whirling orb which "grinds the bright brook into an azure mist."

This tendency to unite "the solid and the etherial" and to give the processes of nature an architectural and geometric stiffening did not make its first appearance in Shelley's Italian poetry, as section two of *Queen Mab* would alone suffice to prove. "White light scattered in strings" recalls Cythna's "flowing hair like strings of flame" (XI.iii), and the picture of a storm in *Ode to the West Wind* may be compared with an earlier one in canto six of *The Revolt of Islam*:

> but the wide sky
> Flooded with lightning was ribbed overhead
> By the black rafters.   (XLVI)

But his travels in Italy were certainly responsible for developing a tendency which had been little more than embryonic and conventional before. The first striking piece of architecture which Shelley saw in Italy was the cathedral at Milan, the garish magnificence of which seems to have palled on most modern observers, but which overwhelmed Shelley when he first saw it.

The cathedral is a most astonishing work of art. It is built of white marble, and cut into pinnacles of immense height, and the utmost delicacy of workmanship, and loaded with sculpture. The effect of it, piercing the solid blue with those groups of dazzling spires, relieved by the serene depth of this Italian Heaven, or by moonlight when the stars seem gathered among those clustered shapes, is beyond anything I had imagined architecture capable of producing.   (J.IX.298)

There are similar passages on Venice, and on Rome with its "domes beyond domes, and palaces, and colonnades interminably, even to the horizon" (J.X.41). The reflection of these experiences in Shelley's later poetry is obvious at a glance. The architectural descriptions in *Queen Mab, Alastor,* and *The Revolt of Islam* show Shelley's susceptibility to this sort of imagery,[11] and it is certainly no less apparent in the *Ode to Liberty,* the fragmentary story *The Colosseum,* and the *Lines Written among the Euganean Hills:*

> Lo! the sun upsprings behind,
> Broad, red, radiant, half-reclined
> On the level quivering line
> Of the waters crystalline;
> And before that chasm of light,
> As within a furnace bright,
> Column, tower, and dome, and spire,

Shine like obelisks of fire,
Pointing with inconstant motion
From the altar of dark ocean
To the sapphire-tinted skies;
As the flames of sacrifice
From the marble shrines did rise
As to pierce the dome of gold
Where Apollo spoke of old.   (100–14)

But more important than the direct uses of architecture are figurative uses such as those we have already observed in the *Ode to the West Wind* and *The Cloud*. In the letters to Peacock we can observe the landscape and the architecture mingling with one another, sometimes literally, sometimes figuratively.

We passed on day after day, until we came to Spoleto, I think the most romantic city I ever saw. There is here an aqueduct of astonishing elevation, which unites two rocky mountains—there is the path of a torrent below, whitening the green dell with its broad and barren track of stones, and above there is a castle, apparently of great strength and of tremendous magnitude, which overhangs the city, and whose marble bastions are perpendicular with the precipice. I never saw a more impressive picture; in which the shapes of nature are of the grandest order, but over which the creations of man, sublime from their antiquity and greatness, seem to predominate.   (J.X.4)

The mingling is particularly close when Shelley is describing the Roman or Greek ruins at or near Rome and Naples.

We visited the Forum and the ruins of the Coliseum every day. The Coliseum is unlike any work of human hands I ever saw before. It is of enormous height and circuit, and the arches built of massy stones are piled on one another, and jut into the blue air, shattered into the forms of over-hanging rocks. It has been changed by time into the image of an amphitheatre of rocky hills overgrown by the wild olive, the myrtle, and the fig-tree, and threaded by little paths, which wind among its ruined stairs and immeasurable galleries: the copsewood overshadows you as you wander through its labyrinths, and the wild weeds of this climate of flowers bloom under your feet. The arena is covered with grass, and pierces, like the skirts of a natural plain, the chasms of the broken arches around. But a small part of the exterior circumference remains—it is exquisitely light and beautiful; and the effect of the perfection of its architecture, adorned with ranges of Corinthian pilasters, supporting a bold cornice, is such as to diminish the effect of its greatness. The interior is all ruin. I can scarcely believe that when encrusted with Dorian marble and ornamented by columns of Egyptian granite, its effect could have been so sublime and so impressive as in its present state. It is open to the sky, and it was the clear and sunny weather of the end of November in this climate when we visited it, day after day.   (J.X.13)

The temples at Posidonia are described in even greater detail. They too seem to be a part of their natural surroundings.

The scene from between the columns of the temple consists on one side of the sea to which the gentle hill on which it is built slopes, and on the other, of the grand amphitheatre of the loftiest Apennines, dark purple mountains, crowned with snow, and intersected there by long bars of hard and leaden-coloured cloud. The effect of the jagged outline of mountains, through groups of enormous columns on one side and on the other the level horizon of the sea, is inexpressibly grand.
                                                             (J.X.31–32)

He wrote Peacock an equally breathless account of Pompeii, and two years later recalled his impressions in the first stanza of the *Ode to Naples:*

> I stood within the city disinterred;
>   And heard the autumnal leaves like light footfalls
> Of spirits passing through the streets; and heard
>   The mountain's slumberous voice at intervals
>   Thrill through those roofless halls;
>
>   .   .   .   .
>
>   Through white columns glowed
>   The isle-sustaining Ocean-flood,
> A plane of light between two heavens of azure:
>   Around me gleamed many a bright sepulchre
> Of whose pure beauty, Time, as if his pleasure
>   Were to spare Death, had never made erasure;
>   But every living lineament was clear

> As in the sculptor's thought; and there
> The wreaths of stony myrtle, ivy and pine,
> Like winter leaves o'ergrown by moulded snow,
> Seemed only not to move and grow
> Because the crystal silence of the air
> Weighed on their life. . . .

In his account to Peacock, Shelley goes on to draw something of a moral from the architecture he has seen in the Greek city of Pompeii.

The Greeks . . . lived in a perpetual commerce with external nature, and nourished themselves upon the spirit of its forms. Their theatres were all open to the mountains and the sky. Their columns, the ideal types of a sacred forest, with its roof of interwoven tracery, admitted the light and wind; the odour and the freshness of the country penetrated the cities. Their temples were mostly upaithric; and the flying clouds, the stars, or the deep sky, were seen above.   (J.X.26)

It is important to realize that, because Shelley never saw Greece, he visualized its cities in terms of the ruins of Pompeii. As a result, when, in the *Ode to Liberty* he describes Athens, he is seeing it in terms of his memory of Pompeii.

> Athens arose; a city such as vision
>   Builds from the purple crags and silver towers
> Of battlemented cloud, as in derision
>   Of kingliest masonry: the ocean floors
> Pave it; the evening sky pavilions it;
>   Its portals are inhabited
>   By thunder zoned winds, each head
> Within its cloudy wings with sun-fire garlanded,—
>   A divine work! Athens, diviner yet,
>   Gleamed with its crest of columns, on the will
> Of man, as on a mount of diamond, set. . . .   (61-71)

Perhaps the most complex mingling of nature and architecture in the letters to Peacock occurs in the description of "the mountainous ruins of the Baths of Caracalla" (C.327), near which Shelley wrote much of *Prometheus Unbound:*

The perpendicular wall of ruin is cloven into steep ravines filled with
flowering shrubs, whose thick twisted roots are knotted in the rifts of
the stones. At every step the aerial pinnacles of shattered stone group
into new combinations of effect, and tower above the lofty yet level
walls, as the distant mountains change their aspect to one rapidly travelling along the plain. . . . These walls surround green and level spaces
of lawn, on which some elms have grown, and which are interspersed
toward their skirts by masses of fallen ruin, overtwined with the broad
leaves of the creeping weeds. The blue canopies it, and is as the everlasting roof of these enormous halls. [He ascends to the thickly wooded
"summit of these piles."] . . . From the midst rise those pinnacles
and masses, themselves like Mountains, which have been seen from below. In one place you wind along a narrow strip of weed grown ruin:
on one side is the immensity of earth and sky, on the other a narrow
chasm, which is bounded by an arch of enormous size, fringed by the
many coloured foliage and blossoms, and supporting a lofty and ir-
regular pyramid, overgrown like itself with the all-prevailing vegetation.
Around rise other crags and other peaks, all arrayed, and the deformity
of their vast desolation softened down, by the undecaying investiture
of nature. Come to Rome. It is a scene by which expression is overpowered; which words cannot convey.   (J.X.38–39)

It is difficult to believe that two years later when Shelley was writing
Adonais he did not have a copy of this letter beside him:

> Go thou to Rome,—at once the Paradise,
> The grave, the city, and the wilderness;
> And where its wrecks like shattered mountains rise,
> And flowering weeds and fragrant copses dress
> The bones of Desolation's nakedness,
> Pass. . . .   (XLIX)

   Perhaps the most striking mixture of nature and architecture in
all Shelley's prose is the expanded description of the Coliseum in
Shelley's fragmentary story of that name.

We see the liquid depth of heaven above through the rifts and the
windows; and the flowers, and the weeds, and the grass and creeping
moss are nourished by its unforbidden rain. The blue sky is above—
the wide, bright, blue sky—it flows through the great rents on high,

and through the bare boughs of the marble rooted fig-tree, and through
the leaves and flowers of the weeds, even to the dark arcades beneath.
. . . Yes, and through the highest rift the noonday waning moon is
hanging, as it were, out of the solid sky, and this shows that the atmosphere has all the clearness which it rejoices me that you feel.

(C.225–26)

The old man of the story defines this ruin as "a nursling of man's
art, abandoned by his care, and transformed by the enchantment of
Nature into a likeness of her own creations" (C.226).

These passages from the letters and *The Coliseum* show unmistakably how Shelley's tendency to see nature in terms of architectural and geometric shapes was strengthened or developed by
what he saw in Italy. It is appropriate that the retreat to which
Shelley suggests that he retire with Emily in *Epipsychidion* is not
merely an island, but a ruined building. Shelley's description of it
is perhaps his most successful attempt to present in poetry something
of what he saw in the ruins of Pompeii, Posidonia, and the Baths of
Caracalla, here transported to his pastoral Aegean isle.

> But the chief marvel of the wilderness
> Is a lone dwelling, built by whom or how
> None of the rustic island-people know;
> 'Tis not a tower of strength, though with its height
> It overtops the woods; but, for delight,
> Some wise and tender Ocean-King, ere crime
> Had been invented, in the world's young prime,
> Reared it, a wonder of that simple time,
> And envy of the isles, a pleasure-house
> Made sacred to his sister and his spouse.
> It scarce seems now a wreck of human art,
> But, as it were, Titanic, in the heart
> Of Earth having assumed its form, then grown
> Out of the mountains, from the living stone,
> Lifting itself in caverns light and high;
> For all the antique and learned imagery
> Has been erased, and in the place of it
> The ivy and the wild vine interknit
> The volumes of their many-twining stems;

Parasite flowers illume with dewy gems
The lampless halls, and, when they fade, the sky
Peeps through their winter-woof of tracery
With moonlight patches, or star-atoms keen,
Or fragments of the day's intense serene,
Working mosaic on their Parian floors.   (483–507)

In this description the island and the house are indistinguishable.
Indeed, the house seems almost to have grown out of the mountains from a seed stored up "in the heart / Of Earth." The architecture of man and the architecture of Nature seem to form two
sides of the same thing, and it is absurd to consider whether the
art of Nature mimics the art of man or vice versa.

Shelley repudiated the idea of a creator God and made fun of
the argument from design; yet, provided the stuff of nature was
given to start with, he was willing in *Adonais* at least to imagine
how

> the one Spirit's plastic stress
> Sweeps through the dull dense world, compelling there
> All new successions to the forms they wear,
> Torturing the unwilling dross that checks its flight
> To its own likeness, as each mass may bear,
> And bursting in its beauty and its might
> From trees and beasts and men into the Heaven's light. (LXIII)

But to go beyond this and imagine a geometer or architect or
sculptor God would have smacked too much of Deism or even of
Paley's Watchmaker. Nevertheless, Shelley's severely patterned universe seems to demand the sort of Newtonian God celebrated in
so much devotional or descriptive verse from Addison to Erasmus
Darwin. That universe with its roofs and floors, its domes and
arches, its pillars and pinnacles, its temples and pavilions, its intersecting lines and implicated orbits and cyclic processes, seems to be
summed up in a phrase which Shelley echoes from the opening of
De Rerum Natura. "I sing of the daedal earth," cries Shelley's Pan.
And, according to the *Ode to Liberty:*

the daedal earth,
That island in the ocean of the world,
Hung in its cloud of all-sustaining air.   (18–20)

Daedalus, we recall, means "cunning worker," and the legendary
Athenian who bore the name was famed as sculptor, architect, and
inventor, his most famous creation being the labyrinth of Crete. The
"daedal" earth would have been a worthy product of so great a
craftsman; and it is the "daedal" qualities of nature that form the
hard core of Shelley's descriptive poetry.

In this fact lies the greatest justification for the charge that Shelley's poetry is too "abstract." He tends to reduce the flesh to a shimmering veil and seize on the forming skeleton beneath. Through a
foreground of motion and process certain stark, ruthlessly reduced
outlines are apparent. Shelley is abstract in the way that Cézanne
is abstract, a way that has very little to do with an opposition between the abstract and the concrete or sensuous. The designs are
visible, but they are at the same time a reduction of the particularity and complexity of the visible world, just as Prometheus and
Cenci and Emily and Adonais are of the ethical world. When we
read Shelley's descriptive poetry (particularly if he is at his best),
we are aware of a drawing out of the abstract relations of the objects described. It is one of the peculiarities of modern criticism
that those features of modern art (the emphasis upon design, selectivity, abstraction) which have seemed most advanced to art
critics have seemed most dated to Shelley's literary critics. Not that
Shelley carries his method to extremes; his closest analogues are
Cézanne, Van Gogh, and, to some extent, Turner. For example, the
first stanza from *Evening: Ponte al Mare, Pisa,* is selective, but still
quite naturalistic; only in the second does the abstraction approach
that of some contemporary art:

There is no dew on the dry grass to-night,
    Nor damp within the shadow of the trees;
The wind is intermitting, dry, and light;
    And in the inconstant motion of the breeze

The dust and straws are driven up and down,
And whirled about the pavement of the town.

.   .   .   .

The chasm in which the sun was sunk is shut
By darkest barriers of enormous cloud,
Like mountain over mountain huddled—but
Growing and moving upwards in a crowd,
And over it a space of watery blue,
Which the keen evening star is shining through.

Shelley's fondness for reducing and abstracting, and the consequent elimination of a good deal of the detail, complexity, and
living wholeness of the scenes and things that he depicts, leaves
him open to objections from a point of view that has been central
to literary criticism since Coleridge. The Romantic belief in the
"organic" is still a central dogma of most contemporary criticism.
But, as Fogle points out in comparing the visual imagery of Keats
and Shelley,

the visual imagery of Keats is, then, for the most part synthetic, while
Shelley's is analytical. One may say that Shelley's view of things is
mechanical, Keats' organic.[12]

This is admirably put. For, despite Shelley's foreground of motion
and process and transformation, his scenes are mixtures, not organic compounds. Coleridge might have called him fanciful, not
imaginative. His cloud moves less through an organic process
than along an assembly line. His visual images do not coalesce into
scenes, they congregate and form up. When, in Act Four of
Prometheus Unbound, Shelley gives us an abstract vision of the
Earth itself, the result is an extraordinary machine. Commentators
have seen both Ezekiel and Milton in the background here.[13] It
has also been plausibly suggested that Shelley is recalling from his
schooldays one of the rotating machines that Adam Walker
brought to Sion House for his series of scientific lectures. At the
same time, Grabo is surely right to see in Shelley's sphere the effects

of current speculation on the atomic and electrical nature of matter.[14] But, whatever its sources, this Platonic form of the earth is the perfect summing up (almost, one might say, the *reductio ad absurdum*) of Shelley's characteristic method of depicting the natural world.

But in stressing the geometrical patterns we should not lose sight of the ether, "Filling their bare and void interstices." [15] As my analyses of the imagery of *Ode to the West Wind, The Cloud,* and *Epipsychidion* will already have suggested, the effect of the skeleton is partly caused by the tension between its outline and the shimmering transformations of the flesh through which our vision is filtered, the "spume that plays / Upon a ghostly paradigm of things," [16] in Yeats's phrase. The Earth, in Panthea's vision, may be

> A sphere which is as many thousand spheres,
> Solid as crystal. *Yet* through all its mass
> Flow, as through empty space, music and light.

The solid flows, the impenetrable admits the etherial. Panthea sees "sphere within sphere"; but "every space between" is "Peopled with unimaginable shapes." The austerity of the vision is never final. To geometry is added color ("Purple and azure, white, green and golden"), mist ("an azure / Of elemental subtlety"), smell ("The wild odour of the forest flowers"), sound ("The music of the living grass and air"), and simple vitality. The outline dominates, but we observe a tension between the skeletal and the etherial, the mechanical and the organic, which is no doubt one aspect of Shelley's Platonism. Not that Shelley's dualism will always translate easily into Plato's. Sometimes the "skeletal" will be Plato's transcendental component, sometimes the "etherial"; sometimes neither.

Lines Written among the Euganean Hills contains a great deal of Shelley's most notable visual imagery. Indeed, Stephen Spender has called it his "lyric masterpiece" for that reason.[17] By analyzing a characteristic passage I can summarize my conclusions about how he focuses and organizes what he sees. Here are some of the finest lines in Shelley:

Noon descends around me now.
'Tis the noon of autumn's glow,
When a soft and purple mist,
Like a vaporous amethyst,
Or an air-dissolved star
Mingling light and fragrance, far
From the curved horizon's bound
To the point of heaven's profound
Fills the overflowing sky.
And the plains that silent lie
Underneath; the leaves unsodden
Where the infant frost has trodden
With his morning-winged feet,
Whose bright print is gleaming yet;
And the red and golden vines,
Piercing with their trellised lines
The rough, dark-skirted wilderness;
The dun and bladed grass no less,
Pointing from this hoary tower
In the windless air; the flower
Glimmering at my feet; the line
Of the olive-sandalled Apennine
In the south dimly islanded;
And the Alps, whose snows are spread
High between the clouds and sun;
And of living things each one;
And my spirit, which so long
Darkened this swift stream of song,—
Interpenetrated lie
By the glory of the sky:
Be it love, light, harmony,
Odour, or the soul of all
Which from heaven like dew doth fall,
Or the mind which feeds this verse
Peopling the lone universe. (285–319)

First, an evanescent, dissolving atmosphere is established, set, however, almost immediately within certain limits, which, although
remote and, in a sense, undefined, are stated with a specious geometric precision. The mist extends from the "curved horizon's

bound" to the "point of heaven's profound." The poet himself is standing on one of the Euganean hills and now drops his gaze from the zenith and the horizon to the plains below. A few sharply defined lines and points of light stand out and are selected from the vast panorama: the gleam of the frost, as clear-cut as a footprint on the crisp leaves, and the criss-cross of the vine-covered trellises, which stand out vividly against the harsh and undefined flux of "the rough, dark-skirted wilderness" behind. Now he starts to focus on the foreground, and gazes first at the grass growing from the nearby tower and pointing like blades into "the windless air," then at a single flower which glimmers at his feet. His panoramic view has moved from the horizon up to the zenith, and then covered a complete semicircle down to a point at his feet. Next, instead of moving his eyes vertically, he moves them horizontally and turns south toward the "line" of the mountains in the distance, with their olive trees clustered like sandals at the base; first the Apennines, and then beyond them the Alps with their snows "spread" between clouds and sun. But the wheel has come full circle, and we return both to the atmosphere with which the passage began and to the poet, who, like all "living things," is "interpenetrated" by "the glory of the sky," which now fades away into the undefinable. This glory may be, Shelley surmises, "love, light, harmony, odour" or even the world soul itself. Then again, it may simply be the mind of the poet "peopling the lone universe." From this brief obeisance to the Newtonian continuum [18] and the Berkeleian mind, he returns once again to the autumn scene.

V

THE CAVE OF
DEMOGORGON

For those who regard *Prometheus Unbound* as an allegory, Act Two presents something of a challenge. The three Oceanides, Asia, Ione, and Panthea, must be assigned their place, as must the ominous, and obviously central, figure of Demogorgon. Moreover (and here the difficulties are most notable), the journey itself must be explained as some sort of moral or intellectual or political process, and the scenes passed through identified. There are also two dreams and some local figures (spirits and fauns) to be considered. A consistent allegorist like Grabo may admit the difficulty of finding the allegorical meaning of some of these things, but he never doubts that the meaning is there to be found, and ultimately he does find it in one way or another.[1] An allegorist of more specialized aims, like Cameron, will be more inclined to pick and choose among the characters and incidents to be interpreted allegorically.[2]

But just as a piece of music may often be fugal without being a fugue, so a narrative poem may often be allegorical without being an allegory. *Prometheus Unbound* uses allegory as one among many techniques, not as the central one to which everything else must be related. Shelley simply does not apply it to Ione and Panthea. It is quite possible, by summarizing the typical features of their acts and words, to come out with some more or less plausible abstractions like "the Spirit of Love in Beauty" and "sympathetic love,"[3] or, by analogy with the *Letter to Maria Gisborne*, to call them Hope and Memory,[4] or, arguing from the obvious identification of Asia with Venus or Love at the end of Act Two, to call

the three sisters Faith, Hope, and Charity.[5] Less specifically, they
may be said to represent merely "degrees of love and perceptiveness
in the human mind." [6] But the main functions of Ione and Panthea
are as commentators, consolers and messengers. Were they omitted
from the play its moral or political significance would be precisely
the same; but there would be less dialogue and more soliloquy, less
variety and contrast of reactions, and, in Act One, more direct
presentation of Prometheus' situation; there would be no dream
mechanism (or a quite different one) in Act Two, scene one, and
no one for Asia to talk to before, during, and after her visit to the
cave of Demogorgon. In Act Three, Ione and Panthea have one
short speech each; in Act Four they simply query or describe what
they see and hear. To Ione Shelley gives the vision of the form of
the Moon and to Panthea that of the form of the Earth. Apart from
the two principals they are the only characters who are generally
present and available to fulfill minor functions in the drama. In
this lies their main *raison d'être*.

When Act Two opens we are with Asia in the lovely Caucasian
Vale, observing the advent of the long delayed spring. Asia has
been expecting a visit from Panthea, the messenger between her
and Prometheus during their separation. But Panthea, as she explains on arrival, has been delayed by a dream in which the love of
Prometheus seemed to flow from him and overwhelm her. As
Asia looks into Panthea's eyes she sees a vision of a smiling and
radiant Prometheus, and immediately recognizes the significance of
this transfiguration. The release of Prometheus must be at hand.

> Say not those smiles that we shall meet again
> Within that bright pavilion which their beams
> Shall build on the waste world? The dream is told.
>
> (II.1.124–26)

But there was another, unrecalled dream, which suddenly appears
between them.

> What shape is that between us? Its rude hair
> Roughens the wind that lifts it, its regard

> Is wild and quick, yet 'tis a thing of air,
> For through its gray robe gleams the golden dew
> Whose stars the noon has quenched not.   (II.i.127-31)

The first dream prophesied the release of Prometheus; the second demands that Asia do her part in making that release possible. The first dream concerned the end and was literal; the second concerns the means and is symbolic. Asia describes it in ominous terms: it is rough and wild and hairy. At the same time it remains a dream, "a thing of air," and through it gleams the promise of the "golden dew." To call the dream "revolution," as Cameron does,[7] is perhaps one-sided, but his word has the right connotations. It suggests the exercise of the fierce and terrible power of Demogorgon.

Panthea now recalls this second, symbolic dream and describes it:

> It passes now into my mind. Methought
> As we sate here, the flower-infolding buds
> Burst on yon lightning-blasted almond tree;
> When swift from the white Scythian wilderness
> A wind swept forth wrinkling the Earth with frost;
> I looked, and all the blossoms were blown down;
> But on each leaf was stamped, as the blue bells
> Of Hyacinth tell Apollo's written grief,
> OH, FOLLOW, FOLLOW!   (II.i.132-40)

This dream both warns and demands. The "lightning-blasted almond tree" bursts into premature bloom, but its rebirth proves abortive: an icy wind nips the blossoms and casts them down. The release of Prometheus must not be thus ineffectual. On the blossoms is an insistent demand, by which, if Asia accepts it, she can prevent the same fate from befalling Prometheus: "Oh, follow, follow!"

These words stir memories in Asia's mind, and she recalls dreams of her own in which she saw such words written on the clouds and mountain slopes or heard them in the wind. She even recalls having seen them in Panthea's eyes. In the distance echoes start to take up the refrain, and, as Asia and Panthea listen or question one another, they sing a series of choruses inviting the two to follow them into the remote caverns and forests.

> In the world unknown
>   Sleeps a voice unspoken;
> By thy step alone
>   Can its rest be broken;
>   Child of Ocean!   (II.1.190–94)

Asia finally makes her decision to "pursue the sound":

> Come, sweet Panthea, link thy hand in mine,
> And follow, ere the voices fade away.   (II.1.188, 207–8)

Ignorant of their destination, the two sisters start their journey to the "world unknown," where exists the most enigmatic figure in the play.

We accompany them on part of the route, first through a dark "Forest intermingled with Rocks and Caverns" and then to "a Pinnacle of Rock among mountains," from which, although we do not see them doing it, they descend down a volcanic chasm to the remote depths of the "Cave of Demogorgon." The route seems appropriate enough and does not demand explanation. The cave of Demogorgon is a remote and ultimate source of power—a power, moreover, which has no particular respect for values, human or divine. The journey to this subhuman power is one of penetration down to the roots of existence. The path through the forest, curtained almost completely from the sky, and pierced only by the occasional starbeams or dewclouds, obviously suggests such penetration through matter to something ultimate and mysterious. The atmosphere is heavy, drugged, voluptuous, sensual, and enervating.

> The path through which that lovely twain
>   Have passed, by cedar, pine and yew,
>   And each dark tree that ever grew,
>   Is curtained out from Heaven's wide blue;
> Nor sun, nor moon, nor wind, nor rain,
>   Can pierce its interwoven bowers.
>
>   .   .   .   .
>
> There the voluptuous nightingales,
>   Are awake through all the broad noonday:

> When one with bliss or sadness fails,
>   And through the windless ivy-boughs,
>   Sick with sweet love, droops dying away
> On its mate's music-panting bosom;
> Another from the swinging blossom
>   Watching to catch the languid close
>   Of the last strain, then lifts on high
>   The wings of the weak melody. . . .   (II.ii.1–6, 24–33)

The last of the three semichoruses suggests (very cryptically indeed) the compulsive force of the natural cycles of birth and death
as they follow their course under the spell of "Demogorgon's mighty
law" (II.ii.43). These cycles differ from the more naturalistic ones
of *The Cloud* and *Ode to the West Wind* mainly by the presence in
the background of the Platonic myth of preexistence and incarnation. Grabo, in his exposition of the passage, is more elaborate and
circumstantial than Shelley, but his summary is basically sound:

The mutations of matter as symbolized in the cloud, depicting the cyclical
history of the hydrogen atom drawn from the sea to the sky and then
home again to its source, are paralleled by the life history of the souls
drawn from the ocean of universal being, individually incarnated and
returning again to their source.[8]

These three semichoruses in the forest have been much allegorized
by commentators. According to Miss Scudder,

Love and Faith are pursuing their journey through all human experience: and first they pass through the sphere of the Senses, or external
life (Semichorus I.); then through that of the Emotions (Semichorus
II.); finally through that of the Reason and the Will (Semichorus III.).[9]

Such a schematic interpretation is not particularly misleading,
but it is unnecessary. For, although the three semichoruses may
be richly elaborated, the details suggest not a sequence of allegorical states on the road to Demogorgon's cave, but something a good
deal simpler. Since Asia and Panthea are journeying to something
deep, ultimate, and subhuman, inevitably their route does not lead
them aloft into the "intense inane" but into a heavy, thick, matter-

clogged world of natural force, inhabited by subhuman fauns (who, like Caliban, speak some of the loveliest poetry in the play) and haunted by spirits, who, if the Second Faun is to be believed, are formed in and return to the ooze at the bottom of "clear lakes and pools" (II.ii.73) and who, in the third semichorus, sing of creation and dissolution. The reference to "Demogorgon's mighty law" is a tentative anticipation of the goal to which the journey is leading. If such a journey is to be taken, what more appropriate route could be found to lead to the "darkness visible" of Demogorgon on his throne? Only, I would suppose, a route into the bowels of the earth itself; and this is precisely where Shelley leads Asia and Panthea at the end of the next scene.

In that scene we find them on a pinnacle of rock with a mighty portal at their feet, out of which "oracular vapour is hurled up" (II.iii.4). The peak is islanded by circles of vapor and beyond that it is surrounded by

> the dark and blooming forests,
> Dim twilight lawns, and stream-illumined caves,
> And wind-enchanted shapes of wandering mist.
>
> (II.iii.25–27)

Far in the distance "icy spires" reflect the dawn. Asia and Panthea seem to be standing at the center of a vast circular panorama; at their feet lies a hole, which, according to the beckoning spirits who appear out of the mist, leads

> To the deep, to the deep,
>   Down, down!
> Through the shade of sleep,
> Through the cloudy strife
> Of Death and of Life;
> Through the veil and the bar
> Of things which seem and are,
> Even to the steps of the remotest throne,
>   Down, down!   (II.iii.54–62)

Before them lies the still center of the circular processes of nature, a point at which the distinction between Death and Life, Appearance and Reality, has not even begun. Out of that ultimate Nothingness something just begins to form itself, like Necessity rising out of Chaos. It is Demogorgon.

In scene four Panthea describes what she sees on the "ebon throne":

> I see a mighty darkness
> Filling the seat of power, and rays of gloom
> Dart round, as light from the meridian sun,
> Ungazed upon and shapeless; neither limb,
> Nor form, nor outline; yet we feel it is
> A living Spirit.   (II.iv.2–7)

Demogorgon, a sort of "darkness visible," exists at the point where nothing becomes something, where chaos achieves form, where anarchy is replaced by law. Asia has reached the womb of life.

In the past, commentators anxious to find a literary source for the name and conception of Demogorgon were inclined to allude briefly to Plato, Milton, and Spenser and leave it at that. More recently a possible direct relation to Boccaccio's *Genealogia Deorum Gentilium* has attracted attention.[10] But the relevant passages in Spenser and particularly in Milton are in need of some reexamination. In Book Four of *The Faerie Queene,* the mother of Priamond, Diamond, and Triamond, anxious to know their fate,

> By wondrous skill and many hidden wayes
> To the three fatall sisters house she went.
> Farre under ground from tract of living went,
> Downe in the bottome of the deepe Abysse,
> Where Demogorgon, in dull darknesse pent
> Farre from the view of gods and heavens bliss,
> The hideous Chaos keepes, their dreadfull dwelling is. (II.xlvii)

In Spenser's home of Demogorgon, as in Shelley's, Chaos, Fate, and Law meet. Not only do the controlling Fates dwell in Demogorgon's Chaos, but Demogorgon himself "keepes" Chaos; he is not subdued to the element he works in, but subdues it. He is both a part of Chaos and above it, like the Demogorgon of *Prometheus Unbound.* A passage from Book One of the *Faerie Queene* is also

suggestive. Duessa meets "griesly Night" (V.xx) coming forth
from her cave and addresses her as

> thou most auncient Grandmother of all,
> More old than Jove, whom thou at first did breede,
> Or that great house of Gods caelestial,
> Which wast begot in Daemogorgon's hall,
> And sawst the secrets of the world unmade. . . .   (V.xxii)

After Duessa's complaint is over, Night excuses herself by saying:

> But who can turn the stream of destiny,
> Or break the chayne of strong necessitee,
> Which fast is tyde to Joves eternall seat?   (V.xxv)

Here Demogorgon's name occurs only in passing. But it is surrounded by a cluster of ideas and images appropriate to Shelley's
emergent god. Spenser depicts his hall of Demogorgon as a place
of birth and the source out of which the unmade secrets of the
world are made. The chain of necessity is, to be sure, under Jove's
throne not Demogorgon's but it may well have suggested "the snake-
like Doom coiled underneath his throne" (II.iii.97) in the song
sung by Spirits during Asia's descent into the cave.

Although I do not doubt that Shelley remembered Spenser's
Demogorgon when he wrote *Prometheus Unbound,* Milton's Demogorgon occurs in a passage which influenced Shelley to a far greater
degree. I shall come back to the cosmology of Book Two of *Paradise Lost,* and its importance to Shelley, later. What needs emphasis
here is the conception of a chaos partly ordered, of a world which
has been partly reclaimed and organized, but whose points of order
are surrounded by the flux out of which they have emerged and
into which they may return: "the Womb of nature and perhaps her
Grave." When the gate of chaos is opened to Satan, Sin, and Death,

> Before their eyes in sudden view appear
> The secrets of the hoary deep, a dark
> Illimitable Ocean without bound,
> Without dimension, where length, breadth, and highth,

And time and place are lost; where eldest Night
And *Chaos,* Ancestors of Nature, hold
Eternal *Anarchy.*

. . . .

Chaos Umpire sits,
And by decision more embroils the fray
By which he Reigns; next him high Arbiter
Chance governs all. Into this wild Abyss,
The Womb of nature and perhaps her Grave,

. . . .

the wary fiend
Stood . . . and look'd a while. . . . (II.890–96, 907–11, 917–18)

However, it is only when Satan is in the midst of chaos that the
name of Demogorgon occurs among a number of minor powers,

when straight behold the Throne
Of Chaos, and his dark Pavilion spread
Wide on the wasteful Deep; with him Enthroned
The Consort of his Reign; and by them stood
Orcus and Ades, and the dreaded name
Of Demogorgon.   (II.959–64)

That this last passage was firmly impressed on Shelley's mind
when he wrote Act Two of *Prometheus Unbound* is obvious from
some lines which are closely based on the earlier part of it:

Say not those smiles that we shall meet again
Within that bright pavilion which their beams
Shall build on the waste world?   (II.i.124–26)

At the same time, in his account of the cave of Demogorgon,
Shelley has eliminated the wild combat and confusion and emphasized the gloom and mystery of what he calls in *The Revolt of Islam* "the womb of inessential Nought" (I.xxvi).[11]

Like a good many distinguished writers, Shelley did not make
any habitual distinction between nonexistence and chaos ("inessential Nought" and "chaos" are interchangeable in *The Revolt*) or

between Chance and Fate. More important, his effective force, Demogorgon or Necessity (we may accept with reservations the familiar term here) is shrouded in mystery and only half emerged from chaos. Fate and Chance meet and cannot be separated. The chain of cause and effect is inscrutable, yet we believe in it. It has

>   neither limb,
>   Nor form, nor outline; yet we feel it is
>   A living Spirit.

Of Demogorgon we may say what he himself says in answer to one of Asia's questions about ultimate authority:

>   If the abysm
>   Could vomit forth its secrets—but a voice
>   Is wanting, the deep truth is imageless;
>   For what would it avail to bid thee gaze
>   On the revolving world? What to bid speak
>   Fate, Time, Occasion, Chance and Change?   (II.iv.114–20)

Demogorgon may be Necessity, but he is not the dogmatic necessity of D'Holbach or of *Queen Mab*. As C. E. Pulos points out, "to the mature Shelley, as to Hume, Necessity is fundamentally an unknown power." [12]

As early as the notes to *Queen Mab* and *A Refutation of Deism*, Shelley showed himself convinced by Hume's destruction of the traditional view of causation.

Hume has shown to the satisfaction of all philosophers that the only idea which we can form of causation is derivable from the constant conjunction of objects, and the consequent inference of one from the other. We denominate that phenomenon the cause of another which we observe with the fewest exceptions to precede its occurrence.   (C.136)

This Humean skepticism remained with Shelley to the end and grew rather than diminished. It is present in *Mont Blanc*, where we find in the mountain itself Demogorgon's most interesting predecessor.

>   All things that move and breathe with toil and sound
>   Are born and die; revolve, subside and swell;

Power dwells apart in its tranquillity,
Remote, serene, and inaccessible:

  . . . .

    The glaciers creep
Like snakes that watch their prey, from their far fountains,
Slow rolling on; there, many a precipice,
Frost and the Sun in scorn of mortal power
Have piled—dome, pyramid and pinnacle,
A city of death, distinct with many a tower
And wall impregnable of beaming ice.
Yet not a city but a flood of ruin
Is there, that from the boundaries of the sky
Rolls its perpetual stream; vast pines are strewing
Its destined path, or in the mangled soil
Branchless and shattered stand; the rocks, drawn down
From yon remotest waste, have overthrown
The limits of the dead and living world,
Never to be reclaimed.

This power exists in remote tranquillity, governing the cycles of nature, but not subject to them, a bridge between waste and waste. The concluding lines of the poem have often been thought to represent a new departure, contradicting the Godwinian picture of Necessity which the mountain is supposed to symbolize. I agree, however, with Pulos that

once we recognize the sceptical quality of Shelley's idea of Necessity, the conclusion of *Mont Blanc* is seen to be not anti-climactic but climactic:

   And what were thou, and earth, and stars, and sea,
   If to the human mind's imaginings
   Silence and solitude were vacancy?

These lines do not express, as Mr. Kapstein believes . . . , a shift of attitude toward Necessity which disrupts the unity of the poem. Rather the lines bring to a suitable climax the scepticism pervading *Mont Blanc* as a whole: that Necessity is an unknown power and any conception of it must be a fiction, a creation of the imagination.[13]

It is, nevertheless, a fiction which Shelley is willing to accept while recognizing its inscrutability.

Demogorgon is not an isolated figure, of course. He is an actor in the drama of the poem and in the drama of history, and Shelley relates him to other actors, powers, and incidents. Before we see him in action, however, he has an extended and cryptic conversation with Asia, in which Asia asks the questions and does most of the talking, while Demogorgon makes brief and deliberately oracular replies. The main subject of conversation is the origin and nature of evil, how it is sustained and when it will be conquered. Asia tries to push him into the familiar theological corner of having to ascribe the creation of evil to a beneficent God. Like the young Shelley trying to trap unsuspecting clergymen, she lulls him into a false sense of security by asking him who made life and the components of human life, such as "thought, passion, reason, will, / Imagination" (II.iv.10–11). To these questions he answers "God." By asking who created our transient awareness of beauty, she even causes him to answer "Merciful God." Then she suddenly turns on him and drives home the crucial point in a speech which reminds us, in its vivid sense of internal evil, of Prometheus' temptation by the Furies:

> And who made terror, madness, crime, remorse,
> Which from the links of the great chain of things
> To every thought within the mind of man
> Sway and drag heavily, and each one reels
> Under the load toward the pit of death;
> Abandoned hope, and love that turns to hate;
> And self-contempt, bitterer to drink than blood;
> Pain, whose unheeded and familiar speech
> Is howling, and keen shrieks, day after day;
> And Hell, or the sharp fear of Hell?   (II.iv.19–28)

Demogorgon avoids the trap by simply asserting: "He reigns." In other words, whoever the maker of evil may be, he is in the ascendancy now. But whether this means Jupiter or something prior to him is left an open question. Although Asia persists, Demogorgon refuses to elaborate on his answer and simply repeats: "He reigns."

Neither Demogorgon nor Shelley is simply evading the issue. Although they both recognize the limitations of human reason and the impossibility of cutting the Gordian knot of ultimate questions, a number of positive conclusions emerge from this scene. A significant point is that Asia contributes them, not Demogorgon. Demogorgon's method resembles nothing so much as that of a subtle and taciturn seminar leader, who, although he contributes very little directly himself, manages to persuade his interlocutors to answer their own questions to his own satisfaction. Even when he does offer an opinion, he seems to Asia merely to be echoing her own thoughts:

> So much I asked before, and my heart gave
> The response thou hast given; and of such truths
> Each to itself must be the oracle.   (II.iv.121–23)

Among Asia's contributions to this scene is a long historical passage, which starts before even the Saturnian age, but concentrates on the career of Prometheus. It contains some things (mostly minor details) which are new to us, but the main lines of the story and its significance are familiar from Act One. Nevertheless, Shelley finds it convenient to reconsider and remind us of the whole matter at this juncture. One important new revelation is that, although the age of Jupiter signalizes a new access of evil, the preceding age of Saturn also involved a significant lapse of a somewhat different kind. The first state seems to have consisted of eternal essences, although in this world not another:

> There was the Heaven and Earth at first,
> And Light and Love; then Saturn, from whose throne
> Time fell, an envious shadow. . . .   (II.iv.32–34)

Shelley is not concerned here with deploring the limitations of time: he emphasizes mainly the joy and vitality of "earth's primal spirits" in the Saturnian age. But whatever the advantages of the Saturnian age, it achieved them at a price. Saturn refused men

> The birthright of their being, knowledge, power,
> The skill which wields the elements, the thought
> Which pierces this dim universe like light,

> Self-empire, and the majesty of love;
> For thirst of which they fainted.   (II.iv.39–43)

Saturnian men, it seems, lived in a state of blissful ignorance. They lacked knowledge and civilization. They also lacked freedom and any conception of love as service (for so I interpret "the majesty of love").

These Prometheus endeavored to supply. First, he put the services of his own knowledge into Jupiter's hands and supported him as a claimant to Saturn's throne. In providing Jupiter with this source of power he made only one stipulation: man must not be enslaved. But when Jupiter has succeeded in seizing the throne, he disregards his promise.

>   Then Prometheus
> Gave wisdom, which is strength, to Jupiter,
> And with this law alone, 'Let man be free,'
> Clothed him with the dominion of wide Heaven.
> To know nor faith, nor love, nor law, to be
> Omnipotent but friendless, is to reign;
> And Jove now reigned; for on the race of man
> First famine, and then toil, and then disease,
> Strife, wounds, and ghastly death unseen before,
> Fell; and the unseasonable seasons drove,
> With alternating shafts of frost and fire,
> Their shelterless, pale tribes to mountain caves;
> And in their desert hearts fierce wants he sent,
> And mad disquietudes, and shadows idle
> Of unreal good, which levied mutual war,
> So ruining the lair wherein they raged.   (II.iv.43–58)

Seeing the misery of man, Prometheus showers on him all the gifts he can invent. Among them are the hope of immortality, to hide "the shape of Death" (II.iv.63); Love to bind together their disunited hearts; fire (and other potentially harmful things, like iron, gold, gems, poisons) adapted to civilized uses; language, which made it possible to think coherently and to see the universe in terms of some order; science, which menaced but did not overthrow the authority of heaven and earth; prophetic songs; music to lift and soothe the spirit; sculpture to idealize the human form; medicine and perhaps vegetarianism; astronomy; seamanship and exploration to bring the various races together in fellowship; and finally cities (like the Greek city of Pompeii) in which nature and civilization were fused into an architectural unity:

> Cities then
> Were built, and through their snow-like columns flowed
> The warm winds, and the azure ether shone,
> And the blue sea and shadowy hills were seen.
> Such, the alleviations of his state,
> Prometheus gave to man, for which he hangs
> Withering in destined pain; but who rains down
> Evil, the immedicable plague, which, while
> Man looks on his creation like a god
> And sees that it is glorious, drives him on,
> The wreck of his own will, the scorn of earth,
> The outcast, the abandoned, the alone?
> Not Jove: while yet his frown shook heaven, ay, when
> His adversary from adamantine chains
> Cursed him, he trembled like a slave. Declare
> Who is his master? Is he too a slave?   (II.iv.94–109)

Jupiter himself, it seems, is not the ultimate source of evil, although he "rains down / Evil" (II.iv.100–1). This, like most of Asia's revelations, is no news to us, although it confirms our understanding of Act One. Jupiter both acts and suffers evil, is both its master and its slave. As Demogorgon says in reply to Asia's question, leaving it up to his questioner as usual,

> All spirits are enslaved which serve things evil:
> Thou knowest if Jupiter be such or no.   (II.iv.110–11)

But Asia wishes to penetrate beyond the secondary realm of Jupiter and Prometheus to something primary; and this is precisely what Demogorgon, and Shelley, is neither able, nor will pretend to be able, to do. When Asia asks what the word God means to

Demogorgon, he simply recognizes it as common usage for Jupiter, "the supreme of living things" (II.iv.113). When Asia, stimulated by her newfound awareness that Jupiter is a slave as well as a master, asks who is the master of Jupiter the slave, Demogorgon refuses to try to probe an ultimate mystery or to believe that if reached it could be made intelligible. He insists, in words I have already emphasized, that "a voice is wanting" and that "the deep truth is imageless." But, although Demogorgon has no deep truth to offer, he does offer a secondary and contingent truth.

> For what would it avail to bid thee gaze
> On the revolving world? What to bid speak
> Fate, Time, Occasion, Chance and Change? To these
> All things are subject but eternal Love.　　　　(II.iv.117–20)

The final statement is cautiously phrased. Demogorgon does not say that Love, even eternal Love, is the master of "Fate, Time, Occasion, Chance and Change." All he says is that these things are not the master of eternal Love. It will become apparent shortly that neither is the master or slave of the other, and the forces of Demogorgon's realm must cooperate with Love if the downfall of Jupiter is to be assured. Neither "Demogorgon's mighty law" nor Love can stand by itself as the molder of the ultimate historical event which Shelley is about to celebrate.[14]

Asia has asked a good many questions, but not the most relevant and practical one. The second dream has yet to shed light on the first. "One more demand," says Asia,

> 　　　　and do thou answer me
> As my own soul would answer, did it know
> That which I ask. Prometheus shall arise
> Henceforth the sun of this rejoicing world:
> When shall the destined hour arrive?　　　　(II.iv.124–28)

In response Demogorgon shows her a procession of the chariots of the Hours. Among them is a dark chariot driven by a ghastly charioteer. "Who art thou? Whither wouldst thou bear me?" asks Asia; and the charioteer replies,

> I am the Shadow of a destiny
> More dread than is my aspect; ere yon planet
> Has set, the darkness which ascends with me
> Shall wrap in lasting night heaven's kingless throne.
>
> (II.iv.145–49)

Demogorgon floats up from his throne and ascends the chariot; "the coursers fly / Terrified" and the chariot moves on among the stars, "blackening the night" (II.iv.153–55). But another chariot awaits Asia, driven by a young hopeful-eyed Spirit, whose "soft smiles attract the soul," and who invites Asia and Panthea to ascend. When the chariot pauses "on the Top of a snowy Mountain" to restore its energy, the Spirit receives a warning from the earth that their flight must be "swifter than fire" (II.v.4). Asia seems to have become impatient as a result of the delay, and is anxious to urge on the chariot with her own breath. "Thou breathest on their nostrils," she says to the Spirit, "but my breath would give them swifter speed." The Spirit, however, has no illusions about this possibility: "Alas! it could not" (II.v.6–7).

The allegory here is obvious enough, except perhaps in some of the details. The two chariots may represent two successive Hours, or, more probably, two aspects of the same Hour: first, the Hour of Jupiter's downfall, and, second, the Hour of Prometheus' release. The second chariot, however, stands apart, at the edge of the main procession, and it does not seem to be intended as one of the regular Hours at all. The downfall of Jupiter has to occur, but it need not involve the release of Prometheus or the advent of the millennium, and might well be simply followed, first, by a counterrevolution and then by the reign of a new Jupiter or even a second reign of the old. It might, in other words, suffer the fate of the French Revolution. Prometheus' regeneration and Asia's journey to the cave of Demogorgon give the overthrow of Jupiter a meaning it need not have. But, fundamental as her role may be, Asia remains a co-operator in the chariot's journey; she needs it as much as it needs her. This is the significance of the brief dialogue between Asia and the Spirit, which I quoted a moment ago. Asia imagines that her

breath might urge the chariot on more quickly, but the Spirit knows
better: "Alas! it could not." Without Asia the chariot would never
arrive at the Caucasian peak to release Prometheus, but her efforts
cannot make it arrive one moment sooner or later. Man cannot
"turn the wheel on which he turns." [15] Asia can take advantage of
the critical moment when it arrives, but she cannot ordain when
that moment will arrive. Quite simply, Love is not enough; it needs
opportunity. [16]

Following Mary Shelley, commentators have identified Asia with
Love, although a number (like Mary Shelley herself) do not stop
there. [17] I have avoided making use of this identification until now,
because only at this point in the play does Shelley make it explicit
to the reader. During the journey in the chariot Asia undergoes
something of an apotheosis. Panthea is overcome by the new
radiance, which is so dazzling as to be almost unendurable. "Some
good change," she says,

> Is working in the elements, which suffer
> Thy presence thus unveiled. The Nereids tell
> That on the day when the clear hyaline
> Was cloven at thy uprise, and thou didst stand
> Within a veined shell, which floated on
> Over the calm floor of the crystal sea,
> Among the Aegean isles, and by the shores
> Which bear thy name,—love, like the atmosphere
> Of the sun's fire filling the living world,
> Burst from thee, and illumined earth and heaven
> And the deep ocean and the sunless caves
> And all that dwells within them, till grief cast
> Eclipse upon the soul from which it came.
> Such art thou now; nor is it I alone,
> Thy sister, thy companion, thine own chosen one,
> But the whole world which seeks thy sympathy. (II.v.18–34)

This traditional account of the birth of Venus is followed by
Asia's quiet praise of the sweetness and universality of love. Suddenly a voice is heard in the air, singing the most famous and

extravagantly praised lyric in the whole play. The intensity of this lyric and the superb conception which it tries to embody do, I think, transmit themselves to most readers, despite the occasional slipshod workmanship and looseness of statement. The voice sings a paean to Asia as the life of life and the light of light. As the very essence of light, she is unbearable to mortal eyes. For us to see her at all, her smiles must be screened by her looks (whatever that means) and her limbs hidden by a shrouding atmosphere. Indeed, we are told in an extraordinary and only partially successful image, she is folded from our sight in the low and tender tones of her voice, through which we are able to feel what we can never see.

> Fair are others; none beholds thee,
>   But thy voice sounds low and tender
> Like the fairest, for it folds thee
>   From the sight, that liquid splendour,
> And all feel, yet see thee never,
> As I feel now, lost forever. (II.v.60–65)

The Voice's account of Asia bears a startling resemblance to Panthea's description of Demogorgon in his cave. If Demogorgon suggests Milton's "darkness visible," Asia certainly more than suggests "light invisible." Both are "imageless"; yet their presence can be felt. And it is this apparently ill-assorted and yet complementary pair who, each in his chariot, journey to initiate the day

> which down the void abysm
> At the Earth-born's spell yawns for Heaven's despotism,
> And Conquest is dragged captive through the deep;
> Love, from its awful throne of patient power
> In the wise heart, from the last giddy hour
> Of dread endurance, from the slippery, steep,
> And narrow verge of crag-like agony, springs
> And folds over the world its healing wings. (IV.554–61)

VI

THE SPHERE OF OUR SORROW

The presentation of Asia in Act Two becomes increasingly meta-physical. And no doubt Shelley is willing to regard Love as a metaphysical essence, or as the ultimate goal of a process. But he is equally interested, and perhaps more intimately interested, in the process itself, in the activity which Asia stimulates. His metaphysical interest in Love is based on an ethical interest in loving, and on a fascinated and even morbid preoccupation with the forces which are opposed to loving.

Shelley's ethical views are basically traditional and even common-place, although he sometimes works them out in fairly individual terms. He is concerned, therefore, less with the opposition between Love and Hate than with the prior and more basic opposition betwe n two kinds of love, one of which is Love proper and the other its debased counterpart. In terms of Christian ethics the two might be charity and cupidity; in terms of more secular ethics, altruism and egoism; in terms of Shelley's eighteenth-century ethical back-ground, benevolence and self-love. It would not be correct to see in this opposition of Love and self-love the center of Shelley's view of good and evil throughout his career. But whenever what we have called Shelley's eighteenth-century radicalism is dominant, this op-position is at the center of the ethical argument.

The process of loving is for Shelley an expansion away from and beyond the self. He describes this process in a number of prose passages, notably in the Preface to *Alastor,* in the essay *On Love,* and in the fragmentary short story *The Coliseum,* as well as in poetic (and less expository) passages. The self, he believes, cannot be content with exploring its own dens. It finds in itself "the chasm of an insufficient void" (C.170). It cannot fulfill itself without communication and sympathy, without, indeed, bursting its own bounds and going beyond itself.

> The great secret of morals is love; or a going out of our own nature, and an identification of ourselves with the beautiful which exists in thought, action, or person, not our own.   (C.282–83)

The enemy is self-love; by which the self, pressed inwards, is reduced to a morbid and degrading contemplation of its own evil. This enemy we have already examined at length in the "trick" of the Cenci family and in the temptations of Prometheus. The expansive escape from the bondage of self, the Love with which Prometheus regenerates himself, we have observed, but taken for granted without any close examination. It needs close examination if we are to see it in the context of Shelley's other long poems.

A glance at the *Shelley Concordance* under *self* and its successive compounds should convince anyone (however crudely) of Shelley's preoccupation. There are thirty-three compounds, excluding the irrelevant *self-same,* the less indicative *selfish* and *selfishness,* and pronouns like *myself* and *ourselves.* If we merge such headings as *self-accusation* and *self-accusing,* the number can be reduced to twenty-seven:

self-accusation	self-despising	self-mistrust
self-anatomy	self-destruction	self-misunderstood
self-compassion	self-empire	self-moving
self-conflicting	self-enshrined	self-murder
self-consuming	self-esteem	self-oblivious
self-contempt	self-impelling	self-offence
self-content	self-important	self-rebuke
self-contention	self-interest	self-sufficing
self-created	self-love	self-torturing

By far the largest number of entries (nine) is under *self-contempt,* to which might be added those under headings like *self-mistrust* and *self-despising*. About half of these entries are from *Prometheus Unbound*. The *Keats Concordance* paints a very different picture. For one thing, there are less than half the number of *self* compounds listed, and never more than one entry under each. Even the less specialized *selfish* and *selfishness* provide an interesting comparison. Keats uses *selfishness* once, *selfish* not at all. Shelley uses *selfish* thirteen times and *selfishness* ten times. *Self-contempt* and its associated words are never used by Keats. Shelley's larger output does not account for such differences. Keats is simply not ethically concerned with the self. He does not despise or repudiate it even when he desires to transcend it.

But this does not mean that Keats is unconcerned with the problem of self, or at least with *a* problem of self. The reader who has gone along with my mechanical comparison of Concordances thus far will perhaps be surprised to discover that if we look at the entries under the root *self,* we discover twenty-seven for Keats and only twenty-four for Shelley. Keats is, of course, very much concerned with the self, not certainly with judging it, but with discovering what it is, or defining it, or simply recognizing it. When we combine with the "orbed drop / Of light" which is love, Keats tells us at the climax of the pleasure thermometer passage in *Endymion,* "Life's self is nourished by its proper pith" (I.806–7, 814). When Saturn awakes in Book One of *Hyperion* he seems to have lost his self.

> I am gone
> Away from my own bosom: I have left
> My strong identity, my real self,
> Somewhere between the throne, and where I sit
> Here on this spot of earth. Search, Thea, search!   (I.112–16)

The problem of self for Keats is the problem of identity; and it is not a single problem for him. As an intelligence in a recalcitrant world, he sees his development as the formation of his real identity.

Do you not see how necessary a World of Pains and troubles is to school an Intelligence and make it a Soul? . . . As various as the Lives of Men are—so various become their Souls, and thus does God make individual beings, Souls, Identical Souls of the sparks of his own essence—.[1]

But, as an admirer of Shakespeare (or perhaps as a diplomatic friend trying to disown some earlier, unguarded remarks), he has no identity, and exists in the identity of others, whether the others are poetic creatures or people in the room whose identity presses on him. Then there is the "habitual self" or the "sole self" to which he reluctantly returns after a transcendent flight and which is no doubt to be distinguished from his real identity.

In the Introduction to Volume Four of their *Poets of the English Language* Auden and Pearson try to define the Romantic hero in terms of self-consciousness:

In the Middle Ages, the quality which man shares with God and which the creatures do not have is a will that can make free choices. What separates man from God is sin: that he can and does choose wrongly, love himself, act selfishly. The function of the poet is to exhibit the human soul tempted by competing loves, and to celebrate the ways in which she can be redeemed.

In the neo-classical period, the divine human quality is reason, the capacity to recognize general laws, and the function of the poet is to celebrate the Rational City and to pour scorn on its enemies.

Toward the end of the eighteenth century—Rousseau is one of the first symptoms—a new answer appears. The divine element in man is held to be neither power nor free will nor reason, but self-consciousness. Like God and unlike the rest of nature, man can say "I."

.   .   .   .

Thus, the subject of the greatest long poem of this period, *The Prelude,* is not a heroic action like the siege of Troy, nor a decisive choice like the Fall of Man, nor a threat to civilization like the Goddess of Dulness, but the Growth of a Poet's Mind.[2]

If these generalizations have any validity, and I think they have more than a little, then Keats and Wordsworth are in the mainstream of the Romantic tradition to a far greater extent than Shelley, who seems more mediaeval or even neoclassical. In these terms

Byron is more typically Romantic than Shelley, for the Byronic hero, although he may be self-torturing and even self-despising and may try to escape from the pressing load of his identity, finds his ultimate compensation in being himself alone. "I am what I am." The tradition of Auden and Pearson would include the Tennyson of *In Memoriam* and *De Profundis,* the Arnold of the Marguerite poems and *The Buried Life,* and T. S. Eliot. Browning, despite his presentation of unique "characters," is well outside it. And Shelley's concern with the moral status of the self and with the perfection of the will, rather than with the establishment of identity and with the growing pattern of consciousness, makes it impossible for him to take a very significant place in the tradition which Auden and Pearson describe.

For Shelley the ability to escape from bondage to the self, the ability to expand beyond the insufficient void which is all that self-love can finally discover, and the realization in action of that ability, is "the great secret of morals." But it depends on the will, and the will may simply not be stimulated to activity. Prometheus' will regenerates itself; and for Shelley the will is capable of this, just as it is capable of degenerating itself. But, although every act of will is no doubt a miracle, and no amount of preparation can be really responsible for it when it occurs, conditions can be more or less favorable, and man is not reduced simply to awaiting "the spark from heaven."

Man can condition his will by exercising his imagination, by peopling his mind with "beautiful idealisms of moral excellence" or by identifying himself with those persons and situations beyond himself which are provided by works of imagination. "My purpose," says Shelley in a most un-Godwinian passage of the Preface to *Prometheus Unbound,*

has hitherto been simply to familiarize the highly refined imagination of the more select classes of poetic readers with beautiful idealisms of moral excellence; aware that until the mind can love, and admire, and trust, and hope, and endure, reasoned principles of moral conduct are seeds cast upon the highway of life which the unconscious passenger tramples into dust, although they would bear the harvest of his happiness.[3] (C.328).

The mind may know what it should do and may be able to produce convincing reasons for doing it, but the will may not respond and man may not be able to do what he knows. He must be passionately and morally involved in the truth he discovers before he can make that truth effective, and poetry, by exercising the imagination of the reader and expanding his mind to include things which are beyond his present moral scope, prepares him for the day when they are no longer beyond him and his will can encompass them in the grasp of love. According to *A Treatise on Morals:*

Imagination or mind employed in prophetically [imaging forth] its objects is that faculty of human nature on which every gradation of its progress, nay, every, the minutest, change depends. (C.189)

Shelley elaborates and develops these ideas in a famous passage from *A Defence of Poetry:*

The whole objection, however, of the immorality of poetry rests upon a misconception of the manner in which poetry acts to produce the moral improvement of man. Ethical science arranges the elements which poetry has created, and propounds schemes and proposes examples of civil and domestic life: nor is it for want of admirable doctrines that men hate, and despise, and censure, and deceive, and subjugate one another. But poetry acts in another and diviner manner. It awakens and enlarges the mind itself by rendering it the receptacle of a thousand unapprehended combinations of thought. . . . The great secret of morals is love; or a going out of our own nature, and an identification of ourselves with the beautiful which exists in thought, action, or person, not our own. A man, to be greatly good, must imagine intensely and comprehensively; he must put himself in the place of another and of many others; the pains and pleasures of his species must become his own. The great instrument of moral good is the imagination; and poetry administers to the effect by acting upon the cause. . . . Poetry strengthens the faculty which is the organ of the moral nature of man, in the same manner as exercise strengthens a limb. (C.282–83)

Imagination is the bridge which can link the intellect and the will. And it is not merely a useful interim companion while the will awaits the "spark from heaven" which can galvanize the will into action. In fact, for Shelley, there is no "spark from heaven." From a Christian point of view, what Shelley lacks is any awareness of the necessity of divine grace. He does not posit any complementary force outside the individual which meets the imaginative impulse from within and transforms self-love into charity. We may recall from the previous chapter that the act of love and the achievement of the millennium were separated by a gap and that the two could only be joined by the "darkness visible" of Demogorgon. There is an analogous gap between the moral knowledge and the moral act, and the link which may serve to unite them is the imagination, which is Shelley's human equivalent for the divine grace which he cannot conceive, at least in Christian terms. Between the knowledge and the act "Falls the Shadow." Shelley can only hope that imagination will narrow the gap, or lessen the darkness.

Prometheus Unbound was written before these ideas had worked themselves out in Shelley's mind,[4] and in it he is therefore concerned with the function of the imagination only tentatively, in the series of songs which succeed Prometheus' temptation by the Furies. The full development of the theory does not come until 1821, by which time the radical hypothesis itself is facing stiff competition in Shelley's mind. His restatement of the moral function of the imagination in the later pages of *A Defence of Poetry* is one of his most vigorous passages, but most of the vigor is expended on the consequences of our imaginative failure rather than on the regeneration to which it is the key.

We have more moral, political, and historical wisdom, than we know how to reduce into practice; we have more scientific and economical knowledge than can be accommodated to the just distribution of the produce which it multiplies. The poetry, in these systems of thought, is concealed by the accumulation of facts and calculating processes. There is no want of knowledge respecting what is wisest and best in morals, government, and political economy, or at least what is wiser and better than what men now practice and endure. But we let "I *dare not* wait upon *I would,* like the poor cat i' the adage." We want the creative faculty to imagine that which we know; we want the generous impulse to act that which we imagine; we want the poetry of life: our calculations have outrun conception; we have eaten more than we can digest. The cultivation of those sciences which have enlarged the limits of the empire of man over the external world, has, for want of the poetical faculty, proportionally circumscribed those of the internal world; and man, having enslaved the elements, remains himself a slave. . . . From what other cause has it arisen that the discoveries which should have lightened, have added a weight to the curse imposed on Adam? Poetry, and the principle of Self, of which money is the visible incarnation, are the God and Mammon of the world. (C.293)

Shelley here returns to the arch-enemy, self-love. It, allied with knowledge, has "circumscribed" the internal world rather than expanded it. "Circumscribed" is a geometric metaphor. Self-love confines by drawing a tight little circle around itself.

The only distinction between the selfish man and the virtuous man is that the imagination of the former is confined within a narrow limit, while that of the latter embraces a comprehensive circumference. (C.189)

Poetry attacks self-love by the way in which it "enlarges the circumference of the imagination" (C.283). Because Lord Bacon was a poet, we are told, his writing

distends, and then bursts the circumference of the reader's mind, and pours itself forth together with it into the universal element with which it has perpetual sympathy. (C.281)

Love (and its herald, imagination) is centrifugal; self-love is centripetal. Love strives to push back, or expand beyond, the circumference. Self-love grows inward and presses upon the center.

It seems inevitable that anyone whose ethics, like Shelley's, are based on the egoism-altruism opposition should sometimes use figures (they are not always sensuous enough to be called images) involving the conflict between center and circumference. Indeed it seems likely for such figures to be part of the staple texture of nineteenth-century verse, even when the poetry lacks Shelley's particular ethical bias. But the circle figure, although an obvious one, is less frequent in nineteenth-century verse than we might guess. It is nothing like as common as the wheel figure, with which it may easily be confused, and which is also of some importance in Shelley. The significant fact about the wheel is, of course, its rotation; and the conflict which it exemplifies is not between expansion and contraction, but between the moving circumference and the still center, between time and eternity. And it is the rotation of the wheel rather than the expansion of the circle that dominates nineteenth-century metaphors.

Keats, for example, although almost entirely unconcerned with moral good and evil (evil for him being generally a matter of various physical pressures),[5] is concerned with the conflict between the poetry of egocentric indulgence and the poetry of humanitarian sympathy, to which the center-circumference—or let us call it simply the circle—figure might be appropriate. But Keats does not use it significantly at all. Circles revolve; the Cave of Quietude is a sort of still center surrounded by violent motion, like Wordsworth's "central peace, subsisting at the heart / Of endless agitation";[6] groups of objects arrange themselves circularly, but any relation between center and circumference is restricted to the "widening circlets" of eyes and the expanding circles around a disturbance in the water, or to the most obvious and ungeometric sort of centrality. Tennyson, whose concern with the contraction and formation of identity, and with the prior or subsequent expansion and dissolution of it, would favor the circle figure, does use it (although not in clearly geometric terms), but to a surprisingly slight degree, whatever his fondness for spinning spheres.

The circle figure and the wheel figure are superficially easy to combine. The result is the vortex or the spiral. But, although the vortex became something of an intellectual catchword in the mid-nineteenth century ("Mind and matter . . . glide swift into the vortex of immensity," [7] says Miss Toppit in Dickens's parody) and was a vivid and important image for Melville, and although the spiral was a useful way of representing real but not always perceptible progress for evolutionists, it is not until the twentieth century in the poetry of Yeats that the vortex and spiral figures are fully developed. The "widening gyres" of *The Second Coming* are rotating around and expanding from the center, which "will not hold." As has been pointed out, the phrasing of this poem shows the influence of *Prometheus Unbound*.[8]

But in Shelley the expanding circles and the rotating wheels do not come together. He never uses the word "vortex" in his poems, and "spiral" occurs once only, as an image for a cypress. There are no "whirlpools" in his poetry after 1818, except for a quite literal one in *A Vision of the Sea*. But the conflict of center and circumference is frequently significant, and, obvious as the figure seems to us, it apparently did not have the importance for Shelley's poetic contemporaries and successors that it did for him. When Shelley forbids us to mourn for Adonais, he goes on to make an extraordinary demand:

> Oh come forth
> Fond wretch! and know thyself and him aright.
> Clasp with thy panting soul the pendulous Earth;
> As from a centre, dart thy spirit's light
> Beyond all worlds, until its spacious might
> Satiate the void circumference; then shrink
> Even to a point within our day and night. . . .   (XLVII)

The self of Adonais has expanded until it circumscribes the universe; if the mourner will follow him in imagination, he will understand why there is no cause to mourn. In the slight but lively prose fragment *Essay on the Devil and Devils*, Shelley's humor plays about a fancy which is somewhat more than fanciful to him:

If the sun is Hell, the Devil has a magnificent abode, being elevated as it were on the imperial throne of the visible world. If we assign to the Devil the greatest and most glorious habitation within the scope of our senses, where shall we conceive his mightier adversary to reside? Shall we suppose that the Devil occupies the centre and God the circumference of existence, and that one urges inwards with the centripetal, while the other is perpetually struggling outwards from the narrow focus with the centrifugal force, and that from their perpetual conflict results that mixture of good and evil, harmony and discord, beauty and deformity, which are the general laws of the moral and material world? Alas, the poor theologian never troubled his fancy with nonsense of so philosophical a form.   (C.272–73)

These are among the more striking examples of the circle figure in Shelley. Perhaps his most interesting use of it to illuminate the workings of the poetic imagination is in the portrait of Wordsworth in *Peter Bell the Third,* which is still one of the most penetrating analyses of Wordsworth's poetic character.

> All things that Peter saw and felt
>   Had a peculiar aspect to him;
> And when they came within the belt
> Of his own nature, seemed to melt,
>   Like cloud to cloud, into him.
>
> And so the outward world uniting
>   To that within him, he became
> Considerably uninviting
> To those, who meditation slighting,
>   Were moulded in a different frame.
>
>   . . . .
>
> He had a mind which was somehow
>   At once circumference and centre
> Of all he might or feel or know;
> Nothing went ever out, although
>   Something did ever enter.   (IV.11–20, 31–35)

Wordsworth does not expand and become what he contemplates outside himself, he absorbs the circumference into the center. "The doorways of his head," to use Tennyson's phrase, are not shut, but they open all one way. Like God, his center is everywhere and his circumference nowhere. Consequently, from Shelley's point of view, Wordsworth has no imagination; his mind may be packed with matter, but the container itself has no circumference worth considering; and he is unable to escape from it.

> He had as much imagination
>   As a pint-pot;—he never could
> Fancy another situation,
> From which to dart his contemplation,
>   Than that wherein he stood.   (IV.36–40)

Wordsworth is not primarily a nature poet for Shelley (as he goes on to suggest in the succeeding stanzas), he is a psychological or introspective poet with an intense apprehension "of his mind's work" and of the inseparable interconnections of thought with sense. Shelley is able to appreciate Wordsworth's skill, as he new creates and refines and combines "by a master spirit's law." But the circumference of Wordsworth's mind is not enlarged, although it might be argued (Shelley does not consider the point) that the reader's is.

Perhaps a more familiar figure for the self-absorbed soul is the contemplation of the self in a mirror, the Narcissus or reflection figure. Our examination of self-contemplation in *The Cenci* has already shown us two notable mirror figures, one when Cenci compares the incestuous offspring of his anticipated union with Beatrice to "a distorting mirror," and another when Giacomo calls Orsino's smooth face "The mirror of my darkest thoughts." In *Alastor,* written five years earlier, the mirror figures suggest a theme of self-love which never really emerges in the poem, although it is referred to in the Preface. The Poet, after dreaming of his visionary maiden, awakens to a world of frustration and meaninglessness, and

> His wan eyes
> Gaze on the empty scene as vacantly
> As the ocean's moon looks on the moon in heaven.   (200–2)

Some time later, when his boat emerges from the whirlpool in the Caucasian cave, he finds himself, wasted in body and mind, in a green cove,

> closed by meeting banks, whose yellow flowers
> Forever gaze on their own drooping eyes,
> Reflected in the crystal calm.   (406–8)

This cove is surrounded by a forest, in which the Poet's wanderings lead him to a well, whose "translucent" water "images all the woven boughs above" in a "liquid mirror."

> Hither the Poet came. His eyes beheld
> Their own wan light through the reflected lines
> Of his thin hair, distinct in the dark depth
> Of that still fountain; as the human heart,
> Gazing in dreams over the gloomy grave,
> Sees its own treacherous likeness there.   (469–74)

All these figures are sinister and reflect Shelley's preoccupation with self-love, although the three from *Alastor* are casual and not sufficiently absorbed into the poem. But the mirror figure is not always so obviously sinister. Indeed, it is one of the most profoundly ambiguous figures in Shelley. And this ambiguity as well as this profundity are most notable when it is used in conjunction with the circle figure.

Literally, a circle can only expand in one direction, which is all directions. It does not need to be given a goal. Its goal is provided by its very form. But Shelley is not always so literal and purely geometric (or pantheistic) as all that. The self must expand outside itself; the center must go beyond the circumference, and there must be a goal for the center to aspire to. If the expansion of the circle is the process of loving, this goal outside the circle is Love itself, the metaphysical essence, whose significance we have so far avoided touching in this chapter.

Where does this goal come from? Is it just something given, to which the self expands, or which meets it halfway? I have already suggested that Shelley lacks a sense of the necessity and reality of divine grace, which enables the self to do that which by itself it cannot do, namely, convert self-love into charity. Does he here assume some equivalent gift, which is not merely the goal but also the means of achieving it? On the whole, he does not, although the difficulty, perhaps even impossibility, of the position he is trying to assume makes him inevitably inconsistent, and although his ideas on the subject are in a permanent state of transition. The goal is not a gift from the outside but a projection from within. The self aspires to an ideal beyond itself, but that ideal is a creation or reflection of the self. It is a soul within the soul and a soul out of the soul, if I may paraphrase the ambiguous title of *Epipsychidion*.

In the Preface to *Alastor* Shelley describes the psychological process as it appeared to him in 1815. It is difficult, however, to disengage the process from a number of other matters with which he was closely concerned at the time, but which are not essential to it in its later development. For example, Shelley contrasts the contemplation of nature and the drinking of the fountains of knowledge with the search for human love. The former are apparently not expansive, sympathetic pursuits, as they are for the later Shelley; the Poet's secluded nature-worship and esoteric speculation are self-centered, and his mind awakes to the need for "intercourse with an intelligence similar to itself" (C.314). The goal here must be human love. Moreover, this goal must be finite. The self-centered protagonist at first sought the infinite and the unmeasured; now he desires a finite image, the earthly perfection of the thing itself. There is no Neoplatonic quest for an ideal; the prototype must be here and now, indistinguishable from the antitype, although the protagonist of the poem seems a good deal less clear about the matter than the author of the Preface. These humanitarian limitations, the extraordinary division between the deluded humanitarians and the mean self-lovers with which the Preface ends, the assumption that the good are destroyed early by their moral impulses, and the skeptical fascination with the doctrine of immortality (more apparent in the poem itself), all these special points must be kept in mind when reading *Alastor* and its Preface. The danger is that we shall read back into them the doctrines of *Epipsychidion* and distort their own distinctive framework. But since *Alastor* engages our attention here solely for the light it sheds on the doctrines of the later poems, and since I do not intend to interpret *Alastor* as a whole poem in its own right, the danger is not serious, particularly if we recognize it.

The time comes, says Shelley, when the "infinite and unmeasured" objects "cease to suffice."

His mind is at length suddenly awakened and thirsts for intercourse with an intelligence similar to itself. He images to himself the Being whom he loves. Conversant with speculations of the sublimest and most perfect natures, the vision in which he embodies his own imaginations unites all of wonderful, or wise, or beautiful, which the poet, the philosopher, or the lover could depicture. The intellectual faculties, the imagination, the functions of sense have their respective requisitions on the sympathy of corresponding powers in other human beings. The Poet is represented as uniting these requisitions and attaching them to a single image. He seeks in vain for a prototype of his conception. Blasted by his disappointment, he descends to an untimely grave.

(C.314)

He creates an image within himself, which he projects outside himself as a finite goal, in this case a quite literal woman, who unites all that he desires intellectually, poetically, and physically. He never reaches the goal, and his final hope that she will greet him on the other side of death is supported neither by the poem nor the Preface. Why does he fail? Is he destroyed by some tragic flaw, or by circumstances beyond his control, or by the unsatisfactory goal he has set himself?

According to Hoffman, he is destroyed by his failure to seek a goal which is really outside himself. The veiled maiden, whose

> voice was like the voice of his own soul
> Heard in the calm of thought,   (153–54)

is simply his own reflection, and like Narcissus he is destroyed by an unattainable love for his own image. Instead of escaping from his "self-centred seclusion" (C.314) he really plunges more deeply into it. Such an interpretation is not absurd; it fits into a well-prepared corner of Shelley's mind, its terms are Shelleyan, and it is consistent with the implications of the mirror images which we have already examined. Shelley might well have written a poem of the sort Hoffman describes, he might even have revised *Alastor* into that poem; but the existing *Alastor* is not it. According to the epigraph which Shelley took from the *Excursion:*

> The good die first,
> And those whose hearts are dry as summer dust
> Burn to the socket.

It is the Poet's goodness that destroys him. His "irresistible passion" pursues him "to a speedy ruin"; but that passion is contrasted with the unsympathizing passions which preceded it. It does not simply continue or develop them. In one sense only is his self-love responsible. His early seclusion makes his later search so frenzied that "blasted by disappointment, he descends to an untimely grave." But those isolated individuals of whom the Poet is an illustrious representative really do move from self-love to Love, and their abandonment to the latter is a result of their awakening to the inadequacy of the former. This sounds like a familiar modern description of ordinary adolescent psychology, although it is perhaps also Platonic. The Poet of *Alastor,* however, is no ordinary mortal. His exceptional sensitivity or, as Shelley calls it, his "too exquisite perception" makes the process particularly intense.

It seems, then, that the Poet is destroyed by his tragic virtues more than his tragic vices. But what alternative is open to him? If you begin by attempting to exist without human sympathy (whether this is a necessary stage in human development or not Shelley fails to specify, and his remarks elsewhere are inconsistent), you either awaken later on to its necessity and perish seeking its object or you remain isolated and dry up.

Among those who attempt to exist without human sympathy, the pure and tender-hearted perish through the intensity and passion of their search after its communities, when the vacancy of their spirit suddenly makes itself felt. All else, selfish, blind, and torpid, are those unforeseeing multitudes who constitute, together with their own, the lasting misery and loneliness of the world. Those who love not their fellow-beings live unfruitful lives, and prepare for their old age a miserable grave.   (C.314–15)

The choice seems to be between slow poison and the ruin of an irresistible passion. The best the Poet can do is choose a not inglorious death inspired by Love, instead of an abject and miserable one inspired by blind selfishness. The scheme of things seems to present him with an insoluble problem. It is less his vices or his virtues that destroy him than life itself, which seems to demand that "the good die first" (C.315). From this point of view, *Alastor* is a tragic poem, like *Oedipus Rex,* because any choice will destroy the Poet, and the more morally admirable the choice, the more certain and speedy the destruction. The elegy which concludes the poem does not blame him for anything, but it does lament the inadequate law of the world.

A final explanation of the Poet's failure may lie in the image itself, which he creates as his goal. At the end of the poem, as the moon disappears and the Poet is absorbed into the black mists of Nature, the vision he has sought seems unattainable and delusive. It does not preside over his death; it is extinguished like the horned moon, whose two lessening points seem intended to remind us of it. The Preface, although it sees the Vision as uniting "all of the wonderful or wise or beautiful, which the poet, the philosopher, or the lover could depicture," is not averse later on to grouping the Poet with those who are "deluded" by a "generous error," "instigated" by a "sacred thirst of doubtful knowledge," or "duped" by an "illustrious superstition" (C.314).

Alastor is a profoundly ambiguous poem, not because it is a good and complex poem, but because Shelley has failed to work it out with sufficient rigor and finality. It is the *Hamlet* of Shelley criticism, and the subject of twice as many recent articles as any other poem of Shelley's,[9] but unlike *Hamlet* it provides very little compensation for the effort of comprehension. The three fragments in which some of its ideas on love are developed and modified (the essay *On Love,* the prose story *The Coliseum,* and the poem *Prince Athanase*) are less disappointing because they promise less.

Although its date remains a matter for controversy, *On Love* was probably written in 1817. It is therefore later than *Alastor,* contemporaneous with *Prince Athanase,* and earlier than *The Coliseum* or *Epipsychidion.* It defines love in terms which are related to those of the Preface to *Alastor,* but some significant differences emerge. First, love of a human being is no longer sharply distinguished from the love of nature or knowledge; these are, at the least, less effective but valuable substitutes for human love:

[Love] is the bond and the sanction which connects not only man with man but with everything which exists. . . . In the motion of the very leaves of spring, in the blue air, there is then found a secret correspondence with our heart.[10]

Second, after some rhetorical questions, Shelley starts the essay with a paragraph not on loving but on being loved, or, more specifically, on the disappointment of being repulsed, and in the rest of the essay he does not forget the importance of mutual sympathy (in *Alastor* or its Preface, whether his love is requited or not is the least of the Poet's worries); third, the lover does not seek a prototype of his vision, as in *Alastor,* but its antitype (he sees "the ideal prototype" within his "intellectual nature"); fourth, the essay, unlike the Preface, does not analyze or classify those who lack sympathy, nor does it criticize the secluded; finally, the theme of the self-destructive love of generous youth is never suggested.

The awakening of love is stimulated "when we find within our own thoughts the chasm of an insufficient void and seek to awaken in all things that are"—here the essay goes well beyond the Preface—"a community with what we experience within ourselves." The three faculties which require completion in another are reason, imagination, and feeling or sense.

If we reason, we would be understood; if we imagine, we would that the airy children of our brain were born anew within another's; if we feel, we would that another's nerves should vibrate to our own. . . .

Similarly in the Preface the vision meets the requirements of "the poet, the philosopher, and the lover," and satisfies "the intellectual faculties," "the imagination," and "the functions of sense." And later in *On Love* the antitype whom the lover seeks is defined in terms of "an understanding," "an imagination," and "a frame whose nerves . . . vibrate with the vibrations of our own." Even the description of the visionary maid in *Alastor* itself corresponds to this threefold division, as Gibson observes.[11]

The genesis of the vision, of the goal toward which the impulses of love must strive, is much more elaborately analyzed in *On Love*. Both the circle figure and the mirror figure are used. The description of that genesis begins by unexpectedly and inconsistently assuming that the will to love, instead of being inspired by the emptiness of its opposite, is born with us and gradually grows to maturity. When it matures,

We dimly see within our intellectual nature a miniature as it were of our entire self, yet deprived of all we condemn or despise, the ideal prototype of every thing excellent or lovely that we are capable of conceiving as belonging to the nature of man. Not only the portrait of our external being but an assemblage of the minutest particles of which our nature is composed; a mirror whose surface reflects only the forms of purity and brightness; a soul within our soul that describes a circle around its proper paradise which pain, and sorrow, and evil dare not overleap.

The prototype is a sort of selective mirror which eliminates those things in ourselves which we condemn or despise and "reflects only the forms of purity and brightness." It is the uncontaminated idea of the self. Indeed it seems to be the self from which self has been eliminated. The mirror figure is used here without any sinister connotations at all, like the "lie-consuming mirror" of Truth in one of the great choral stanzas of *Hellas*. It is the opposite of the distorting mirror which Cenci sees degrading the image of Beatrice, the "mirror of my darkest thoughts" which Giacomo sees in the "smooth and ready countenance" of Orsino, the mirror which Shelley attributes to Byron in a letter to Peacock:

He is not yet an Italian and is heartily and deeply discontented with himself; and contemplating in the distorted mirror of his own thoughts the nature and the destiny of man, what can he behold but objects of contempt and despair?   (J.X.12)

or of the sinister glass of Desire in the fragment *Love, Hope, Desire, and Fear:*

> Desire presented her [false] glass, and then
>   The spirit dwelling there
> Was spellbound to embrace what seemed so fair
>   Within that magic mirror;
>   And, dazed by that bright error,
> It would have scorned the [shafts] of the avenger. . . .

In *Prince Athanase* the mirror figure recurs, but its meaning is somewhat different. Athanase, like the Poet of *Alastor,* is wise but secluded.

> His soul had wedded wisdom, and her dower
> Is love and justice, clothed in which he sate
> Apart from men, as in a lonely tower,
>
> Pitying the tumult of their dark estate.   (I.31–34)

Unlike the Poet's, his isolation, though lonely, does not seem self-centered. His "love and justice" may be remote, but they easily surpass the Poet's. And, we are told,

> With those who toiled and wept, the poor and wise,
> His riches and his cares he did divide.   (I.41–42)

But his "cares" turn out to be impenetrable. Beneath the mild surface lurk hidden and destructive passions, which he does not understand and which others cannot share.

> What was this grief, which ne'er in other minds
>
> A mirror found, he knew not—none could know;
> But on whoe'er might question him he turned
> The light of his dark eyes, as if to show
>
> He knew not of the grief within that burned. . . .   (I.75–78)

But, although Athanase finds no mirror in other minds, he half finds one in nature:

> How many a one, though none be near to love,
>
> Loves then the shade of his own soul, half seen
> In any mirror, or the spring's young minions,
> The winged leaves amid the copses green.   (II.117–20)

Whatever sinister connotations this figure may have to us are not underlined by Shelley, but that it could have such connotations for Shelley in 1817 is brought out unmistakeably by a remarkable parallel figure in canto eight of *The Revolt of Islam*. Cythna attacks the sailors' anthropomorphic conception of God by depicting it as mere self-worship:

> What is that Power? Some moonstruck sophist stood,
> Watching the shade from his own soul upthrown
> Fill Heaven and darken Earth, and in such mood
> The Form he saw and worshipped was his own,
> His likeness in the world's vast mirror shown.   (vi)

This would be an innocent dream, Cythna says, if the Power were not depicted as vindictive. Athanase is no "moonstruck sophist," but his psychological process is described in similar terms.

The selective mirror of *On Love* is described as "a soul within our soul that describes a circle around its proper paradise which pain, and sorrow, and evil dare not overleap." This circle figure is not an expansive one. Like that at the end of *Lines Written among the Euganean Hills,* it is a magic circle which includes the good and excludes the evil, and I doubt if it can be classed among the circle figures we have been considering. At the same time, although expanding so as to surround something and absorbing it within an exclusive circle are different processes, they end up at the same place. This can be observed in Shelley's development of the circle figure in *The Coliseum*. The old man of that story says to his daughter:

The internal nature of each being is surrounded by a circle, not to be surmounted by his fellows; and it is this repulsion which constitutes

the misfortune of the condition of life. But there is a circle which comprehends as well as one which mutually excludes, all things which
feel. And, with respect to man, his public and his private happiness consists in diminishing the circumference which includes those resembling
himself, until they become one with him and he with them.   (C.227)

Here Shelley seems to be revising his figure, but he is still saying
much the same thing.

Moving again from the process to the goal, we recall that, whereas
the Poet of *Alastor* sought for a prototype, the lover of *On Love*
seeks the antitype of the prototype he has dimly seen in his selective
mirror. *On Love* is dualistic, while *Alastor* is not. In *Alastor* the
Poet sees a woman in a dream and spends the rest of his life looking
for her. He does not seek an embodiment or earthly equivalent of
an otherworldly form. He seeks the thing itself, which is simply the
human object he finds most desirable. Even if he were to find her in
the next world, she would be no different from what she would be
in this. The image within his mind and the original which he seeks
outside it are not on separate levels of existence. *Alastor* is anything
but Platonic. It is humanistic or even naturalistic. *On Love* differs
significantly. Here the goal is an ideal against which human cor-
respondences are measured.

To this we eagerly refer all sensations, thirsting that they should resemble or correspond with it. The discovery of its antitype; . . . this
is the invisible and unattainable point to which Love tends; and to attain
which, it urges forth the powers of man to arrest the faintest shadow
of that without the possession of which there is no rest nor respite to
the heart over which it rules.

The prototype is unattainable, but we are able to find more or less
equivalent shadows.

We can also lose our way and become disillusioned among supposed equivalents. Mary Shelley sketches Shelley's idea for the
uncompleted *Prince Athanase:*

The idea Shelley had formed of Prince Athanase was a good deal
modelled on *Alastor*. In the first sketch of the poem, he named it
Pandemos and Urania. Athanase seeks through the world the One whom

he may love. He meets, in the ship in which he is embarked, a lady who appears to him to embody his ideal of love and beauty. But she proves to be Pandemos, or the earthly and unworthy Venus; who, after disappointing his cherished dreams and hopes, deserts him. Athanase, crushed by sorrow, pines and dies.   (J.III.146)

She quotes a note of Shelley's: "On his deathbed, the lady *who can really reply* to his soul comes and kisses his lips" (J.III.146). Even here there is no assertion that the goal is otherworldly, but if Mary Shelley's summary can be trusted, Shelley seems to have translated *Alastor* into terms far more Platonic than the earlier Preface would have allowed, or than the poem itself used. The influence of Peacock in 1817 is bearing fruit. The Pandemos-Urania opposition is of course Platonic, and quite irrelevant to *Alastor*. Equally irrelevant is the betrayal by the false Venus. The Poet of *Alastor* not only failed to recover the reality, he failed even to meet a delusive substitute. He is as far from shadows as from reality. Mrs. Shelley also attributes to the plan of the poem a dualism of "ideal" and "embodiment" which may be just casual phraseology, but may also represent a dualism in the projected poem. The poem, says Dowden, "stands in conception midway between 'Alastor' and 'Epipsychidion'." [12] The last stage in this development would be, I suppose, Shelley's famous remark to Mr. Gisborne:

I think one is always in love with something or other; the error—and I confess it is not easy for spirits cased in flesh and blood to avoid it—consists in seeking in a mortal image the likeness of what is perhaps eternal.   (J.X.401)

Alastor has by now been left far behind. An empirical dualism of subject and object has become a transcendental dualism of Time and Eternity. The naturalistic concern with human sympathy has been replaced by a pessimistic Platonism. In a way, however, the wheel has come full circle. One sets up the human image, the other the divine form. Neither allows any commerce between Time and Eternity. *Epipsychidion* does, as we shall observe before long.

VII

PAVILIONED UPON CHAOS

Act Three of *Prometheus Unbound,* originally the final act, did not satisfy Shelley as a conclusion for his drama. And the modern reader may well find something unresolved about it, despite the ecstatic report of the Spirit of the Earth. Prometheus, after his release, is surprisingly melancholy, and his withdrawal with Asia to pastoral contemplation certainly does not contribute to the social and political emphasis of the poem. Prometheus describes their simple dwelling in a passage which has something of the hovering balance, the sharp transparency, and the fluidity of the best descriptive passages in *Epipsychidion.* But it turns in a somewhat unexpected direction.

> There is a cave,
> All overgrown with trailing odorous plants,
> Which curtain out the day with leaves and flowers,
> And paved with veined emerald; and a fountain
> Leaps in the midst with an awakening sound.
> From its curved roof the mountain's frozen tears,
> Like snow, or silver, or long diamond spires,
> Hang downward, raining forth a doubtful light;
> And there is heard the ever-moving air
> Whispering without from tree to tree, and birds,
> And bees; and all around are mossy seats,
> And the rough walls are clothed with long soft grass;
> A simple dwelling, which shall be our own;
> Where we will sit and talk of time and change,
> As the world ebbs and flows, ourselves unchanged.
> What can hide man from mutability? (III.ii.10–25)

Surely at this moment, a turning point in human history, these resigned lamentations strike a strange and even ominous note.

The note is partly determined by the necessities of the legend.
Prometheus, in so far as he is himself a representative of the human
will and its capacity for regeneration, belongs to time and is himself
involved in the ebb and flow. But Prometheus is also the hero of a
legend and an immortal god. Part of the action of Act Three consists in his own personal release and reunion with Asia. He will
continue to aid his favorite, man, and plans to discover "arts, though
unimagined, yet to be" (III.ii.56), but he is free of the conditions
of existence in time. Therefore, as Prometheus moves from human
representative to legendary god, the melancholy disparity between
time and eternity also moves into the foreground where it now
belongs. The contrast which Prometheus draws between human
mutability and his own unchanging condition, is exactly parallel to
that which Shelley draws between our mutability and the immortality
of the Witch of Atlas:

> We, the weak mariners of that wide lake,
> Wheree'er its shores extend or billows roll,
> Our course unpiloted and starless make
> O'er its wild surface to an unknown goal;
> But she in the calm depths her way could take
> Where in bright bowers immortal forms abide,
> Beneath the weltering of the restless tide.   (498-504)

If Prometheus' resumption of his role as an immortal and his
retirement to pastoral immortality were the only reason for these
melancholy thoughts on such a glorious day, we might expect
them to subside when the center of attention starts to move away
from Prometheus. But they remain visible in the background. The
Earth describes the renovating effects on her of the new era:

> The dew-mists of my sunless sleep shall float
> Under the stars like balm; night-folded flowers
> Shall suck unwithering hues in their repose;
> And men and beasts in happy dreams shall gather

> Strength for the coming day, and all its joy;
> And death shall be the last embrace of her
> Who takes the life she gave, even as a mother,
> Folding her child, says, "Leave me not again."   (III.ii.100-7)

This minimizes the importance of death, but the word has been spoken, and, as we may remember from Act One, words and language are particularly important in conversation with the Earth. Asia is shocked.

> Oh, mother! wherefore speak the name of death?
> Cease they to love, and move, and breathe,
> Who die?   (III.ii.108-10)

The Earth responds with a characteristic equivocation, which serves also to reemphasize the difference between mortals and immortals:

> It would avail not to reply;
> Thou art immortal and this tongue is known
> But to the uncommunicating dead.   (III.ii.110-12)

Nevertheless she does reply, and denies the evil of death in a famous (and traditional) metaphor:

> Death is the veil which those who live call life;
> They sleep and it is lifted.   (III.ii.113-14)

In other words, it is really life that is deathlike. With its end we start to live indeed.

But this defense has really made matters worse, and the Earth fails to improve things by saying that at least in the meantime we have the beauties of nature. When the Earthly Paradise is going to be described, it is no help to contrast it in advance with the superiority of unchanging immortality and even to describe it as a deathlike veil. The climax of the poem is about to be reached, and the poet is quietly undermining it for us, although he tries to repair the damage as soon as it is done.

But perhaps all this will be forgotten when the Spirit of the Hour appears to tell the immortals about the visible effects of the downfall of Jupiter. The Spirit does forget it for most of his ecstatic speech, but it recurs at the very end, minimized but unmistakable.

> The loathsome mask has fallen, the Man remains,—
> Sceptreless, free, uncircumscribed,—but man:
> Equal, unclassed, tribeless and nationless,
> Exempt from awe, worship, degree, the King
> Over himself; just, gentle, wise;—but man:
> Passionless? no: yet free from guilt and pain,
> Which were, for his will made, or suffered them,
> Nor yet exempt, tho' ruling them like slaves,
> From chance, and death, and mutability,
> The clogs of that which else might oversoar
> The loftiest star of unascended heaven,
> Pinnacled dim in the intense inane.   (III.iv.193–204)

"But man." This statement of limitations at first sounds like a positive virtue as it echoes "the man remains." But the positive statements start to be challenged by the negative. Being man has its disadvantages, even if regenerate man manages almost to compensate for them. Guilt and pain may be conquered by the will, but man is still not free from "chance, and death, and mutability." Man does hold these inescapable enemies in subjection, but they still exist, and it is difficult to decide exactly what is meant by "ruling them like slaves," unless it simply means the application of scientific discoveries which control disease, and thereby prolong life, but do not finally destroy mutability. And the last three lines of the act (what were to be the last three lines of the poem) are negative. I wonder how many of those who remember or quote the lines,

> The loftiest star of unascended heaven,
> Pinnacled dim in the intense inane,

remember that this heaven is "unascended," that clogs hold man from attaining it, and that it is therefore a challenge to a further conquest which exists beyond the millennium and for which Demogorgon's final exhortation is not enough. We must not over-

emphasize this counterpoint in a minor key, which Shelley minimized but did not eliminate from Act Three of *Prometheus
Unbound;* but it must not be forgotten, for it is capable of undermining the whole structure, if allowed a free hand.[1]

There are really two enemies, or groups of enemies. On the one
side are the unregenerate will, hate, self-contempt, and revenge, with
their earthly embodiments: the tyrant, the priest, the slave, and the
loveless man. On the other are chaos, mutability, decay, change,
chance, and death, with their embodiments: the glory that *was*
Greece, degenerate Christianity, dead love, and time itself. One is
positive evil, the perverse activity of the human will, the other
negative evil, the inescapable limitations of earthly existence. In
the essay *On the Devil and Devils,* Shelley distinguishes between
two ways of describing the activities of the evil principle or the
Devil: one Manichaean and the other Greek.

The Manichaean philosophy respecting the origin and government of
the world, if not true, is at least an hypothesis conformable to the
experience of actual facts. To suppose that the world was created and
is superintended by two spirits of a balanced power and opposite dis-
positions is simply a personification of the struggle which we experience
within ourselves, and which we perceive in the operations of external
things as they affect us, between good and evil. The supposition that
the good spirit is, or hereafter will be, superior, is a personification of
the principle of hope and that thirst for improvement without which
present evil would be intolerable. . . .
But the Greek philosophers abstained from introducing the Devil.
They accounted for evil by supposing that what is called matter is
eternal and that God in making the world made not the best that he,
or even inferior intelligence, could conceive; but that he moulded the
reluctant and stubborn materials ready to his hand into the nearest
arrangement possible to the perfect archetype existing in his contemplation. In the same manner as a skilful watchmaker, who, if he had
diamonds, and steel, and brass, and gold, can construct a timepiece of
the most accurate workmanship, [but] could produce nothing beyond
a coarse and imperfect clock if he were restricted to wood as his material.

(C.265–66)

This is a rough and ready distinction, and Shelley's own version of the Greek view does not suggest the eternity of matter, but with some qualifications we may identify these two views as the intertwining and conflicting strands which make up Shelley's conception of evil. The Universe, he tells us (in the midst of the attack on Christianity which succeeds these speculations), is a place

> where evil and good are inextricably entangled, and where the most admirable tendencies to happiness and preservation are forever baffled by misery and decay.   (C.266)

In these two parallel clauses we see the Manichaean and the Greek (or, as I would prefer, the radical and the Platonic) loosely allied with one another. The picture of the Creation and the Fall in *The Revolt of Islam* also sets them clearly beside one another:

> Know then that from the depth of ages old
> Two Powers o'er mortal things dominion hold,
> Ruling the world with a divided lot,
> Immortal, all-pervading, manifold,
> Twin Genii, equal Gods—when life and thought
> Sprang forth, they burst the womb of inessential Nought.

> The earliest dweller of the world alone
> Stood on the verge of chaos. Lo! afar
> O'er the wide wild abyss two meteors shone,
> Sprung from the depth of its tempestuous jar—
> A blood-red Comet and the Morning Star
> Mingling their beams in combat. As he stood
> All thoughts within his mind waged mutual war
> In dreadful sympathy—when to the flood
> That fair Star fell, he turned and shed his brother's blood.
>   (I.xxv, xxvi)

The radical dominates the Platonic here, but both are present. With the Creation, Good and Evil rise out of chaos and enter the breast of the first man. In their war within him the Spirit of Evil is victorious, and man slays his brother. At the moment of this "primal eldest sin" the Spirit of Good descends into chaos. The two evil

principles are present, and the Spirit of Good falls victim both to
the Spirit of Evil and to Inessential Nought. The Spirit of Evil, whose
intermittent victory *The Revolt of Islam* chronicles, is defined by a
number of names: on the one hand,

> Death, Decay,
> Earthquake and Blight, and Want, and Madness pale,
> Winged and wan diseases, an array
> Numerous as leaves that strew the autumnal gale,

and, on the other,

> without whom all these might not avail,
> Fear, Hatred, Faith and Tyranny, who spread
> Those subtle nets which snare the living and the dead
>
> (I.xxix)

The ultimate victory of the Spirit of Good in *The Revolt of Islam*
is Platonic, not radical. Tyranny is again victorious in this world, but
Laon and Cythna have been translated to Eternity, where the Spirit
of Good awaits them in his temple.

Whereas the conflict with positive evil could be depicted as between
love and self-love or the circumference and the center, the conflict
with negative evil could be depicted as between eternity and time
or civilization and decay. Shelley's architectural bent and his experience in Italy often inspired him to present this last figure more
specifically as a city, group of buildings, or even a single structure,
decaying and disintegrating. The images of Venice, Rome, and
Naples (with its Baian towers "quivering within the waves' intenser day") impressed themselves on him, and the crumbling of
civilization's proud structures fused in his mind with the threat to
the formal structure of the eternal values, the Palace of Thought.

In *Lines Written among the Euganean Hills,* which registers
vividly the impact of Italy (and, in particular, of Venice), the radical
and the Platonic are again juxtaposed. Italy is threatened by the
Austrian usurpers, by its own slave mentality, and by the mutual
evil of "the despot's rage, the slave's revenge."

Many domed Padua proud
Stands, a peopled solitude,
Mid the harvest-shining plain,
Where the peasant heaps his grain
In the garner of his foe,
And the milk-white oxen slow
With the purple vintage strain,
Heaped upon the creaking wain,
That the brutal Celt may swill
Drunken sleep with savage will;
And the sickle to the sword
Lies unchanged, though many a lord,
Like a weed whose shade is poison,
Overgrows this region's foison,
Sheaves of whom are ripe to come
To destruction's harvest home.
Men must reap the things they sow,
Force from force must ever flow,
Or worse; but 'tis a bitter woe
That love or reason cannot change
The despot's rage, the slave's revenge.   (215-35)

But the earlier and later parts of the poem have a different emphasis. Shelley sees the columns, towers, domes, and spires of Venice "shine like obelisks of fire" in the light of the rising sun, and then reflects:

Sun-girt City! thou hast been
Ocean's child, and then his queen;
Now is come a darker day,
And thou soon must be his prey,

. . . .

A less drear ruin then than now,
With thy conquest-branded brow
Stooping to the slave of slaves
From thy throne among the waves,
Wilt thou be, when the sea-mew
Flies, as once before it flew,
O'er thine isles depopulate,

> And all is in its ancient state,
> Save where many a palace-gate
> With green sea-flowers overgrown
> Like a rock of ocean's own,
> Topples o'er the abandoned sea
> As the tides change sullenly.   (115–18, 121–33)

This figure of inevitable decay is assimilated very uneasily to the account of oppression and slavery which follows, although the pessimism of the poem makes it more appropriate here than it would have been in, say, Act One of *Prometheus Unbound*. Moreover, the figure of the decaying city is ultimately replaced by its rival within the Platonic framework, the island surrounded by "the deep, wide sea of human misery," and the poem ends as it began, with the author's bark seeking the flowering but unchanging island, which is also, however, the circle of love. In that island he will find

> the love which heals all strife,
> Circling, like the breath of life,
> All things in that sweet abode
> With its own mild brotherhood.
> They, not it, would change; and soon
> Every sprite beneath the moon
> Would repent its envy vain,
> And the earth grow young again.   (366–73)

This poem is something of a seedbed for Shelley's Italian period. It can prepare us for the cities under the sea or sinking into the sea, the cities surrounded by wildernesses, the decaying cities, the buildings perched on an abyss, the island eternities set in the sea of time, and the garden paradises subject to decay, which populate so many of the later poems.

> Go thou to Rome,—at once the Paradise,
> The grave, the city, and the wilderness.
>
> .   .   .   .
>
> And gray walls moulder round, on which dull Time
> Feeds, like slow fire upon a hoary brand.

Then the rain came down, and the broken stalks
Were bent and tangled across the walks;
And the leafless network of parasite bowers
Massed into ruin, and all sweet flowers. . . .

Unfathomable Sea! whose waves are years,
    Ocean of Time, whose waters of deep woe
Are brackish with the salt of human tears!
    Thou shoreless flood, which in thy ebb and flow
Claspest the limits of mortality, . . .
        Treacherous in calm, and terrible in storm,
            Who shall put forth on thee,
            Unfathomable Sea? [2]

On the whole, these quotations are characteristic of the later poems. The trend is from the radical to the Platonic. We have already observed this in passing, when we traced the development of Shelley's view of love from *Alastor* beyond *Epipsychidion*. A balance of some sort is achieved in *Lines Written among the Euganean Hills,* in the *Witch of Atlas,* and in *Prometheus Unbound,* but the apocalypse has overpowered the millennium in *Adonais, Epipsychidion, Hellas, The Triumph of Life,* and even *A Defence of Poetry.* Yet the radicalism never disappears. It may be obscured by the bulk of the Platonism, but, under favorable conditions, it will spring up vigorously again, as in *A Philosophical View of Reform.*

Two of Shelley's favorite passages of poetry seem to have mingled with the imagery of decaying architecture in which his Platonic conceptions often clothed themselves. One is Prospero's meditation on mutability in Act Four of *The Tempest:*

And, like the baseless fabric of this vision,
The cloud-capp'd towers, the gorgeous palaces,
The solemn temples, the great globe itself,
Yea, all which it inherit, shall dissolve,
And, like this insubstantial pageant faded,
Leave not a rack behind. We are such stuff
As dreams are made on, and our little life
Is rounded with a sleep.   (151-58)

The other is Satan's journey through Chaos, the importance of which for Shelley we have already observed in discussing Demogorgon. The cosmology of this passage made vivid to Shelley the picture of a universe emerging out of chaos, in which certain reclaimed and solidified portions (like the earth itself) are the precariously poised centers of order, and are always menaced by the surrounding chaos, "the Womb of nature and perhaps her Grave." It was for nineteenth-century poets the poetic equivalent of the nebular hypothesis, although its antecedents went back to Hesiod. Shelley did not believe in creation by the fiat of a creator God, but he was impressed by

> this wild Abyss,
> The Womb of nature and perhaps her Grave,
> Of neither Sea, nor Shore, nor Air, nor Fire,
> But all these in their pregnant causes mixt
> Confus'dly, and which thus must ever fight,
> Unless th' Almighty Maker them ordain
> His dark materials to create more worlds . . .

and by

> the Throne
> Of Chaos, and his dark Pavilion spread
> Wide on the wasteful Deep.   (II.910–16, 959–61)

Two words which stuck in his mind from these two passages and which sometimes betray the source of his inspiration are "inherit" from *The Tempest* and "pavilion" from *Paradise Lost,* both of which he misuses from the point of view of their source. The "it" which precedes "inherit" becomes not its object but its subject, and the pavilion spread on Chaos becomes not the abode of Chaos but the reclaimed abode of order emerging from, and always threatened by, the Chaos beneath, like Venice on the water. The following speech from *Hellas* mingles echoes from the two passages, as well as from John of Gaunt's address to England, and puts them to the service of some of Shelley's favorite Platonic and Berkeleian ideas. The whole is a vigorous, although not particularly distinguished,

statement both of his obsessive sense of the insubstantiality and impermanence of this universe in Time and of his reliance on a world
of eternal thought, which alone has being, and of which this world
of becoming can only provide "idle shadows."

> Sultan! talk no more
> Of thee and me, the future and the past;
> But look on that which cannot change—the One,
> The unborn and the undying. Earth and Ocean,
> Space, and the isles of life or light that gem
> The sapphire floods of interstellar air,
> This firmament pavilioned upon chaos,
> With all its cressets of immortal fire,
> Whose outwall, bastioned impregnably
> Against the escape of boldest thoughts, repels them
> As Calpe the Atlantic clouds—this Whole
> Of suns, and worlds, and men, and beasts, and flowers,
> With all the silent or tempestuous workings
> By which they have been, are, or cease to be,
> Is but a vision; all that it inherits
> Are motes of a sick eye, bubbles, and dreams;
> Thought is its cradle and its grave, nor less
> The future and the past are idle shadows
> Of thought's eternal flight—they have no being;
> Nought is but that which feels itself to be.   (766–85)

The figures of this rather incoherent passage are seen to have under-
gone some remarkable modifications or even reversals when we compare them with their sources. The ramparts which in *Richard II*
protected England from outside enemies here prevent the escape of
Thought into Chaos. The Womb and Grave of Nature are no longer
the surrounding Chaos, but the surrounding Thought which gives
Chaos meaning, the Cradle and Grave of life. Even "Our little
life is rounded with a sleep" shares, if less strikingly, in the transformation by which the surrounding and the surrounded are mingled
and interchanged. We shall never be certain in *Hellas* whether to
expect Chaos founded on Thought or Thought founded on Chaos.
    The figure of the structure threatened by disintegration is ac-

companied in *Hellas* by the figure of the wheel, to which it is closely
related. Life is at the mercy both of chaos and decay and of endless
cycles which solve nothing. History may finally not arrive anywhere
but just repeat itself forever. No work of Shelley's is more obsessed
with Time and its categories. Like the Satan of the Prologue, it
sees "but the Past in the To-come." The eternal reality of Thought
is asserted, but it is the rise and fall of generations which dominate
the foreground.

But *Hellas* ought not to be dominated by figures such as these.
Its occasion demanded a radical not a Platonic play, a play of the
active will not of the embattled structure of Thought, a linear not a
cyclical view of history. Where *Hellas* succeeds simply as poetry
(in some of the choruses and occasionally in the scenes with Ahasuerus and the Spirit of Mahomet), its success contributes very little
to its ostensible purpose as a tribute to the cause of Greek victory and
independence. One wonders what Prince Mavrocordato would have
thought of the final chorus.

The mingled thread of the unfinished Prologue to *Hellas* provides
an appropriate background to the finished play. It has the same
texture of figures, the same Platonic frame of reference (ineffectively
counteracted by rhetorical outbursts reminiscent as much of *Queen
Mab* as of Act One of *Prometheus Unbound*). It depicts a meeting
of "the senate of the Gods," in which the fate of Greece is debated.
A herald of eternity sets the scene, a chorus hymns the gathering of
the gods, and three speakers (Christ, Satan, and Mahomet) begin
the debate before the fragment is over. The Greeks were Christians,
and Shelley's sympathies were with the Greeks, so that Christ's
speech becomes a sympathetic one, asserting the relation of Platonism and the Greek spirit to Christianity and prophesying the
rebirth of Greece. Satan's reply is in the manner of the Furies in
Prometheus Unbound and looks forward to an endless succession
of Famine, Pestilence, Superstition, War, Anarchy, Tyranny, and so
forth. Mahomet, whose speech survives in three fragments of five,
four, and two lines, might in a complete Prologue have been more

than just an inspirer of tyrants. He might also have been an instrument for criticizing the shortcomings of Christianity, which Shelley had not forgotten, despite his support for the Christians against the Turks. "Be thou a curse," says Mahomet,

> on them whose creed
> Divides and multiplies the most high God.   (178-79)

Shelley, no less than Mahomet, was opposed to the conception of the Trinity.

But it is not the structure or argument but the texture of the unfinished Prologue that we are concerned with here. The place where the gods meet is

> the roofless senate-house, whose floor
> Is Chaos, and the immovable abyss
> Frozen by his steadfast word to hyaline.   (2-4)

Even the senate-house of the gods, then, is built on Chaos, which is frozen into a solid crystal floor by the decree of God. The gods themselves ("hierarchs and kings," as the Herald calls them), who sway the present from their thrones "pinnacled on the past," also

> sit
> Pavilioned on the radiance or the gloom
> Of mortal thought. . . .   (7, 8, 9-10)

Such god-sustaining "mortal thought" (11) arises in a mist which obscures its divine origin. The earth, from which it arises, is doomed to ultimate destruction, but "the swift decree / Yet hovers" (14-15). In the meantime, under the impulse of the "atmosphere of living spirit," which ebbs and flows, and "rolls from realm to realm / And age to age" (22, 24-25), the generations succeed one another in due order. The Herald goes on to outline the history of Greece and announce the impending crisis which faces the decision of the assembly of the gods. But before the advocates debate, a chorus intervenes, describing the coming together of the gods in terms of figures similar to those in the Herald's opening speech. This chorus is an unrevised and loosely written fragment. It depicts the roofless, crystalline senate-house, in which "Golden worlds revolve and shine" as they fly "From every point of the infinite" (60, 62). Toward it "in pavilioned chariots" move "the Giant Powers" (67, 69). Before the chorus ends with the appearance of Satan, Christ, and Mahomet, a two-line fragment intervenes:

> A chaos of light and motion
> Upon that glassy ocean.　　　　　(71–72)

When Christ begins to speak, he first distinguishes among the ingredients of evil and describes how they are mixed in mortal destiny. On the one hand there are the two fountains, of Discord (i.e. War) and Slavery, and on the other an unnamed third power, the "fiercest and mightiest," who mixes the urns of Discord and Slavery and adds as his own contribution "Chaos and Death and slow Oblivion's lymph" (84, 85). It hardly needs pointing out that Christ's division corresponds to that between radical evil and Platonic evil which we have already observed in Shelley's thought. Christ then swears that Greece shall rise again. He swears first by his own agony in the garden and his pity on those who were moved to revenge (i.e., his Promethean, or radical, experiences) and second

> 　　　　　by Plato's sacred light,
> Of which my spirit was a burning morrow—
> By Greece and all she cannot cease to be. . . .　　(94–96)

The climax of the passage sees Greece reborn out of Chaos.

> 　　　　　　She shall arise
> Victorious as the world arose from Chaos!
> And as the Heavens and the Earth arrayed
> Their presence in the beauty and the light
> Of thy first smile, O Father, as they gather
> The spirit of thy love which paves for them
> Their path o'er the abyss, till every sphere
> Shall be one living Spirit, so shall Greece—.　　(112–119)

At this point Satan interrupts him with a speech strongly reminiscent of the temptations of the Furies in *Prometheus Unbound,* but on a notably inferior level. The fragment continues with Christ's repudiation of Satan as proud and time-ridden, unable to see Eternity beyond the cycles of history. "Thou seest but the Past in the To-come" (161).

This Prologue, as I have already suggested, is in its emphasis similar to *Hellas* as a whole. The radical evil, so brilliantly depicted in *Prometheus Unbound,* is not forgotten, but it is continually being edged out of the way by the Platonic evil of limitation in Time and by references to historical cycles, rolling worlds, ebb and flow, thrones or buildings on Chaos, crystalline floors paving Chaos, foundations solid or fluctuating, and the like. In *Hellas* proper this emphasis is particularly notable in the choruses and in Mahmud's scenes with Ahasuerus and the shade of Mahomet. Familiar choral passages immediately come to mind:

> Worlds on worlds are rolling ever
>   From creation to decay,
> Like the bubbles on a river,
>   Sparkling, bursting, borne away.
> But they are still immortal
> Who, through birth's orient portal
> And death's dark chasm hurrying to and fro,
>   Clothe their unceasing flight
>   In the brief dust and light
> Gathered around their chariots as they go. . . .
>
> (197–206)

> Temples and towers,
>   Citadels and marts, and they
> Who live and die there, have been ours,
>   And may be thine, and must decay;
> But Greece and her foundations are
> Built below the tide of war,
> Based on the crystalline sea
> Of thought and its eternity;
> Her citizens, imperial spirits,

> Rule the present from the past;
> On all this world of men inherits
>   Their seal is set.   (692–703)

The telltale word "inherits" betrays Shelley's memory of Prospero's "cloud-capped towers," although he is actually attempting to refute Prospero's argument. As a final choral illustration, here is the great vision of Greece resurrected in a world beyond time:

> If Greece must be
> A wreck, yet shall its fragments reassemble,
> And build themselves again impregnably
>   In a diviner clime,
> To Amphionic music, on some Cape sublime
> Which frowns above the idle foam of time.   (1002–7)

Ahasuerus is an immortal mortal, poised between Time and Eternity. His scene with Mahmud is similarly poised. Long before he enters we hear of him from Hassan:

> The Jew of whom I spake is old, so old
> He seems to have outlived a world's decay;
>
>   . . . .
>
>   but from his eye looks forth
> A life of unconsumed thought which pierces
> The present, and the past, and the to-come.
> Some say that this is he whom the great prophet
> Jesus, the son of Joseph, for his mockery,
> Mocked with the curse of immortality.
> Some feign that he is Enoch; others dream
> He was pre-adamite, and has survived
> Cycles of generation and of ruin.   (137–38, 146–54)

When Ahasuerus appears to Mahmud, the latter addresses him as "an adept" in "Greek and Frank philosophy" (741, 742) and as one who sees

> The birth of this old world through all its cycles
> Of desolation and of loveliness,
> And when man was not, and how man became

> The monarch and the slave of this low sphere
> And all its narrow circles. . . .   (746–50)

(Note that the wheel figure and the circle figure are juxtaposed here, as nowhere else in Shelley.)

Ahasuerus does two things for Mahmud: first, he subjects the confused monarch to a discourse on the permanence of mind and the dream-like impermanence of this world; second, he shows him a vision of the terrors of the future, which are only a repetition of the terrors of the past. We have already examined Ahasuerus' main speech on mutability; he prepares for the vision of the future with another:

> All is contained in each.
> Dodona's forest to an acorn's cup
> Is that which has been or will be, to that
> Which is—the absent to the present. Thought
> Alone, and its quick elements, Will, Passion,
> Reason, Imagination, cannot die;
> They are what that which they regard appears,
> The stuff whence mutability can weave
> All that it hath dominion o'er—worlds, worms,
> Empires, and superstitions. What has thought
> To do with time, or place, or circumstance?
> Wouldst thou behold the future?—ask and have!
> Knock and it shall be opened—look and lo!
> The coming age is shadowed on the past
> As on a glass.   (792–806)

The coming age, as it appears to Mahmud, is war and ruin. Ahasuerus draws the moral:

> Thou mayst behold
> How cities, on which empire sleeps enthroned,
> Bow their towered crests to mutability.
>
> . . . .
>
> The Past
> Now stands before thee like an Incarnation
> Of the To-Come.   (844–46, 852–54)

Before leaving he calls up the Phantom of Mahomet the Second to Mahmud.

In the scene which follows, Mahomet sees his own glory and the empire of Mahmud descending into the blank deep. His throne is surrounded by the wrecks of the earlier power which fell when he arose. Now he sees Islam itself in the autumn of its cycle, waiting for wolfish winter to strip its foliage, and for a new power to be born out of its decay. But Mahomet is resigned to the cycles of history and does not complain. He simply looks forward to Mahmud's descent into the world of death, where they will rule over the ruins of Islam together. I quote Mahomet's speech at length, because it is perhaps the finest in the play and an outstanding example of Shelley's Virgilian mood:

                                        I come
          Thence whither thou must go! The grave is fitter
          To take the living than give up the dead;
          Yet has thy faith prevailed, and I am here.
          The heavy fragments of the power which fell
          When I arose, like shapeless crags and clouds,
          Hang round my throne on the abyss, and voices
          Of strange lament soothe my supreme repose,
          Wailing for glory never to return.
          A later empire nods in its decay;
          The autumn of a greener faith is come;
          And wolfish change, like winter, howls to strip
          The foliage in which Fame, the eagle, built
          Her aerie, while Dominion whelped below.
          The storm is in its branches, and the frost
          Is on its leaves, and the blank deep expects
          Oblivion on oblivion, spoil on spoil,
          Ruin on ruin. Thou art slow, my son;
          The Anarchs of the world of darkness keep
          A throne for thee, round which thine empire lies
          Boundless and mute; and for thy subjects thou,
          Like us, shalt rule the ghosts of murdered life,
          The phantoms of the powers who rule thee now—
          Mutinous passions and conflicting fears,

> And hopes that sate themselves on dust and die,
> Stripped of their mortal strength, as thou of thine.
> Islam must fall, but we will reign together
> Over its ruins in the world of death;
> And if the trunk be dry, yet shall the seed
> Unfold itself even in the shape of that
> Which gathers birth in its decay.   (861–91)

Mahmud wishes to know the exact hour when "Destruction must accomplish / Her consummation" (901–2). Mahomet has just told Mahmud that is impossible to know, when a cry of "victory!" is heard. The Greeks have been defeated. Mahmud wakes from his trance, and the voice crying "victory!" (912, 914) is heard again.

Psychologically this is the critical moment of the play, whose dramatic line (as distinct from its lyrical background) is the development of Mahmud. The Mahmud of the first half of the play is a Shelleyan tyrant who worships power and whose cruelty is equaled only by his fear. He sees his empire crumbling about him and is gradually being overwhelmed by despair. Then he speaks to Ahasuerus and the Phantom of Mahomet. They are beyond Time and the cyclical flux in which Mahmud is vainly struggling to preserve his empire. Ahasuerus recognizes in the crystalline sea of thought a lasting basis which cannot be destroyed by the dream of time. The Phantom of Mahomet prophesies the fall of Islam and the descent of Mahmud to a throne in "the world of darkness." Mahmud is impressed by his two visitors and undergoes something of a conversion. It is not, however, a radical conversion, like the conversion of Prometheus, but a Platonic one. Mahmud feels no pity or love; he does not expand beyond the prison of his self-love. He is simply able to look at the cycles of history in which he is involved and accept the inevitable downfall of his empire with resignation. He comes to accept, with Ahasuerus, the fact that earthly phenomena are in themselves worthless. Their value lies in what they give or teach the mind of man. The victory which the voice is announcing is a delusion, and it leads to the despair which he (like Prometheus,

but in an entirely different way) is now able to conquer. Here is
Mahmud's last speech, as he revives to the sound of offstage cries:

> Weak lightning before darkness! poor faint smile
> Of dying Islam! Voice which art the response
> Of hollow weakness! Do I wake and live?
> Were there such things? or may the unquiet brain,
> Vexed by the wise mad talk of the old Jew,
> Have shaped itself these shadows of its fear?
> It matters not!—for nought we see or dream,
> Possess, or lose, or grasp at, can be worth
> More than it gives or teaches. Come what may,
> The future must become the past, and I
> As they were, to whom once this present hour,
> This gloomy crag of time to which I cling,
> Seemed an Elysian isle of peace and joy
> Never to be attained.—I must rebuke
> This drunkenness of triumph ere it die,
> And dying, bring despair. Victory! poor slaves!   (915–30)

When Mahmud has left, the offstage voice of victory makes an
exulting speech of revenge, and the rest of the play (ll. 940–1101)
is choral, except for three further interruptions by the voice of victory.

The chorus is, of course, composed of Greek Christian slaves. They
are appalled by the news of Greek defeat, yet console themselves
with stories of persecuted peoples who yet survived and with dreams
of a reborn Greece somewhere in the future. According to Shelley's
Preface, in these lyrics he has

> wrought upon the curtain of futurity, which falls upon the unfinished
> scene, such figures of indistinct and visionary delineation as suggest the
> final triumph of the Greek cause as a portion of the cause of civilization
> and social improvement.   (C.331)

This is true enough, but only part of the truth. Reading this passage
and then turning to the concluding choruses of *Hellas,* one discovers
some surprising things. The Greek slaves are less obviously concerned with social improvement in this world and less certain of the
triumph of civilization than Shelley's prose suggests. This difference

can be partly explained on dramatic grounds. After all, these slaves are stimulated to utterance by the bloodthirsty cries of victory which announce the apparent defeat of their cause. That their visionary hopes should be mixed with pessimistic fears and a distrust of this world is hardly surprising. Shelley has himself pointed out in a note on an earlier chorus that the sentiments expressed are in character with "the popular notions of Christianity" (C.333). At the same time, these final choruses surely represent in general the final position of the play as a whole, and their prophecies are what the reader is intended to look forward to as he finishes reading. The ambiguities of their meaning are more, I think, than dramatic necessities, they are involved in the point of view of the play as well as in the point of view of the Greeks.

But it would be a mistake to go to the other extreme and reject Shelley's own account of the conclusion of *Hellas*. This is a political drama, and, although it may stray from its purpose, that purpose is not forgotten. A stanza like the following is less otherworldly than a casual glance might suggest:

> Darkness has dawned in the East
> On the noon of time;
> The death birds descend to their feast,
> From the hungry clime,
> Let Freedom and Peace flee far
> To a sunnier strand,
> And follow Love's folding star
> To the Evening land!   (1023-30)

A commentator like K. N. Cameron is justified, I think, in keeping Shelley's "young Atlantis," "Hesperus," and "Evening land" on the ground and not in some timeless otherworld. Here is his blunt note on "young Atlantis":

. . . the United States; so also "the Evening land" (1030), that is, the land in the west, and other references here and in *Charles the First*, iv. The attitude of the Chorus in this concluding section is that even if liberty perishes in Greece and Europe, it still lives in America and has powers to develop to greater heights throughout the world ("Another Athens . . .").[3]

Shelley is undoubtedly thinking of the United States, as the parallel passage from *Charles the First* makes quite clear. But the following passage goes well beyond such a reference:

> If Greece must be
> A wreck, yet shall its fragments re-assemble,
> And build themselves again impregnably
>   In a diviner clime,
> To Amphionic music on some Cape sublime,
> Which frowns above the idle foam of time.   (1002-7)

This reassembling is beyond Time, and what is built is the eternal pattern of Hellas. The passage is reminiscent of the earlier vision of the Form of Greece:

> But Greece and her foundations are
> Built below the tide of war,
> Based on the crystalline sea
> Of thought and its eternity.

As for the "kingless continents, sinless as Eden" and the "Paradise islands of glory" (1047, 1052), they are certainly the North American continent and its attendant islands, but they are also close relations of *Epipsychidion*'s island Paradise, where Time culminates in its own annihilation. These islands

> Burst, like morning on dream, or like Heaven on death,
>   Through the walls of our prison;
> And Greece which was dead is arisen.   (1057-59)

Whether the dream we awake from is Time, whether the Heaven is simply metaphorical, whether the arising of Greece is out of Time or within the cycles of Time, Shelley does not say. The Greek slaves, it seems, look to the rebirth of Greece, both in and out of Time, the second if not the first.

Cameron's inclusion of the final chorus among the prophecies of Greece's rebirth in the United States may seem like a pretty crude explication. But he is surely right, for this final chorus at least, to emphasize that what the Greek slaves anticipate is an even greater Hellas on this earth. To be sure, it is not simply the United States. The slaves are willing to strengthen their courage by citing the example of the rebellion of "young Atlantis"; they can see America as an idyllic harbor for refugees from the darkening East; they can use it as a springboard from which to rise to their vision of a new Hellas; but they cannot console themselves for defeat merely by seeing America as the successor of Greece. On the other hand, Woodberry's note on "Evening land" goes too far (in the opposite direction from Cameron's) when it asserts:

Here and in the following lines, America appears to furnish the elements of the idealized new age, which soon changes imaginatively into the glorification of a newly arisen ideal Greece.[4]

This "brighter Hellas"[5] is not "ideal" in a Platonic sense, nor, indeed, as the chorus ultimately makes clear, even in the sense of the man in the street. Of course, the disappearance in a phosphorescent decay of the "faiths and empires" of the past "Like wrecks of a dissolving dream" and the succession of comparative adjectives ("brighter Hellas," "waves serener far," "fairer Tempes," "sunnier deep," "loftier Argo") does seem to transport this Hellas well beyond any limited new Greece of history; but fundamentally the last chorus envisions a millennial Greece, about which hangs only a slight aura of the other world. Like the millennium of *Prometheus Unbound*, this new Hellas is subject to "chance, and death, and mutability" (III.iv.201), as becomes obvious in later stanzas.

The first two stanzas are idyllic. Beginning with stanza three, the idyll starts to show some flaws.

> A loftier Argo cleaves the main,
>   Fraught with a later prize;
> Another Orpheus sings again,
>   And loves, and weeps, and dies.
> A new Ulysses leaves once more
> Calypso for his native shore.

The stories of Greece which Shelley remembers are not purely idyllic, although only in the lines about Orpheus is this made explicit. In stanza four, however, the jarring notes dominate, and the chorus cries out,

> Oh, write no more the tale of Troy,
>   If earth Death's scroll must be!
> Nor mix with Laian rage the joy
>   Which dawns upon the free;
> Although a subtler Sphinx renew
> Riddles of death Thebes never knew.

Greek literature for Shelley means not merely Plato but Homer and the Greek dramatists. A new Greece (if we press the parallel) means another ten years' siege of Troy. It means another Theban cycle, including the horrors of Oedipus and the other successors of Laius. And if the waves are serener and the deep is sunnier, so also will the Sphinx be subtler, and her modern riddles of death harder to answer than her Theban predecessor's. After this disrupting stanza, the Chorus abruptly returns to the idyllic side of its vision, but only for a moment.

> Another Athens shall arise,
>   And to remoter time
> Bequeath like sunset to the skies,
>   The splendor of its prime;
> And leave, if nought so bright may live,
> All earth can take or Heaven can give.

What begins in hope ends in melancholy. After announcing the rising of the new Athens, the Chorus turns quickly to its sunset and the splendor which it bequeathes at the end of its cycle. Its brightness can not last and even the bequeathal of its splendor is dependent not merely on the permanent values of Heaven, which are all that survive its temporal demise, but also on the capacity of earth to absorb that splendor. The Chorus again turns back hopefully to the religious superiority of the new Greece, "more bright and good" than the paganism and Christianity of the past. It sees

Greece repudiating the worship of Mammon and Mars and accepting that of Pity and Beauty.

> Saturn and Love their long repose
> Shall burst, more bright and good
> Than all who fell, than One who rose,
> Than many unsubdued;
> Not gold, not blood, their altar dowers,
> But votive tears and symbol flowers.

But the obsessive doubts will not be overcome.

> Oh, cease! must hate and death return?
> Cease! must men kill and die?
> Cease! drain not to its dregs the urn
> Of bitter prophecy.
> The world is weary of the past,
> Oh, might it die or rest at last!

The joyous prophecy of rebirth must also, it seems, be a bitter prophecy of death. The wheel will rotate; "hate and death" will return. The final cry of the play is for death or rest. No answer to the cry or resolution to the conflicting doubts and hopes is offered. The only answer which the play has suggested elsewhere is that death (not within Time but out of Time) is the gateway to rest, because men can rest only in the contemplation of that which is eternal. But *Hellas* does not end by insisting, like *Adonais:*

> Die,
> If thou wouldst be with that which thou dost seek!   (LII)

Such a cry is possible in a consolatory elegy, where the dead must seem to have an advantage over the living. As the conclusion for a tribute to the Greek cause, it is unthinkable. Nevertheless, it seems to be the far-off event toward which *Hellas* is moving.

Among the political poems which mingle a radical argument with a Platonic texture, the most successful is the *Ode to Liberty,* written as a tribute to the Spanish uprising of January, 1820. The texture of *Hellas* undermined its purpose; the similar texture of the *Ode to Liberty* is kept in stricter control, and a sense of the futility of history is not allowed to reflect on the value of the liberty which the poem celebrates. The wheel shows itself on the sunny side, and Chaos is willing to be the instrument of Eternity.

> Athens arose; a city such as vision
>   Builds from the purple crags and silver towers
> Of battlemented cloud, as in derision
>   Of kingliest masonry: the ocean floors
> Pave it; the evening sky pavilions it;
>   Its portals are inhabited
>   By thunder-zoned winds, each head
> Within its cloudy wings with sun-fire garlanded,—
>   A divine work! Athens, diviner yet,
>   Gleamed with its crest of columns, on the will
>   Of man, as on a mount of diamond, set;
>   For thou wert, and thine all-creative skill
> Peopled, with forms that mock the eternal dead
>   In marble immortality, that hill
>   Which was thine earliest throne and latest oracle.
>
> Within the surface of Time's fleeting river
>   Its wrinkled image lies, as then it lay
> Immovably unquiet, and forever
>   It trembles, but it cannot pass away!
> The voices of thy bards and sages thunder
>   With an earth-awakening blast
>   Through the caverns of the past;
> Religion veils her eyes; Oppression shrinks aghast.
>   A winged sound of joy, and love, and wonder,
>   Which soars where Expectation never flew,
>   Rending the veil of space and time asunder!
>   One ocean feeds the clouds, and streams, and dew;
> One sun illumines heaven; one spirit vast
>   With life and love makes chaos ever new,
>   As Athens doth the world with thy delight renew.   (61–90)

The imagery of the first of these stanzas is Shelley's Platonic imagery, but the architecture (complete with Shakespeare's cloud towers and Milton's pavilion) is set not on the crystalline foundation of Thought,

but on that aspect of man's mind which is central to Shelley's millennial radicalism: "the will of man." This Athens is gone, but it
has achieved the "marble immortality" of its surviving art. The
second stanza is dominated by another figure characteristic of Shelley's Platonism, the city under the water, obscured by the wrinkling
surface of "Time's fleeting river," but indestructible. This city inspires the present with its voices from the past. It rends "the veil
of space and time asunder," not by destroying time, but by its continuing presence in the mind of man and its capacity for renewing
the future, despite its material decay centuries before. The final lines
of the stanza do not set the eternal Spirit of Good irreconcilably
against the depredations of time. The "one spirit . . . makes chaos
ever new," and one of its instruments is the renewing vitality of
Athens. In all this there is no pessimistic opposition between the
forms and the flux, nor is the natural cycle simply deplored. Shelley's
radical ethics and his Greek metaphysics cooperate vigorously in
the service of Liberty.

A similar cooperation can be seen in the picture of the republican
city-states of Italy.

> And many a warrior-peopled citadel,
> Like rocks which fire lifts out of the flat deep,
>> Arose in sacred Italy,
>> Frowning o'er the tempestuous sea
> Of kings, and priests, and slaves, in tower-crowned majesty;
>> That multitudinous anarchy did sweep
>>> And burst around their walls, like idle foam,
>> Whilst from the human spirit's deepest deep,
>>> Strange melody with love and awe struck dumb
> Dissonant arms; and Art, which cannot die,
>> With divine wand traced on our earthly home
>> Fit imagery to pave heaven's everlasting dome.   (124-35)

Here, the city rising out of the deep, braving the tempest and surrounded by the bursts of idle foam, suggests the already quoted lines
from *Hellas,* in which the Greek slaves imagine the fragments of
their country reassembling above the sea of Time.

But in the *Ode to Liberty* Shelley's Platonic imagery is used for radical purposes. The citadel is not an eternal beacon in the sea of Time, but a center of resistance surrounded by the enemies of Liberty and by the "multitudinous anarchy" in which these "kings, and priests, and slaves" flourish. The "idle foam" is in both passages, but in one it is the foam of Time and in the other the foam of anarchy, which for Shelley is the greatest foe of Liberty and the seedbed of oppression. These Italian citadels, like Athens, partake of the eternity of Art, without being themselves eternal.

The last three stanzas are a fitting summary of the thought of the poem and subside into a beautifully controlled conclusion.

> He who taught man to vanquish whatsoever
>   Can be between the cradle and the grave
> Crowned him the King of Life. Oh, vain endeavor!
>   If on his own high will, a willing slave,
> He has enthroned the oppression and the oppressor.
>   What if earth can clothe and feed
>   Amplest millions at their need,
> And power in thought be as the tree within the seed?
>   Oh, what if Art, an ardent intercessor,
>   Driving on fiery wings to Nature's throne,
>   Checks the great mother stooping to caress her
>   And cries: Give me, thy child, dominion
> Over all height and depth? If Life can breed
>   New wants, and wealth from those who toil and groan,
>   Rend of thy gifts and hers a thousandfold for one.   (241–55)

The first five lines are a superb statement of Shelley's radical creed that the destiny of man depends upon the will of man. The next three state the optimistic side of Shelley's Platonism: that the eternal power of thought can direct (even if it cannot start or stop) the cycles of history, and the last seven suggest the fructifying and civilizing power of Art, as it ascends to the throne of Nature and demands dominion over Life. The Spirit who utters the central stanzas of the *Ode* now readdresses Liberty herself and calls on her to lead Wisdom out of the recesses of man's mind:

Come thou, but lead out of the inmost cave
  Of man's deep spirit, as the morning-star
Beckons the sun from the Eoan wave,
  Wisdom. I hear the pennons of her car
Self-moving, like cloud charioted by flame;
      Comes she not, and come ye not,
      Rulers of eternal thought,
  To judge with solemn truth life's ill-apportioned lot?
    Blind Love, and equal Justice, and the Fame
      Of what has been, the Hope of what will be?
    O Liberty! if such could be thy name
      Wert thou disjoined from these, or they from thee—
  If thine or theirs were treasures to be bought
    By blood or tears, have not the wise and free
    Wept tears, and blood like tears?   (256–70)

Observe that the syntax in this and the previous stanza has become negative and interrogative and concessive. Shelley does not
state directly that all depends on man's will, he says that all is lost
if man does not exercise properly the freedom of his will. The rest
of the stanza is dominated by a series of "if" clauses: "what if
earth . . . ?" "what if Art . . . ?" In the next stanza the Spirit
hears the approach of Wisdom's chariot, but the syntax does not
become more positive. Interrogatives and negatives and subjunctives
dominate it: "comes she not, and come ye not . . . ?" "if such
could be thy name . . . ;" "If thine or theirs were treasures to be
bought . . . ;" "have not the wise and free / Wept tears . . . ?"
The union of Wisdom and Liberty seems very hypothetical in this
stanza.

The voice stops singing.

The solemn harmony

Paused, and the Spirit of that mighty singing
  To its abyss was suddenly withdrawn;
Then as a wild swan, when sublimely winging
  Its path athwart the thunder-smoke of dawn,
Sinks headlong through the aerial golden light
  On the heavy sounding plain,

When the bolt has pierced its brain;
As summer clouds dissolve unburdened of their rain;
As a far taper fades with fading night,
As a brief insect dies with dying day,—
My song, its pinions disarrayed of might,
Drooped; o'er it closed the echoes far away
Of the great voice which did its flight sustain,
As waves which lately paved his watery way
Hiss round a drowner's head in their tempestuous play.

(270–85)

Except for the perfunctory and infelicitous phrasing of the last two lines, this is a worthy conclusion to the poem. It sets the millennial hopes of the *Ode* in their limiting framework but does not discredit the glowing account of Liberty's activity, upon which the *Ode* centers. The "beautiful idealisms of moral excellence" were displayed and the possibility of their reattainment was asserted; then the difficulties and uncertainties of their attainment were gradually drawn to the foreground; now finally the possibility of failure emerges, or human inability to sustain its effort. The swan sings only before death, and the poet's own raptures must subside, now unsupported by the inspired voice of the Spirit. The poem dies away amid imagery of dissolving clouds, fading tapers, and dying day. At last the echoes close over the poet's head like the water closing over the head of a drowning man; and the poem is done. Chaos is come again, but Liberty seems untouched, not merely on its eternal throne but in its presence here and now. The end of the *Ode to Liberty* does not envisage the death of the world but the sleep of exhaustion after strenuous efforts on behalf of the goddess.

But, as my comments have suggested, if only in passing, the *Ode* is about Imagination almost as much as about Liberty. Stanzas two to five (from the state of nature to Periclean Athens) stand the Hobbesian thesis on its head and depict the state of nature as a state of Tyranny and Priestcraft, and civilization as the child of Liberty. Among the chief consequences of civilized Liberty is the stimulation of Art and Verse. Moreover, the history of Liberty, the praise of its powers, the demand for its rebirth—all this is not the whole poem, but a play within a play. The outer play is the story of a prophetic voice which inspires the poet with its singing but suddenly withdraws, leaving his song to droop, "its pinions disarrayed of might." In the end the *Ode* is about the poet's inability to sustain his prophetic imagination.

Two notions of the interaction of Art and Liberty are involved in the poem. In the one, Liberty inspires Art; in the other, Art inspires Liberty. Shelley's stress on both activities is, of course, one of the central paradoxes of *A Defence of Poetry*. I suppose it can be resolved in historical terms, although not without a few loose ends. Originally Liberty precedes and stimulates great Art. But Art is long and Liberty is short. When Liberty has died, Art survives in the monuments of the past and even in the fragmentary episodes of the degenerate present; it hoards the spark of Liberty in an "unextinguished hearth" and ultimately heralds rebirth.

But Art heralds something more than Liberty, or even the millennium, in *A Defence of Poetry*. That essay, with its disconcerting eclecticism, gives us a great many imaginations, including the synthetic imagination, the folk imagination, the sympathetic and expansive imagination, and the Platonic or apocalyptic imagination. The last two are both versions of the prophetic imagination. The first strengthens our capacity for love and assists us to comprehend kinds of moral excellence which are beyond our present reach. As such it prepares us to be better people in a better society; ultimately, to be the regenerate links in the total millennium. But the imagination is prophetic in a second way:

Not that I assert poets to be prophets in the gross sense of the word, or that they can foretell the form as surely as they know the spirit of events. . . . A poet participates in the eternal, the infinite and the one; as far as relates to his conceptions, time and place and number are not.
(C.279)

[A poem] is the creation of actions according to the unchangeable forms of human nature as existing in the mind of the creator, which is itself the image of all other minds. (C.281)

[Poetry] strips the veil of familiarity from the world and lays bare the naked and sleeping beauty, which is the spirit of its forms.   (C.295)

In these passages Shelley comes close to saying that the imagination itself destroys space and time in order to reveal the pure eternity of the Platonic forms. This act of imagination is apocalyptic, it heralds not merely the millennium but the conquest of time. In the *Ode to Liberty* the imagination seems prophetic in the second sense as much as in the first, which may be why the Voice from the deep, increasingly aware of the limitations of man's historical lot, is unable to sustain its utterance for the benefit of the poet. The art of republican Italy

> With divine wand traced on our earthly home
> Fit imagery to pave heaven's everlasting dome,   (134–35)

and the voices of Athens' bards and sages are

> A winged sound of joy, and love, and wonder,
> Which soars where Expectation never flew,
> Rending the veil of space and time asunder!   (84–86)

But I do not mean to suggest any obvious disorder among the components of this poem, which I regard as the best Romantic poem of its kind, rivaled only by Coleridge's *France: an Ode*.[6] The timeful and the timeless seem to complement one another; the play within the play is rounded out by the play itself.

The *Ode to Naples*, written as a tribute to the Neapolitan revolution of July, 1820, is a much less successful poem. The ruined Greek city of Pompeii is described in the first stanza and Baiae with its underwater caves in stanza two, but these descriptions are just decorative displays of some of Shelley's favorite figures. The poem is a hymn of hate and revenge against unjust oppressors, written in a nerveless and ejaculatory rhetoric that tightens up on very few occasions. It belongs to the world of the unregenerate Prometheus:

> Spirit of Beauty! at whose soft command
> The sunbeams and the showers distil its foison
> From the earth's bosom chill;

> Oh, bid those beams be each a blinding brand
> Of lightning! bid those showers be dews of poison!
>   Bid the Earth's plenty kill!

Once only is the rhetoric sufficiently vigorous to be compared to
that of the *Ode to Liberty*. Shelley describes the advance of the
Austrian "Anarchs of the North" in hard and rugged verse:

> Hear ye the march as of the Earth-born Forms
>   Arrayed against the ever-living Gods?
> The crash and darkness of a thousand storms
>   Bursting their inaccessible abodes
>   Of crags and thunder-clouds?
> See ye the banners blazoned to the day,
>   Inwrought with emblems of barbaric pride?
> Dissonant threats kill Silence far away,
>   The serene Heaven which wraps our Eden wide
>   With iron light is dyed,
> The Anarchs of the North lead forth their legions
>   Like Chaos o'er creation, uncreating;
> An hundred tribes nourished on strange religions
> And lawless slaveries,—down the aerial regions
>   Of the white Alps, desolating,
>   Famished wolves that bide no waiting,
> Blotting the glowing footsteps of old glory,
> Trampling our columned cities into dust,
>   Their dull and savage lust
>   On Beauty's corpse to sickness satiating—.

I refrain from quoting the inept couplet which concludes the stanza.

We have observed the undercurrent of melancholy which comes
over the millennial exultation in *Prometheus Unbound* at certain
moments when the limitations of existence in time are seen in relation to the immortality of Prometheus and to the intense inane behind the death-like veil of life. We have traced this relationship
or contrast in a number of later works, particularly *Hellas,* and
examined some of the figures by which it is expressed, particularly
the architecture of time or eternity with its foundations of chaos
or crystal. We are now in a better position to appreciate two passages

from *Prometheus Unbound*. One (from Act Two) is Asia's vision
of reunion with Prometheus, seen in Panthea's eyes:

> There is a change; beyond their inmost depth
> I see a shade, a shape: 'tis He, arrayed
> In the soft light of his own smiles, which spread
> Like radiance from the cloud-surrounded moon.
> Prometheus, it is thine! depart not yet!
> Say not those smiles that we shall meet again
> Within that bright pavilion which their beams
> Shall build o'er the waste world?   (II.i.119–26)

The other (from Act Three) is the Earth's picture of the temple
and cave to which Prometheus and Asia are retiring and to which
a spirit "in the likeness of a winged child" (III.iii, *direction*) is directed to lead them.

>   Run, wayward,
> And guide this company beyond the peak
> Of Bacchic Nysa, Maenad-haunted mountain,
> And beyond Indus and its tribute rivers,
> Trampling the torrent streams and glassy lakes
> With feet unwet, unwearied, undelaying,
> And up the green ravine, across the vale,
> Beside the windless and crystalline pool,
> Where ever lies, on unerasing waves,
> The image of a temple, built above,
> Distinct with column, arch, and architrave,
> And palm-like capital, and overwrought,
> And populous with most living imagery,
> Praxitelean shapes, whose marble smiles
> Fill the hushed air with everlasting love.   (III.iii.152–66)

This, as Hungerford points out, is the temple of Prometheus, supposed to have existed near Plato's Academy (just as the neighboring
cave which the Earth mentions later is probably the cave at Colonus
in Sophocles' play) : [7]

> It is deserted now, but once it bore
> Thy name, Prometheus; there the emulous youths

Bore to thy honor through the divine gloom
The lamp which was thine emblem; even as those
Who bear the untransmitted torch of hope
Into the grave, across the night of life,
As thou has borne it most triumphantly
To this far goal of Time. Depart, farewell!
Beside that temple is the destined cave.   (III.iii.167–75)

But what *is* "this far goal of Time"? Is it the millennium achieved by the regeneration of the moral Prometheus, still subject to the limitations of time and the possibility of a further turn of the wheel, or is it the temple "filled with everlasting love" and sustained by "unerasing waves," beside which the immortal Prometheus will enjoy his eternal union with Asia? Is the goal radical or Platonic? The last act should answer these questions.

VIII

THIS FAR GOAL
OF TIME

Shelley's radical and Platonic goals may be uneasy bedfellows at times, but it is quite possible (as Christianity has found) to work out some sort of compromise between them. The most obvious way of accommodating both is to make one follow the other. First comes the millennium, or the second coming on this earth. This heralds the final stage of the apocalypse, in which death is swallowed up in eternity. The millennium and the apocalypse [1] are simply the two stages in which the two enemies of mankind (Sin and Death) are successively conquered.

A rapid glance at Act Four of *Prometheus Unbound* may suggest that Shelley's plan follows this pattern. Aware, after the completion of Act Three, that the conquest of the will still leaves Time to be conquered (an awareness that he has been unable to keep out of the millennial rejoicings), Shelley decides as an "afterthought" (an Epimetheus to complete the work of his Prometheus [2]) to depict in Act Four the apocalyptic ascent to "the intense inane." But this rapid glance would be misleading. Shelley may have had this idea in the back of his mind, one might even say that he ought to have proceeded on a plan like the one I have outlined, but, in fact, Act Four is more an appendix to the millennium than a leap into eternity.

The funeral chorus of the Dead Hours, to be sure, does seem to be making the very leap that we have just denied Shelley.

> Here, oh, here!
> We bear the bier

> Of the father of many a cancelled year!
>   Spectres we
>   Of the dead Hours be;
> We bear Time to his tomb in eternity.
>
>   Strew, oh strew
>   Hair, not yew!
> Wet the dusty pall with tears, not dew!
>   Be the faded flowers
>   Of Death's bare bowers
> Spread on the corpse of the King of Hours!   (IV.9–20)

This seems definite enough. But the death of Time would mean the death of "Demogorgon's mighty law," the permanent order of recurrence and pattern which gives meaning to Time. Demogorgon, despite his boast to Jupiter, is eternal only by courtesy and default. The cycles of Demogorgon must die with Death and Time. But at the conclusion of Act Four Demogorgon reappears and points out that the eternity which man seems to have entered is fragile and not necessarily eternal at all. The serpent's tail may not stay in its mouth. Time's attempt to surround, clasp, and contain eternity may be frustrated by an infirm eternity. The wheel may turn again, and, if it does, Demogorgon says, the millennium will have to be rewon by the same virtues of steadfastness and forgiveness which produced Prometheus' victory at the beginning of Act One.

Our interpretation of the chorus of Hours is further complicated by the possibility that by Time Shelley here only means past time, and that, in fact, the chorus is only an elegy over the grave of the Hours which composed Jupiter's reign. When Ione asks, "what dark forms are they?" Panthea replies:

> The past Hours weak and gray,
> With the spoil which their toil
>   Raked together
> From the conquest but One could foil.   (IV.30–34)

When Ione asks where they have gone, Panthea replies, "To the dark, to the past, to the dead" (IV.39). At the end of *Hellas,* we may remember, the Chorus cries:

> The world is weary of the past,
> Oh might it die or rest at last!

The world itself may have to die, if we are to be freed of the past. But in *Prometheus Unbound* it seems to be just the past which dies, not the world or the time in which it exists.

Act Four of *Prometheus Unbound* is, then, basically a celebration of the millennium, not the final conquest of Time and Chaos. At the same time, it might be possible to regard Act Four as existing in some indefinable world poised between time and eternity. Certainly the positive efforts of Act Four seem to be directed toward Platonic ends, and the terms or points of reference in which Act Four exists are Platonic, despite the fact that Heaven still remains "unascended."

This is not very surprising. Under Jupiter, thought was thwarted. The gifts of Prometheus could be misdirected by the unregenerate. Now the arts and sciences of the past, not to mention those which Prometheus will give man in the future, can be applied without danger to pushing back the natural frontiers. But this "thought" is for Shelley a part of the eternal. What the Promethean age can achieve, therefore, is the gradual conquest of chaos by thought, or of time by eternity. The final conquest is only possible outside of time altogether, but here and now man can reduce the limitations of earthly existence and expand the borders of the kingdom of thought.

After the dead hours have passed away and the new hours sing of their awakening,

> the Spirits of the human mind,
> Wrapped in sweet sounds, as in bright veils, approach.
>
> (IV.81–82)

The new hours ask these Spirits (who have swift feet, wings like thought, and eyes like love) where they come from. They reply:

> We come from the mind
> Of humankind. . . .

From that deep abyss
Of wonder and bliss,
Whose caverns are crystal palaces;
From those skyey towers
Where Thought's crowned bowers
Sit watching your dance, ye happy Hours!

. . . .

From the temples high
Of Man's ear and eye,
Roofed over Sculpture and Poesy;
From the murmurings
Of the unsealed springs,
Where Science bedews his daedal wings.

(IV.93–94, 99–116)

They are not pure thought, as these and other passages make clear,
but Thought and Love. The Thought can now accomplish the intellectual aims of Prometheus because of the Love.

The Spirits go on to sing of their future accomplishments:

Our spoil is won,
Our task is done,
We are free to drive, or soar, or run;
Beyond and around,
Or within the bound
Which clips the world with darkness round.

We'll pass the eyes
Of the starry skies
Into the hoar deep to colonize;
Death, Chaos and Night,
From the sound of our flight,
Shall flee, like mist from a tempest's might.

And Earth, Air and Light,
And the Spirit of Might,
Which drives round the stars in their fiery flight;
And Love, Thought and Breath,
The Powers that quell Death,
Wherever we soar shall assemble beneath.

And our singing shall build
In the void's loose field
A world for the Spirit of Wisdom to wield;
We will take our plan
From the new world of man,
And our work shall be called the Promethean.   (IV.135–58)

The world is here seen as a reclaimed area surrounded by Chaos. The function of these Spirits is to move not merely "within" and "around" but "beyond" "the bound / Which clips the world with darkness round." They must "colonize" "the hoar deep" and scatter "Death, Chaos and Night"; and wherever they soar the enemies of Death ("Love, Thought and Breath"—i.e., Life) shall support them. By this means they shall build up in the Chaos of "the void's loose field" a world which "the Spirit of Wisdom" can rule. This great work "shall be called the Promethean." If the process these Spirits describe can be called an apocalypse, it is certainly a gradual one. Eternity slowly permeates the fabric and finally, one supposes, Time simply drops out, just as in Blake, when the city of Golgonooza is complete, the scaffolding of Time vanishes and we are left with the City of God.[3] But so long as Time remains, the work can be undone. And Demogorgon returns at the end of the play to underline this fact.

The union of Love and Thought which characterizes the Promethean age dominates the rest of the act. First one comes to the foreground and then the other. They are alike in their urge to subdue Chaos. Thought orders Chaos and colonizes "the hoar deep"; Love too brings together with the strong chain of sympathy the formerly scattered atoms and creates a newly coordinated cosmos out of them.

We whirl, surging loud, round the gathering sphere
Till the trees, and the beasts, and the clouds appear
From its chaos made calm by love, not fear.   (IV.169–71)

The analogy with magnetism and electricity, examined by Grabo,[4] arises naturally from this function of Love.

But the phrase "the gathering sphere" brings us unexpectedly back to a familiar figure, which we may not have associated with Shelley's Platonic world: the center and the circumference. The wheel figure has been crowding the circle figure from our attention. We have been considering "cycles / Of desolation and of loveliness"[5] rather than centrifugal and centripetal forces. The wheel is, of course, still important in Act Four of *Prometheus Unbound*, particularly in Panthea's description of the Spirit of the Earth and its sphere "upon a thousand sightless axles spinning" (IV.248). The geological passage with which Panthea continues is also cyclical and depicts the remains of successive civilizations, as they are pierced and illuminated by the beams of light from the Spirit's forehead.

> The beams flash on
> And make appear the melancholy ruins
> Of cancelled cycles; anchors, beaks of ships;
> Planks turned to marble; quivers, helms, and spears,
> And gorgon-headed targes, and the wheels
> Of scythed chariots, and the emblazonry
> Of trophies, standards, and armorial beasts,
> Round which death laughed, sepulchred emblems
> Of dead destruction ruin within ruin!
> The wrecks beside of many a city vast,
> Whose population which the earth grew over
> Was mortal, but not human; see, they lie,
> Their monstrous works, and uncouth skeletons,
> Their statues, homes and fanes; prodigious shapes
> Huddled in gray annihilation, split,
> Jammed in the hard, black deep. . . .   (IV.287–302)

But the colonization of Chaos employs quite naturally the circle figure, although in two sharply different ways. We have already seen the Promethean spirits envisaging an expansion of the bounds of the universe when they soar

> Beyond and around,
> Or within the bound
> Which clips the world with darkness round,

and build a new world in "the void's loose field." In this use of the figure, the Promethean impulse (Knowledge inspired by Love) is centrifugal. But order itself is more easily viewed as centripetal. It pulls together the scattered atoms of Chaos and maintains oases in the midst of the loose void, just as Love itself defeats isolation by mingling one person with another or by coordinating into a group the independent units of society.

This second use of the circle figure sees the Promethean world or worlds, constantly expanding although they may be, as held together by the centripetal forces of magnetism and electricity and as constantly menaced by the possible encroachments of the surrounding Chaos. There is always the possibility that it is Chaos rather than the Imprometheans who will do the colonizing. The "abysses" and "wildernesses" which Shelley is so appallingly fond of joining in rhyme are being held back, but the danger is not over. The Promethean age cannot forget the possibility that

> Things fall apart; the centre will not hold.
> Mere anarchy is loosed upon the world.[6]

Here centrifugal force is the enemy. The bonds that hold the world together may burst and disperse it into Chaos.

Such a use of the circle figure is most apparent in the love duet of the Earth and the Moon. Much of this ecstatic duet celebrates (in some of Shelley's least distinguished verse) Love's interpenetration of the natural phenomena of both planets. The Earth also has something to say about the Enemy of this Love. He describes Jupiter himself in terms of the surrounding Chaos from the threat of which the magnetic force of Love affords a protection:

> Sceptred curse,
> Who all our green and azure universe
> Threatenedst to muffle round with black destruction,
>
> . . . .
>
> All I bring forth, to one void mass battering and blending,
>
> Until each crag-like tower, and storied column,

Palace, and obelisk, and temple solemn,
My imperial mountains crowned with cloud, and snow, and fire,

. . . .

Were stamped by thy strong hate into a lifeless mire:

How art thou sunk, withdrawn, covered, drunk up
By thirsty nothing, as the brackish cup
Drained by a desert-troop, a little drop for all;
And from beneath, around, within, above,
Filling thy void annihilation, love
Bursts in like light on caves cloven by the thunder-ball!

(IV.338–40, 343–46, 349–55)

Jupiter, who seems to be identified with "void annihilation," is drunk up by "thirsty nothing"—consumed by himself it would seem!

The Earth describes how Love, released by the overthrow of Jupiter, is now accomplishing its destined tasks. It destroys "Thought's stagnant Chaos" (IV.380); it replaces the mirror which distorts to evil by the mirror which reflects the true world of Love; it binds men together into

a chain of linked thought,
Of love and might to be divided not,
Compelling the elements with adamantine stress;
As the sun rules even with a tyrant's gaze
The unquiet republic of the maze
Of planets, struggling fierce toward heaven's free wilderness.

(IV.394–99)

It controls the will of man, no longer a prey to "mean passions, bad delights, / And selfish cares" as it sails

through waves which dare not overwhelm,
Forcing life's wildest shores to own its sovereign sway.

(IV.406–7, 410–11)

It inspires the development of the arts and sciences, like astronomy and poetry:

> Language is a perpetual Orphic song,
> Which rules with daedal harmony a throng
> Of thoughts and forms, which else senseless and shapeless were.
>
> (IV.415-17)

All this and much more does Love accomplish. I draw attention only in passing to the radical aspect of Love's deeds, such as the substitution of the good for the evil mirror and the direction of the will of man, and turn instead to Love's war with Chaos.

Poetry's task here is not the preparation of the expansive will by exercises in sympathy, but the ordering of Chaos. It is still the agent of Love, but the Love of Shelley's Platonic frame of reference instead of his radical. The Earth sees the human community held together by Love, in terms of the solar system ruled by the Sun but threatened by centrifugal, disintegrating forces which struggle "fierce toward heaven's free wilderness." The Moon's final lyric in praise of the Love which binds her to the Earth again mentions the void from which his Love is protecting her.

> Brother, wheresoe'er thou soarest
> I must hurry, whirl and follow
> Through the heavens wide and hollow,
> Sheltered by the warm embrace
> Of thy soul from hungry space. . . .   (IV.476-80)

The duet of the Earth and the Moon is succeeded by the final episode of the play: the reappearance of Demogorgon, who addresses the universe in a series of invocations: first the Earth and the Moon, then Gods, the dead, Genii, living things outside of Man, and finally Man himself, in a sort of neo-Platonic chain of being. The Gods, rulers of the planets,

> possess
> Elysian, windless, fortunate abodes
> Beyond Heaven's constellated wilderness.   (IV.530-32)

That is, they exist beyond Chaos and Time in some unchanging realm. The dead are either a part of nature or have passed out of

existence (no translation to Eternity seems to be envisaged here);
the "elemental Genii"

> have homes
> From man's high mind even to the central stone
> Of sullen lead; from Heaven's star-fretted domes
> To the dull weed some sea-worm battens on. (IV.539–42)

These are, presumably, the chemical elements out of which all
bodies are formed, from lead and weeds to the stars and the brain
of man. The "spirits, whose homes are flesh" (IV.544) include
beasts, birds, fish, and planets, but also, apparently, lightning, wind,
meteors, and mists. Finally Demogorgon addresses

> Man, who wert once a despot and a slave,
> A dupe and a deceiver, a decay,
> A traveller from the cradle to the grave
> Through the dim night of this immortal day. (IV.549–52)

Demogorgon here divides man's past into three categories: man
the despot and the slave (now regenerate through the efforts of
Prometheus); man the dupe and the deceiver (now able to pursue
truth in the scientific and artistic paradise of the Promethean age);
and, finally, man the decay, formerly caught in the cradle to grave
cycles of the dim night which precedes the "immortal day."

This last invocation of Demogorgon's brings us face to face again
with the problem with which we began our discussion of Act Four.
Demogorgon not only places man the despot and slave, or dupe and
deceiver, in the past, but man the decay as well. Man, who was
once a traveler in the natural cycle from the cradle to the grave,
is now apparently in the full light of immortality. Or is "immortal
day" not to be taken literally and to be interpreted simply as "never-
to-be-forgotten"?

Demogorgon's series of invocations is succeeded by his final address. Its first stanza summarizes the nature and significance of
Prometheus' regeneration, and the third returns to the same radical
theme in unmistakable terms. The second stanza, however, is equiv-

ocal. Here "Gentleness, Virtue, Wisdom, and Endurance" are the
seals which bar "the pit over Destruction's strength," i.e. they pro-
tect man from Chaos or the Abyss—from the destructive side of
Demogorgon's mighty law itself. The wheel is being held still, the
pit is being closed off, the serpent's tail is in its mouth. But Eternity
herself, it seems, is subject to infirmity.

> And if, with infirm hand, Eternity,
> Mother of many acts and hours, should free
> The serpent that would clasp her with his length,
> These are the spells by which to reassume
> An empire o'er the disentangled doom.

Not only is she potentially infirm, Eternity is also the "Mother of
many acts and hours," not certainly beyond Time.[7] I suspect that
Eternity is here being used very loosely. Man would like the earthly
paradise never to come to an end, but this sort of "Eternity" may
be denied it. If so, the Promethean age may be recovered by a
new exercise of the Promethean virtues. Demogorgon's final speech
is therefore more simply radical than it appears at first sight. But a
disrupting alloy of Platonism still remains in the second stanza of
the address, as it more emphatically does in the preceding invocation.

We have not been able to answer the question: when, in or out
of history, does the last act of *Prometheus Unbound* occur? The
ambiguity is ineradicable. In fact, *Prometheus Unbound* (and I
include the whole play as well as the last act) is profoundly transitional in its thematic structure. In this it has a good deal in common
with some greater works, including *Troilus and Criseyde* and *Paradise Lost*. One might argue that any long work is transitional and
that the best we can do in defining its frame of reference is to decide where it is coming from, where it is going to, and (as far as
possible) where it has got to on the way. Perhaps we can now turn
to the task of charting the position of *Epipsychidion* and *Adonais*,
which are on the same road as *Prometheus Unbound,* or, more accurately, on parallel roads which meet only in Eternity.

It has been obvious to everyone that *Epipsychidion* falls into three sections of approximately equal length: (1) an invocation to Emily and an explanation of the meaning of the speaker's love for her (ll. 1–189); (2) an idealized history of his life and feelings with respect to love (ll. 190–387); (3) an *invitation au voyage,* in which the speaker depicts himself and Emily united in the future on some Ionian isle (ll. 388–591). There is also a brief epilogue (ll. 592–604).

The invocation to Emily, who is identified with the human perfection of the goal toward which the process of Love aspires, makes extensive use of the figure of the veil. We have not looked at this figure before, but it has been so extensively examined by other students of Shelley that a brief summary of its significance should be enough to prepare us for its use in *Epipsychidion*. Shelley's various uses of the figure overlap a good deal, but it is, nevertheless, important to make certain distinctions.

In Act Three of *Prometheus Unbound* the Spirit of the Earth recalls that, before the millennium, he had observed,

> among the haunts of human kind,
> Hard-featured men, or with proud, angry looks,
> Or cold, staid gait, or false and hollow smiles,
> Or the dull sneer of self-loved ignorance,
> Or other such foul masks, with which ill thoughts
> Hide that fair being whom we spirits call man. (III.iv.40–45)

But now the "foul disguise" or "loathsome mask" has fallen;

> The painted veil, by those who were, called life,
> Which mimicked, as with colors idly spread,
> All men believed or hoped, is torn aside.
>   (III.iv.70, 193, 190–92)

For Shelley good is prior to evil. The regenerate will remains under the cover of the unregenerate will, and only awaits the removal of the disguise to assert itself. Good is essential; evil is accidental. Some commentators to the contrary, this is not a sentimental Romantic heresy; it belongs to the mainstream of Christian tradition, although by his denial of the doctrine of grace Shelley places it in a non-Christian setting.

Unfortunately, the wording of the last quotation is reminiscent of a different use of the veil figure, earlier in Act Three. This earlier passage is already familiar to us:

> Death is the veil which those who live call life;
> They sleep and it is lifted. (III.iv.113–14)

In both these quotations we may see the veil (with A. T. Strong) as a symbol of life.[8] But in the first the life symbolized is the morally unregenerate life before the millennium, which unregenerate man supposed was the only life possible; in the second it is life in the sense of mortality, and belongs to regenerate as well as unregenerate man. In the first the veil is what separates man from the millennium; in the second it is what separates man from Eternity.

In both uses, what the veil conceals is good, and the veil itself is evil. But sometimes this moral opposition is less clear-cut. A notorious example is the feeble sonnet *Lift Not the Painted Veil*, which, despite verbal similarities, has very little to do with the passages we have quoted from *Prometheus Unbound*.

> Lift not the painted veil which those who live
> Call Life; though unreal shapes be pictured there,
> And it but mimic all we would believe
> With colors idly spread,—behind, lurk Fear
> And Hope, twin Destinies, who ever weave
> Their shadows o'er the Chasm sightless and drear.

Here the veil is deceptive, but what lies behind it may be even more so, and it is perhaps better to remain with known illusions than to confront unknown reality. The poem ends by depicting the disappointment of one who lifted it:

> A Spirit that strove
> For truth, and like the Preacher found it not.

Such skepticism is characteristic of Shelley the thinker, but he was inclined to minimize it in his poetry.

An equivocal use of the veil figure characteristic of Shelley both as poet and theorist is to represent it as a tempering which makes the eternal bearable. As Blake puts it, "Time is the Mercy of Eternity." [9]

> For she was beautiful; her beauty made
>   The bright world dim, and everything beside
> Seemed like the fleeting image of a shade;
>   No thought of living spirit could abide,
> Which to her looks had ever been betrayed,
>   On any object in the world so wide,
> On any hope within the circling skies,
> But on her form, and in her inmost eyes.
>
> Which when the Lady knew, she took her spindle
>   And twined three threads of fleecy mist, and three
> Long lines of light, such as the dawn may kindle
>   The clouds and waves and mountains with; and she
> As many star-beams, ere their lamps could dwindle
>   In the belated moon, wound skilfully;
> And with these threads a subtle veil she wove—
> A shadow for the splendor of her love.   (xii, xiii)

Such is the Witch of Atlas' consideration for mortal weakness. The lyric "Life of Life" in *Prometheus Unbound* describes Asia's brilliance as similarly adapted to the reception of mortal organs by various screens, shrouds, or vests. In *Epipsychidion,* Emily's "radiant form of Woman" veils

> All that is insupportable in thee
> Of light and love and immortality.   (21–23)

One of the few things about the Vision in *Alastor* that suggests an otherworldly ideal is

> Her glowing limbs beneath the sinuous veil
> Of woven wind. . . .   (176–77)

The fact that the veil can be seen both as a mask to be torn off and as a necessary garment for an Eternal Form to wear if it is to be borne by mortal eyes, points up a central paradox in the work

of any poet who works within a merely Platonic frame of reference.
The deep truth is imageless, and in our ultimate perception of it

> the light of sense
> Goes out, but with a flash that has revealed
> The invisible world: [10]

At the same time, poetry is inextricably bound up with the mortal
image. Poetry is simply one more figure in the veil, and as such is
inevitably inadequate and distorting. But how else is one to attract
attention to what is beyond the veil except through the veil itself?
The veil of poetry may be inadequate, but it may also be necessary.

As a result of this ambiguous attitude toward the Platonic veil,
neither Shelley's defense of poetry nor his disgust with language
is likely to be unqualified or lasting. In *A Defence of Poetry* Shelley
compares poets to artists of other kinds. The former have definite
advantages. They are mirrors not veils.

The former is as a mirror which reflects, the latter as a cloud which en-
feebles the light of which both are mediums of communication. (C.280)

Poetry lifts the veil from the hidden beauty of this world. . . . (C.282)

But poetry, after all, does employ images, the very things which
obscure the truth, not to mention words, for which Shelley often
shares the contempt of the Enlightenment. Somehow the image
must defeat itself. Shelley tries to explain this in a number of ways:

A poem is the very image of life expressed in its eternal truth. There is
this difference between a story and a poem, that a story is a catalogue
of detached facts which have no other bond of connection than time,
place, circumstance, cause, and effect; the other is the creation of actions
according to the unchangeable forms of human nature as existing in
the mind of the creator, which is itself the image of all other minds.
(C.281)

Perhaps, indeed, some sort of veil is necessary for mortal perception.

. . . a poet considers the vices of his contemporaries as the temporary
dress in which his creations must be arrayed and which cover without

concealing the eternal proportions of their beauty. An epic or dramatic personage is understood to wear them around his soul, as he may the ancient armor or modern uniform around his body while it is easy to conceive a dress more graceful than either. The beauty of the internal nature cannot be so far concealed by its accidental vesture, but that the spirit of its form shall communicate itself to the very disguise and indicate the shape it hides from the manner in which it is worn. A majestic form and graceful motions will express themselves through the most barbarous and tasteless costume. Few poets of the highest class have chosen to exhibit the beauty of their conceptions in its naked truth and splendor; and it is doubtful whether the alloy of costume, habit, &c., be not necessary to temper this planetary music for mortal ears.   (C.282)

Shelley even suggests later that the process of reading, both by an individual and by the successive ages which respond to a poem, is like peeling off layer after layer, without any possibility of reaching the center. "Veil after veil may be withdrawn and the inmost naked beauty of the meaning never exposed" (C.291). But Platonism does not make it easy to achieve a close relation between the mortal image and the eternal form. Any cooperation between them is little more than a marriage of convenience. Perhaps it is for this reason that Shelley's most effective statement of their relation is in Christian rather than Platonic terms. "Imagination is as the immortal God which should assume flesh for the redemption of mortal passion" (C.324). But such terms are hardly characteristic.

Even in *A Defence of Poetry* the capacities of the poet (as distinct from those of poetry) are not regarded as unlimited, although the limitations are not simply due to the necessity of images.

When composition begins, inspiration is already on the decline, and the most glorious poetry that has ever been communicated to the world is probably a feeble shadow of the original conceptions of the poet.

(C.294)

Later on in the same paragraph he attributes the necessity of self-criticism, and of conventional links between inspired passages, to "the limitedness of the poetical faculty itself" (C.294). But sometimes it is the very use of images or words which limits poetry. In the essay *On Love,* when Shelley writes the passage about the "soul within our soul that describes a circle around its proper paradise," he adds in a footnote: "These words are metaphorical. Most words are so —— No help!" (C.277). For the Shelley of the end of *Adonais,*

> Flowers, ruins, statues, music, words, are weak
> The glory they transfuse with fitting truth to speak. (LII)

And at the end of *Epipsychidion,* there is a sudden surge of despair about the possibility of making poetry soar to the empyrean:

> Woe is me!
> The winged words with which my soul would pierce
> Into the height of love's rare Universe,
> Are chains of lead around its flight of fire. (587–90)

The Platonic point of view can be much more destructive of poetry's pretensions than it is in Shelley. A reference to Book Ten of *The Republic* suffices to prove that. But Platonism at least reminds Shelley of the limited, approximate nature of poetic figures and even modifies his method of using them. The first section of *Epipsychidion* has some critical comments on the "gray style" of Time and his need to employ young Love as a teacher. The poet himself prays Emily to repair the shortcomings of his mortal and erring poem:

> I pray thee that thou blot from this sad song
> All of its much mortality and wrong. (35–36)

What Shelley seems to have learned from this emphasis on the mortality of his poetic medium is that, since no figure is adequate, the poet's best chance of defining his metaphysical target is to surround it with approximate ones. He must converge on the target from a variety of angles. In a rejected passage of *Epipsychidion* Shelley makes this point explicitly:

> Free love has this, different from gold and clay,
> That to divide is not to take away,
> Like ocean, which the general north wind breaks

> Into ten thousand waves, and each one makes
> A mirror of the moon—like some great glass,
> Which did distort whatever form might pass,
> Dashed into fragments by a playful child,
> Which then reflects its eyes and forehead mild;
> Giving for one, which it could ne'er express,
> A thousand images of loveliness.   (J.II.377)

Shelley attempts to present the goal of his desire in the first section of *Epipsychidion* by means of this technique of varied approximation. Emily herself is the perfect figure of the eternal goal. His own figures will be imitations of that most successful imitation. On the whole, this first section is less good than the second, and much less than the third. Its multitude of figures is very uneven but includes, at the same time, a number of extremely effective ones:

> See where she stands! a mortal shape indued
> With love and life and light and deity,
> And motion which may change but cannot die;
> An image of some bright Eternity;
> A shadow of some golden dream; a Splendor
> Leaving the third sphere pilotless; a tender
> Reflection of the eternal Moon of Love,
> Under whose motions life's dull billows move;
> A metaphor of Spring and Youth and Morning;
> A vision like incarnate April, warning,
> With smiles and tears, Frost the Anatomy
> Into his summer grave.   (112–23)

Here the succession of figures is more adequate than any one of them and reaches a climax in the April image, whose loveliness gave T. S. Eliot "a regretful pleasure." [11] Sometimes the series is more huddled, and the figures reduced even to a series of parallel words:

> Seraph of Heaven! too gentle to be human,
> Veiling beneath that radiant form of Woman
> All that is insupportable in thee
> Of light and love and immortality!

> Sweet Benediction in the eternal Curse!
> Veiled glory of this lampless Universe!
> Thou Moon beyond the clouds! thou living Form
> Among the Dead! thou Star above the Storm!
> Thou Wonder, and thou Beauty, and thou Terror!
> Thou Harmony of Nature's art! thou Mirror
> In whom, as in the splendor of the Sun,
> All shapes look glorious which thou gazest on!   (21–32)

One is liable to become somewhat impatient with the insistent
parallel constructions:

> She met me, Stranger, upon life's rough way,
> And lured me toward sweet death; as Night by Day,
> Winter by Spring, or Sorrow by swift Hope,
> Led into light, life, peace.   (72–75)

One may even be tempted to reduce the one hundred and eighty-
nine lines to an anthology of the closer approximations or the more
felicitously phrased ones:

> An antelope,
> In the suspended impulse of its lightness,
> Were less etherially light . . . ;   (75–77)

> We—are we not formed, as notes of music are,
> For one another, though dissimilar;
> Such difference without discord as can make
> Those sweetest sounds, in which all spirits shake
> As trembling leaves in a continuous air?   (142–46)

> In her mild lights the starry spirits dance,
> The sunbeams of those wells which ever leap
> Under the lightnings of the soul—too deep
> For the brief fathom line of thought or sense.   (87–90)

But by our anthology we are making the brief fathom-line even
briefer. Shelley's conception, if he is to be true to it, must necessarily be diffuse. Unless we define the poem as equivalent to its most
striking details, we need to take the slack with the taut. In any
case, it is all relative. Shelley's target will allow no bulls-eyes.

The last forty-two lines of this section are less figurative than discursive. But, although the angle of approach and the matter approached are different, the conclusions are equally pluralistic. The variety of inadequate figures which surrounded Emily are succeeded by an argument on the infinite divisibility of Love. That Shelley saw the artistic problem and the erotic problem as basically the same is confirmed by the rejected passage quoted earlier. Man cannot contemplate one object of Love and try to make it the only representation of the whole. He thereby simply chains himself to a single inadequate figure. Moreover, since none of these figures is simply a part of the whole, but each *is* the whole in limited mortal terms, "to divide is not to take away." In fact, since the whole does not exist in mortal terms at all, but is imageless and beyond our grasp, each part is greater than the whole, which in Time is non-existent or expressible purely in negatives. The infinite divisibility of Love is, of course, one of its great advantages over the foes arrayed against it, which are inescapably bound up with Time and can be diminished by division.

> If you divide suffering and dross, you may
> Diminish until it is consumed away;
> If you divide pleasure and love and thought,
> Each part exceeds the whole; and we know not
> How much, while any yet remains unshared,
> Of pleasure may be gained, of sorrow spared.
> This truth is that deep well, whence sages draw
> The unenvied light of hope; the eternal law
> By which those live, to whom this world of life
> Is as a garden ravaged, and whose strife
> Tills for the promise of a later birth
> The wilderness of this Elysian earth.   (180–91)

The terms of this obscure passage are unmistakably Platonic, but some of the thought also suggests a translation into the language of *The Republic* of certain radical preoccupations. We may remember that the expansive soul, whose imagination strengthens its capacity to love, extends its circumference to include a variety of objects

with which it can sympathize. The good man "must put himself
in the place of another and of many others" (C.283).

> Love is like understanding that grows bright
> Gazing on many truths; 'tis like thy light,
> Imagination! which from earth and sky,
> And from the depths of human fantasy,
> As from a thousand prisms and mirrors, fills
> The Universe with glorious beams, and kills
> Error, the worm, with many a sun-like arrow
> Of its reverberated lightning. Narrow
> The heart that loves, the brain that contemplates,
> The life that wears, the spirit that creates
> One object, and one form, and builds thereby
> A sepulchre for its eternity.   (162–73)

The first section of *Epipsychidion* is static. The second is, roughly
speaking, a dynamic equivalent of the first. It begins with an imageless revelation of the goal, the soul out of his soul toward which the
speaker is striving.

> On an imagined shore,
> Under the gray beak of some promontory
> She met me, robed in such exceeding glory
> *That I beheld her not.*[12]   (197–200)

As a consequence of this revelation, he keeps hearing intimations
of her in nature, art, and philosophy,

> In the words
> Of antique verse and high romance, in form,
> Sound, color, in whatever checks that Storm
> Which with the shattered present chokes the past,
> And in that best philosophy, whose taste
> Makes this cold common hell, our life, a doom
> As glorious as a fiery martyrdom. . . .   (209–15)

"That best philosophy," by the way, seems to be not Platonism, but
the radical philosophy of Demogorgon's last speech in *Prometheus
Unbound.*

This Being, "the lodestar of my one desire" (219), is, of course, evanescent. She disappears, concealed by the shadow of life itself, "the dreary cone of our life's shade" (228). Where is she to be recovered? There seem to be two possibilities: in some eternal world beyond the grave, or in "the very world which is the world of all of us." The poet's first reactions seem to place the Being beyond Time or at least within the consuming fire:

> I flitted, like a dizzy moth, whose flight
> Is as a dead leaf's in the owlet light,
> When it would seek in Hesper's setting sphere
> A radiant death, a fiery sepulchre. . . .   (220-23)

These lines occur just before her disappearance, but the poet continues to look in the same direction after she has passed:

> And as a man with mighty loss dismayed,
> I would have followed, though the grave between
> Yawned like a gulf whose spectres are unseen.   (229-31)

But a voice suddenly brings him back to this world by insisting that "the Phantom is beside thee whom thou seekest" (233), and for the rest of this section the search is carried out in the here and now.

> I went forth, with hope and fear
> And every gentle passion sick to death,
> Feeding my course with expectation's breath,
> Into the wintry forest of our life;
> And struggling through its error with vain strife,
> And stumbling in my weakness and my haste,
> And half bewildered with new forms, I passed
> Seeking among those untaught foresters
> If I could find one form resembling hers. . . .   (246-54)

He finds, of course, a good many forms, the numerous images, variously inadequate, by which an imageless Being must be represented in a world of images. That for each of these forms Shelley is thinking of a specific human being I do not doubt, but here I am not concerned with their biographical identification but with their relation to the Being and to one another. First there is a False Florimell, whose "touch was as electric poison" (259); not just an inadequate human image, but a fraud and a deception. She is followed by the Moon, the Tempest, the Planet, Emily and the Comet.

Carlos Baker, in an original and stimulating analysis of the poem, reduces these figures to three: the Comet, the Moon and the Sun (Emily). These (and the partly analogous trio, Ione, Panthea, and Asia) he supposes to represent the Platonic triple soul; and the central section of the poem is "the odyssey of a creative soul" as it ascends through three aspects of Love. "For the purposes of clarity," says Baker,

it may be well to set down the equation at which Shelley arrived, with the caution that the equivalences are only approximate.
1. Plato's immortal soul, "akin to the soul of the Universe" $><$ Shelley's Epipsyche $><$ Shelley's concept of Imagination $><$ Shelley's Sun-symbol.
2. Plato's higher mortal soul $><$ Shelley's concept of Reason $><$ Shelley's Moon-symbol.
3. Plato's appetitive soul $><$ Shelley's concept of unruly Emotion (perhaps desire) $><$ Shelley's Comet-symbol.[13]

But Baker, without any attempt to argue the point, assumes that the Planet of line 313 is identical with the Comet of line 368, which is asked to "float into our azure heaven again." That Shelley should suppose a Planet and a Comet to be the same thing is to me totally unbelievable. As for the Tempest, which Shelley both capitalizes and refers to by the personal interrogative "who," Baker simply removes the capital and supposes that nothing is meant but a casual metaphor. But why try to reduce the number of figures to three? There are necessarily a good many of them—more, we can take it, than are specifically represented. The odyssey ends with a picture of three of them circling around the poet.

Unfortunately for the schematic critic, there is another complication. The objects toward which the poet's desires are directed cannot simply be divided into two classes: the temporal and the eternal, with the varied figures on one side and the Platonic form on the other. Emily fits very uneasily into either class. She is not the eternal form, but neither is she just one particularly successful figure among others of the same general kind. Emily, like the world of Act Four of *Prometheus Unbound,* suggests an undefinable middle term. She is "the Vision veiled from me / So many years" (343–44)—the thing itself. Yet she is only a metaphor, an image, a shadow, "an Incarnation of the Sun" (335). If we are thinking of the earth, Emily's superiority makes her seem eternal. If we are thinking of heaven, her temporal existence makes her seem simply a figure. She is the impossibly perfect imitation in Time of Love's goal out of Time. The other figures are not so much inadequate imitations of the Eternal Form as inadequate imitations of her.

Any Christian theologian could recognize at sight all the approaches along which Shelley tries to define the status of Emily. He has been through it all in trying to define the status of the Son in relation to the Father. But another poet may provide a better analogy than a theologian. I am, of course, thinking of Dante and Beatrice. But the difference is as important as the analogy. Dante's Beatrice is possible because Dante's Platonism has been transformed by his Christianity. The timeless can enter time for Dante and not simply be degraded by it. Shelley's Platonic frame of reference, however, denies such interpenetration. In the plain prose of Shelley's letters, Emily can only illustrate the error of "seeking in a mortal image what is perhaps eternal" (J.X.401). But Shelley wishes to have his cake and eat it too. He makes Emily something more than the terms of his poem will allow. Emily must be both a figure and more than a figure. In spite of himself Shelley touches the possibility that Eternity may be fulfilled in Time. He touches it and moves back.

Just as our discussion of Act Four of *Prometheus Unbound* resolved itself into an attempt to place the Promethean Age, so our discussion of *Epipsychidion* has resolved itself into an attempt to place Emily. In the last section of the poem Shelley seems to have done the placing for us. He provides Emily with a local habitation, to which she is invited to retire, and describes it at length. This Ionian isle is Emily's destined home and the place where she can be indissolubly united to the poet.

It seems at first to be simply an Earthly Paradise, "a far Eden of the purple East," "Beautiful as a wreck of Paradise," a pastoral survival of "the age of gold" (417, 423, 428). The Fall has not touched it or its pleasure house, reared by

> Some wise and tender Ocean-King, ere crime
> Had been invented, in the world's young prime.   (487–88)

This is to be their "home in life" (536). Although a naturally "favored place," it is subject to the cycles of Time, and years will "heap / Their withered hours, like leaves, on our decay" (461, 536–37). Its immortality is "a green and golden immortality" (469) (that is, a renewal of nature so continual as to seem unchanging), or the immortality of the arts they bring with them,

> with which high spirits call
> The future from its cradle and the past
> Out of its grave, and make the present last
> In thoughts and joys which sleep, but cannot die,
> Folded within their own eternity.   (520–24)

But the isle is more than a Saturnian Paradise making the best of temporal existence. Its "sweet airs" (445) combine into a "deep music";

> And every motion, odor, beam, and tone,
> With that deep music is in unison,
> Which is a soul within the soul; they seem
> Like echoes of an antenatal dream.   (453–56)

So far we are on familiar ground. "Every motion, odor, beam, and tone" is an echo of a world before birth into mortality, a figure of preexistence, to which the reminiscent "soul within our soul" re-

sponds, despite its burial in mortality. The isle too has its Epipsychidion, figured forth in the life of its surface ("felt, not seen"):

> Yet, like a buried lamp, a Soul no less
> Burns in the heart of this delicious isle,
> An atom of the Eternal, whose own smile
> Unfolds itself, and may be felt, not seen,
> O'er the gray rocks, blue waves, and forests green,
> Filling their bare and void interstices.   (477–82)

Is union with Emily possible on the Ionian isle? Must the buried
lamp remain buried? "Be this our home in life," says Shelley,

> and when years heap
> Their withered hours, like leaves, on our decay,
> Let us become the overhanging day,
> The living soul of this Elysian isle,
> Conscious, inseparable, one.   (536–40)

This union through the soul of the isle is placed in the future, in
the time of decay. "Meanwhile," says Shelley (and I draw particular attention to the word),

> We two will rise, and sit, and walk together
> Under the roof of blue Ionian weather. . . .   (540–42)

The rest of the third section tries to show what union will be
possible, meanwhile. The two wander about their home,

> Possessing and possessed by all that is
> Within that calm circumference of bliss,
> And by each other.
>
>   .   .   .   .
>
> Our breath shall intermix, our bosoms bound,
> And our veins beat together; and our lips,
> With other eloquence than words, eclipse
> The soul that burns between them. . . .   (549–51, 565–68)

So far their union has been mainly physical; notably so, if the
obscure phrase I have just quoted be taken literally. But this is only

the beginning. Their spheres expand with their expanding passion
and finally become one sphere.

> We shall become the same, we shall be one
> Spirit within two frames, oh! wherefore two?
> One passion in twin-hearts, which grows and grew,
> Till like two meteors of expanding flame
> Those spheres instinct with it become the same,
> Touch, mingle, are transfigured; ever still
> Burning, yet ever inconsumable;
> In one another's substance finding food,
> Like flames too pure and light and unimbued
> To nourish their bright lives with baser prey,
> Which point to Heaven and cannot pass away;
> One hope within two wills, one will beneath
> Two overshadowing minds, one life, one death,
> One Heaven, one Hell, one immortality,
> And one annihilation. . . .   (573–87)

The passage moves progressively farther away from the Ionian isle,
indeed from time and space themselves. The lovers' flames do a
good deal more than just "point to Heaven," as one line, with exceptional moderation, suggests. The sphere expands until it bursts
and is annihilated. The ultimate union is apocalyptic and cannot be
contained in any earthly receptacle. The Emily who is more than a
figure can be possessed and possessing only in more than an
Earthly Paradise. This world must be scattered to the four winds
and Time swallowed up in Eternity before she and the poet can
be transfigured; "ever still / Burning, yet ever inconsumable." [14]

But we may be surprised to remember that this apotheosis is all
"meanwhile." Shelley has prepared us for a dualism of millennium
and apocalypse. When he comes to depict his union with Emily on
the isle, however, he is unable to stay on the ground. His "meanwhile" soars beyond this world, because an Emily who is more
than a figure does not belong in any "meanwhile." As the Muses
sing in the epilogue,

> Love's very pain is sweet,
> But its reward is in the world divine,
> Which, if not here, it builds beyond the grave.   (596–98)

Or, as *Adonais* puts it, with a good deal more forthrightness, "No more let Life divide what Death can join together" (LIII).

Shelley's charming little Italian prose fragment, *Una Favola*, presents the search for the far goal of Love in the form of a late Medieval or early Renaissance allegory. In this fable a youth is awakened by Love, of whom he becomes a follower. Love is surrounded by veiled figures, none of whom will unveil themselves to the youth save one called Life. This figure, however, is "more false than any Siren, for by her counsel Love abandoned him . . ." (C.359) The other veiled figures now unveil and are revealed as "each more hideous and terrible than the other" (C.360), as they mock the suffering youth. Weary of suffering, he at length comes to the house of the sister of Life, whose name is Death, and of whom he becomes enamored. But, after enchanting him with her charms, she refuses to satisfy his desires and flees into the forest. The youth pursues her for a number of years, but in vain. One day, as he lies weeping in the grass, a lady appears, full of pity for him.

And his love of Death was suddenly changed into hate and suspicion, for this new love was so potent that it overcame every other thought. This compassionate lady at first loved him for mere pity; but love grew up swiftly with compassion, and she loved him for Love's own sake, no one beloved by her having need of pity any more. This was the lady in whose quest Love had led the youth through that gloomy labyrinth of error and suffering, haply for that she esteemed him unworthy of so much glory, and perceived him too weak to support such exceeding joy. After having somewhat dried their tears, the twain walked together in that same forest, until Death stood before them, and said, "Whilst, O youth, thou didst love me, I hated thee, and now that thou hatest me, I love thee, and wish so well to thee and thy bride that in my kingdom, which thou mayest call Paradise, I have set apart a chosen spot, where ye may securely fulfil your happy loves." And the lady, offended, and perchance somewhat jealous by reason of the past love of her spouse, turned her back upon Death, saying within herself, "What would this lover of my husband who comes here to trouble us?" and cried, "Life! Life!" and Life came, with a gay visage, crowned with a rainbow, and clad in a various mantle of chameleon skin; and Death went away weeping and, departing, said with a sweet voice, "Ye mistrust me, but I forgive ye, and await ye where ye needs must come, for I dwell with Love and Eternity, with whom the souls whose love is everlasting must hold communion. . . ."   (C.360)

A few lines later the fragment breaks off, and we never learn if the youth and the lady ultimately leave Life and join Death and Love and Eternity.

In *Adonais* the form of the pastoral elegy enables Shelley to say finally what *Epipsychidion, Hellas, Una Favola,* and Act Four of *Prometheus Unbound* left half said or said and denied in the same breath. Its certainty stems from the perfect adaptation of the form to the sort of uncompromising Platonism which Shelley could not accept wholeheartedly elsewhere, but which the chosen form here allows or impels him to accept.

IX

FROM HEAVEN
OR NEAR IT

In considering the nature of a particular poem, we need to be aware of what the poem allows as well as what the poet wants. Shelley's creative impulse may have wanted *Hellas* to stand just outside heaven's gate, a tribute to the structure of thought pinnacled beyond Time, but the occasion and purpose of the poem wanted something else, as the Notes make clear. The poem as completed mediates between these demands. But, whereas in *Hellas* the occasion and purpose hold back Shelley's drive toward a goal beyond history, in *Adonais* they goad him on. The purpose of *Hellas* limits the stretch of Shelley's imagination, the form of *Adonais* extends it. Or, if this seems overstated, the form of the pastoral elegy (without demanding it) at least assists Shelley to take up a more uncompromising position than he might otherwise have chosen for himself. Granted the Platonic and apocalyptic echoes of the "name of death" in Shelley's mind, and the opportunities provided by the genre, the end of *Adonais* seems predictable.

Predictable, but not inevitable. One opportunity Shelley certainly missed, blinded perhaps by the absence of any historical and social content in his material, as well as by his apocalyptic vision of death. The end of an elegy (since Christianity, at any rate) seeks two things: first, to make the death of the person elegized seem victory not defeat; second, to revive the mourners, to show the new life that is possible for them, the direction and achievement that remain for them here and now. (The pastoral convention, when employed, and the consequent emphasis on the natural year, ensure that these elegiac goals will be seen in relation to the cyclic pattern of death and rebirth.) Obviously here is an opportunity for Shelley to distinguish between and relate his Platonic and radical goals: the apocalypse and the millennium. One could be the immediate goal of Adonais, the other, of the mourners. But once he is convinced that the center of the poem is simply the swallowing up of death in victory, this opportunity is lost. The two elegiac goals become the same goal, and the survivors no less than the victim are mainly concerned with the pursuit of death.

But the poem reaches its end only after a good many preparations and even false scents. The loss of Adonais must be made to seem important; the mourners must exhibit their sorrow; and, in particular, the chief mourner must appear and reveal her relation to the death of Adonais, so that, having recognized her, we may move on.

Shelley's choice of the name Urania has caused a great deal of critical misunderstanding. It is to be hoped that Earl Wasserman's recent article [1] will prevent future critics from falling into the trap that Shelley's carelessness has prepared for them. Shelley knew, of course, of the Platonic distinction between the Pandemian and Uranian Aphrodite. Indeed, Mary Shelley tells us that *Prince Athanase,* when completed, was intended to hinge on this distinction (J.III.146). We might easily suppose, therefore, that when Shelley, in his version of the Venus and Adonis story, called Venus Urania, he was consciously lifting her from the natural sphere, drawing attention to the fact that his Venus was heavenly not earthly, eternal not temporal. But, in fact, the choice of the name Urania seems to have depended on something quite different. Keats is a poet, and the woman who loves him should be identified with his Muse. By a fortunate coincidence the name Urania has traditionally been given not merely to Venus but also to one of the Muses, the one, indeed, for whose assistance Milton had asked in writing *Paradise Lost.*[2] Shelley's use of the name arose from this coincidence. No other reason seems relevant.

That the Urania of *Adonais* remains an earth mother and not an otherworldly goal would always have been clear, I think, but for the Platonic associations of the name. For Shelley speaks of her as "the mighty Mother" and "that living Might," and she herself laments: "But I am chained to Time, and cannot thence depart!" Her "secret Paradise" is not in the "intense inane." Wasserman's conclusion is justified:

Clearly, Shelley is not attributing to Urania a spiritual immortality. As the goddess of organic life, she is "immortal" only in being chained to all of that time in which the Many change and pass. She belongs to timefulness, not timelessness. . . . Obviously, by being yoked to Time she is opposed to, not identified with, the One, which is an Eternity outside time, an Eternity that "remains." [3]

Naturally, when the poem moves beyond Time, Urania drops out, despite the efforts of critics to put her back in. The Venus and Adonis story, cyclic in its assumptions, is inadequate to express what Shelley says in the last stanzas of the poem. In fact, its inadequacy is a major theme.

Adonais has died, as all things must, however admirable:

> he is gone where all things wise and fair
> Descend; oh, dream not that the amorous Deep
> Will yet restore him to the vital air;
> Death feeds on his mute voice, and laughs at our despair.   (III)

Indeed, Adonais, as a human being, is at a special disadvantage in the natural world. Man's life is linear, and death comes as the end of the line. The rest of nature, bound to the wheel of death and rebirth, can say: "If Winter comes, can Spring be far behind?" Man as an individual can only contrast the productive death of the natural cycle with the finality of his own death. This pessimistic contrast is a recurrent theme of the pastoral elegy, as George Norlin has pointed out; [4] an early stage through which it often moves. The theme has been most common since the Renaissance, but it already found unequivocal expression in Moschus' *Lament for Bion:*

Alas, when the mallows perish in the garden, and the green celery, and the luxuriant, curling dill, they later come to life again and grow in another year; but we, the great, the mighty, the wise men, when once we die, unhearing we sleep in the hollow earth, a right long sleep without end or awaking.[5]

In "November" of the *Shepheardes Calendar* the death of Dido leads to similar reflections:

> Whence is it, that the flouret of the field doth fade,
> And lyeth buried long in winters bale:
> Yet soon as spring his mantle doth displaye,
> It floureth fresh, as it should never fayle?
> But thing on earth that is of most availe,
> As virtues braunch and beauties budde,
> Reliven not for any good.

This contrast is most likely to be strong when the author's frame of reference allows very little commerce between the natural and human (or natural and divine) levels. The Christian humanist, for whom the rebirth of nature must figure forth (even if imperfectly and without an ethical imperative) the rebirth of man, will not take it too much to heart, and in *Lycidas* it is suggested only to be repudiated. The "false surmise" (153) that the flowers strewn on the corpse of Lycidas prefigure his destiny turns out not to be false. Nineteenth-century naturalism may also work against the contrast. The second section of *In Memoriam* suggests it in passing, but Tennyson's main problems are different. Nature, seen from a sufficient distance, may not be cyclic at all. Evolution is linear. The death of the species denies the ultimate reality of rebirth. The danger, therefore, is not man's separation from the pattern of nature, but his conformity to it. The cyclic foreground of nature is an illusion; in the background, for man as well as beast, is the void. But for Cowper, a Calvanistic Evangelical certain of damnation, the contrast between the cyclic history of nature and the linear history of man is tragic and almost inescapable. His great new year's letter to Newton of January 13, 1784, is a kind of pastoral elegy *manqué:*

It is an alleviation of the woes even of an enlightened man, that he can wish for death, and indulge a hope, at least, that in death he shall find deliverance. But, loaded as my life is with despair, I have no such comfort as would result from a supposed probability of better things to come, were it once ended. . . . The weather is an exact emblem of my mind in its present state. A thick fog envelops everything, and at the same time it freezes intensely. You will tell me that this cold gloom will be succeeded by a cheerful spring, and endeavour to encourage me to hope for a spiritual change resembling it;—but it will be lost labour. Nature revives again; but a soul once slain lives no more. The hedge that has been apparently dead, is not so; it will burst into leaf and blossom at the appointed time; but no such time is appointed for the stake that stands in it. It is as dead as it seems, and will prove itself no dissembler. The latter end of next month will complete a period of eleven years in which I have spoken no other language. It is a long time for a man, whose eyes were once opened, to spend in darkness; long enough to make despair an inveterate habit; and such it is in me.[6]

Cowper, of course, is recalling the lament of Job:

For there is hope of a tree, if it be cut down, that it will sprout again, and that the tender branch thereof will not cease. Though the root thereof wax old in the earth, and the stock thereof die in the ground; yet through the scent of water it will bud, and bring forth boughs like a plant. But man dieth, and wasteth away; yea, man giveth up the ghost, and where is he? [7]

If nature is reborn and man is not, then for the sensitive man "April is the cruellest month" (as a modern pastoral elegy puts it), or, as we learn from *Adonais,* "grief returns with the revolving year." Such an elegy will not find any consolation in nature's "high requiem" over the human "sod" or be tempted into idealizing nature's cyclical permanence ("Thou wast not born for death, immortal bird!").

Shelley develops his version of the theme in some of the finest stanzas of the poem:

> Ah woe is me! Winter is come and gone,
> But grief returns with the revolving year;
> The airs and streams renew their joyous tone;
> The ants, the bees, the swallows reappear;
> Fresh leaves and flowers deck the dead Seasons' bier;
> The amorous birds now pair in every brake,
> And build their mossy homes in field and brere;
> And the green lizard, and the golden snake,
> Like unimprisoned flames, out of their trance awake.

> Through wood and stream and field and hill and Ocean,
> A quickening life from the Earth's heart has burst
> As it has ever done, with change and motion,
> From the great morning of the world when first
> God dawned on Chaos; in its stream immersed
> The lamps of Heaven flash with a softer light;
> All baser things pant with life's sacred thirst;
> Diffuse themselves; and spend in love's delight,
> The beauty and the joy of their renewed might.   (XVIII, XIX)

So much for "baser things." But the organic life of spring seems
to affect even the mortal remains of Adonais. "Touched by this
spirit tender," the corpse

> Exhales itself in flowers of gentle breath;
> Like incarnations of the stars, when splendour
> Is changed to fragrance,   (XX)

these "flowers" mock and deny the reality of death. But the mockery
is ironic. In fact, man is no more than an atom intensified into
momentary life, and his doom is to be quenched and chilled into
the repose of mere lifelessness.

> Nought we know, dies. Shall that alone which knows
> Be as a sword consumed before the sheath
> By sightless lightning?—th' intense atom glows
> A moment, then is quenched in a most cold respose.   (XX)

Observe the metaphysical terminology (as well as the images) in
which Shelley states this tragic contrast. The objects of Thought are
apparently indestructible; only the Thought which comprehends

them is consumed. The sheath remains, the sword passes, destroyed by a blind, irrational force. And all the cycles of nature seem to do for man is to increase his sense of the inescapable monotony of human loss.

> Great and mean
> Meet massed in death, who lends what life must borrow.
> As long as skies are blue, and fields are green,
> Evening must usher night, night urge the morrow,
> Month follow month with woe, and year wake year to sorrow.   (xxi)

Or, in the bare statement of Cowper, "I should rejoice indeed that the old year is over and gone, if I had not every reason to prophesy a new one similar to it." [8]

But a funeral elegist (even, to some extent, Bion and Moschus) will concern himself with possible consolations or compensations as well as with the loss itself. Even on the earthly level there are ways in which a man's death is not the end of him, and the elegy can test such compensations and the sort of perpetuation which they offer. Of these the most commonly invoked are survival in memory, survival in creations, (institutions, works of art, children) and material survival in nature. The first two are often combined, and (excluding children) we may put them both under the broad heading of fame, a subject about which elegies have traditionally had a good deal to say.

If by fame we mean no more than survival in the grief-stricken memory of the mourners, Shelley has little consolation to offer.

> Alas! that all we loved of him should be,
> But for our grief, as if it had not been,
> And grief itself be mortal!   (xxi)

But temporal fame of a less immediate and personal kind is certainly possible, as we learn in an earlier stanza. In the first stanza of the poem Shelley asks the Hour of Adonais' death to rouse the Hours of the Future and teach them to preserve "his fate and fame" until eternity. Later he claims that Milton reigns "the third

among the sons of light" (IV). But such fame is subject to the
chances and vicissitudes of temporal existence, and an inglorious
Milton may fail to rise, or may set prematurely, like Keats.

> Not all to that bright station dared to climb;
> And happier they their happiness who knew,
> Whose tapers yet burn through that night of time
> In which suns perished; others more sublime,
> Struck by the envious wrath of man or God,
> Have sunk, extinct in their refulgent prime;
> And some yet live, treading the thorny road,
> Which leads, through toil and hate, to Fame's serene abode.   (v)

Shelley, no more than Milton, is satisfied with Fame as a "plant
which grows on mortal soil," although he would like the Future
to bestow it on Keats. The "night of time" is an inadequate medium
for the "sons of light."

But inadequate earthly consolations are not what Shelley intends
to offer Adonais. As all critics have observed, the transcendental
side of Shelley's Platonic dualism suddenly takes over the direction
of the poem in stanza thirty-eight and remains dominant until the
end. The only significant consolations are otherworldly, and death
is the gateway to them. It is not death that deserves to be regretted,
but "the eclipsing curse / Of birth" (LIV) and the life which stains
and masks with its sordid and unreal shadows the "pure spirit"
issuing from the "burning fountain" (XXXVIII). It is we who decay,
not Adonais, who has "outsoared the shadow of our night" (XL).
He has left our living death behind and through death has rejoined
the life of Eternity.

> Peace, peace! he is not dead, he doth not sleep—
> He hath awakened from the dream of life—
>
> . . . .
>
> He lives, he wakes—'tis Death is dead, not he;
> Mourn not for Adonais.   (XXXIX, XL, XLI)

This is a Platonic opposition of the most uncompromising sort. To
be born is to be degraded, and a "portion of the Eternal" (XXXVIII)

fulfills its destiny only by returning to the fountain which it would
have been better never to have left.

We might expect such a repudiation of time to be characteristic
of the pastoral elegy. Presumably the consolations of an elegy will
emphasize the advantages of death and the disadvantages of life.
But, in fact, although the former are almost inescapable (if consolation is attempted at all), the latter are surprisingly infrequent.
We do not find them, for example, at the end of *Lycidas* or *Thyrsis*.
Moreover, Shelley differs strikingly in praising death not merely
for the sake of Adonais, but for the sake of the mourners as well,
including the poet himself. "What Adonais is, why fear we to
become?"

> The One remains, the many change and pass;
> Heaven's light forever shines, Earth's shadows fly;
> Life, like a dome of many-coloured glass,
> Stains the white radiance of Eternity,
> Until Death tramples it to fragments.—Die,
> If thou wouldst be with that which thou dost seek!
>
> . . . .
>
> 'Tis Adonais calls! oh, hasten thither,
> No more let life divide what Death can join together. (LI, LII, LIII)

Since Virgil's Tenth Eclogue, one of the most common ends for
the pastoral elegy and its relatives is a return to the necessities of
daily life, in particular, to the attending of the flocks. "But now
the sun is driving his horses down from the height of the firmament,
urging us to offer the river's water to our flocks." [9] "Tomorrow to
fresh woods and pastures new." *In Memoriam* ends with an epithala-
mium and an anticipation of the child of the future. But *Adonais*
ends as "The massy earth and sphered skies are riven!" (LV), and
no return is possible or desirable.

The English cemetery at Rome provides suitable images with
which to surround the victory of the white radiance over the
many-coloured dome. The disintegrating architecture in which Shel-

ley's contempt of time liked to clothe itself is everywhere. Early in
the poem Rome is already called

> that high Capital, where kingly Death
> Keeps his pale court in beauty and decay; (VII)

now it is a sepulcher, where "ages, empires, and religions . . . /
Lie buried in the ravage they have wrought" (XLVIII). Amid these
ruins of time, Keats

> is gathered to the kings of thought
> Who waged contention with their time's decay,
> And of the past are all that cannot pass away. (XLVIII)

Characteristically the natural and architectural images mingle in
Shelley's picture of a ruined Paradise:

> Go thou to Rome,—at once the Paradise,
> The grave, the city, and the wilderness;
> And where its wrecks like shattered mountains rise,
> And flowering weeds, and fragrant copses dress
> The bones of Desolation's nakedness
> Pass. . . . (XLIX)

At last we arrive at the cemetery itself, whose

> grey walls moulder round, on which dull Time
> Feeds, like slow fire upon a hoary brand. (L)

But, pointing to heaven from the center of this decay, is the pyramid
of Cestius, a Shelleyan pavilion rising out of chaos, like solidified
fire.

> And one keen pyramid with wedge sublime,
> Pavilioning the dust of him who planned
> This refuge for his memory, doth stand
> Like flame transformed to marble. (L)

Beneath it (among others) lies the grave of Adonais.
"What Adonais is, why fear we to become?" (LI) asks the poet.
Earth has no claim on us, nor works of art:

Rome's azure sky,
Flowers, ruins, statues, music, words are weak
The glory they transfuse with fitting truth to speak. (LII)

Life is no more than a postponed departure; "thou shouldst now depart!" (LIII). The victory of Shelley's Platonism has given *Adonais* a unity and certainty of purpose that *Prometheus Unbound* and *Hellas* and *Epipsychidion* lack. Whether that unity makes it of more value as a poem may be questioned. The elements which prevent unity may be of more value than unity itself.

But those elements may not have been dispersed with quite so much rigor as we have suggested. Even after death, the truth for Adonais is not entirely imageless; nor is Time the only enemy the poem attacks.

 One way of exposing the temporal residue is to see the extent to which the earthly and inadequate consolations of the first thirty-seven stanzas are transformed in the last eighteen. If the "night of time" boasted a good many "sons of light" (however subject to eclipse), we may expect to learn of a "fame in Heaven" which is analogous to earthly fame, but not subject to eclipse. Thus we move from "the firmament of time" and "earthly doom" to "an Heaven of Song":

> The splendours of the firmament of time
> May be eclipsed, but are extinguished not;
> Like stars to their appointed height they climb,
> And death is a low mist which cannot blot
> The brightness it may veil. When lofty thought
> Lifts a young heart above its mortal lair,
> And love and life contend in it, for what
> Shall be its earthly doom, the dead live there
> And move like winds of light on dark and stormy air.
>
> The inheritors of unfulfilled renown
> Rose from their thrones, built beyond mortal thought,
> Far in the Unapparent. Chatterton
> Rose pale, his solemn agony had not
> Yet faded from him; Sidney, as he fought

And as he fell and as he lived and loved
Sublimely mild, a Spirit without spot,
Arose; and Lucan, by his death approved:
Oblivion as they rose shrank like a thing reproved.

And many more, whose names on Earth are dark
But whose transmitted effluence cannot die
So long as fire outlives the parent spark,
Rose, robed in dazzling immortality.
"Thou art become as one of us," they cry,
"It was for thee yon kingless sphere has long
Swung blind in unascended majesty,
Silent alone amid an Heaven of Song.
Assume thy winged throne, thou Vesper of our throng!"

(XLIV, XLV, XLVI) 44-46

These are surely the most unsatisfactory stanzas of the last eighteen, not merely in themselves but in relation to what has preceded them. In order to have heavenly fame, we obviously must have personal immortality. But the immortality which the previous six stanzas have granted Adonais consists primarily of reunion with the One. The "pure spirit" has flowed back to the "burning fountain," and thereby lost its mortal identity. Now, however, having moved beyond the "firmament of time" (in Shelley's metaphysical terminology, from the Apparent to the Unapparent), Adonais joins his poetic peers and shines from the sphere which has long awaited him. Not merely has Time been conquered, but Oblivion as well.

The old familiar problem returns. Where is this "Heaven of Song"? If it is otherworldly, it does not allow differentiation. Earth divides, Heaven unites. Chatterton and Sidney and Lucan and Keats are all merged in the One. It also can have no commerce with either Oblivion or Memory. There is no one to remember and no time to forget. If it is earthly, a part of the "firmament of time," it is subject to the chances and vicissitudes of Time. What Shelley has in fact given Adonais is an immortality of fame presented in terms of mortal memory and identity. In a later passage,

> For he is gathered to the kings of thought
> Who waged contention with their time's decay
> And of the past are all that cannot pass away,

by stressing immortality and forgetting about fame or even identity, Shelley avoids the present difficulty.

An earthly consolation which we mentioned earlier but were unable to illustrate from the first thirty-seven stanzas of *Adonais* is material survival in Nature (a pretty thin consolation, but among the few available to a Swinburne or a Meredith). There is, nevertheless, some evidence of it in *Adonais* (however transformed) among the heavenly consolations. For, although Time may be at an end for Adonais, the One to which he returns is still involved in Time. Any modern reader of Dante knows what difficulties Christian eschatology can get into in trying to cope with the interval between the death of the individual and the death of Time. Platonic eschatology (which is non-Platonic in the sense that it does not grant the eternity of matter) has analogous problems. Since the One is still engaged in its supposedly distasteful job of coercing Nature into some shadow of the Divine Beauty, Adonais, who has returned to the One, must also be involved in Nature.

> He is made one with Nature: there is heard
> His voice in all her music, from the moan
> Of thunder, to the song of night's sweet bird;
> He is a presence to be felt and known
> In darkness and in light, from herb and stone,
> Spreading itself where'er that Power may move
> Which has withdrawn his being to its own;
> Which wields the world with never wearied love,
> Sustains it from beneath, and kindles it above.   (XLII)

The last two lines introduce a somewhat jarring echo of Christianity. In merely Platonic terms, while the natural may be impelled by love of the divine, the divine can hardly be expected to love the natural. Indeed, the whole passage depicts the Platonic descent with a joyous energy that contrasts oddly with what is said of the "eclipsing curse / Of birth" or "the world's slow stain" elsewhere in the poem.

> He is a portion of the loveliness
> Which once he made more lovely: he doth bear
> His part, while the one Spirit's plastic stress
> Sweeps through the dull dense world, compelling there
> All new successions to the forms they wear;
> Torturing th' unwilling dross that checks its flight
> To its own likeness, as each mass may bear;
> And bursting in its beauty and its might
> From trees and beasts and men into the Heaven's light. (XLIII)

Moreover, the phrase "as each mass may bear" allows the "dull dense world" and "th' unwilling dross" some variety of density at least. The virtue allowed them may be negative, but, at any rate, some things are less "unwilling" than others. More positively, we are told in a later stanza that Love

> Burns bright or dim, as each are mirrors of
> The fire for which all thirst.   (LIV)

The variety and plenitude of the world of Time, if it does nothing else, prevents matter from being equally dense throughout.

But Adonais, in addition to Immortality in the One and participation in its difficult work on the dull or polished mirrors of Time (something which he shares with any other "portion of the Eternal") is also given another kind of earthly continuance in the images of Nature. A poet participates in such images in a way that has very little to do with Death and Immortality at all. If the voice of Keats is heard in the "song of night's sweet bird," it is presumably because he wrote the *Ode to a Nightingale* and thereby transformed Nature for the receptive reader. Nature imitates Art. In two senses Keats is

> a portion of the loveliness
> Which once he made more lovely.

There is a further, quite different way in which the Platonic framework loses something of its purity. In the last eighteen stanzas the enemy, no doubt, is "dull Time." But what about "the unpastured dragon in his den" (xxvii) who slew Adonais? What about the poison he was given to drink (for Shelley uses a number of objects to represent what in the legend would be the boar)? Just before the shift to Platonic consolations occur the two stanzas attacking the "deaf and viperous murderer" (xxxvi), as Shelley calls the critics of Keats. This murderer

> felt, yet could escape the magic tone
> Whose prelude held all envy, hate and wrong,
> But what was howling in one breast alone. . . .   (xxxvi)

A famous statement from *A Defence of Poetry* may be relevant here: "The great instrument of moral good is the imagination; and poetry administers to the effect by acting on the cause" (C.283). But, unresponsive to poetry, this murderer is incapable of benefiting from its moral stimulus and discharges his hate and envy on the young and defenseless Adonais. His reward from Shelley is a towering curse:

> Live thou, whose infamy is not thy fame!
> Live! fear no heavier chastisement from me,
> Thou noteless blot on a remembered name!
> But be thyself, and know thyself to be!
> And ever at thy season be thou free
> To spill the venom when thy fangs o'erflow:
> Remorse and Self-contempt shall cling to thee;
> Hot Shame shall burn upon thy secret brow,
> And like a beaten hound tremble thou shalt—as now.   (xxxvii)

Our lapse into another world is now unmistakable. Shelley's curse on the murderer is simply a version of Prometheus' curse of Jupiter:

> I curse thee! let a sufferer's curse
> Clasp thee, his torturer, like remorse!
>
> · · · ·

Heap on thy soul, by virtue of this Curse,
  Ill deeds, then be thou damned, beholding good;
Both infinite as is the universe,
  And thou, and thy self-torturing solitude.
    An awful image of calm power
    Though now thou sittest, let the hour
    Come, when thou must appear to be
    That which thou art internally.
  And after many a false and fruitless crime,
Scorn track thy lagging fall thro' boundless space and time.

(I.286–87, 292–301)

The main difference is that Jupiter is to be punished by being revealed to others for what he is, as well as to himself, whereas the
murderer is to be punished purely by the horrors of self-contemplation.

But, although in *Adonais* we recognize the terms of Prometheus'
curse (not to mention the terms in which the Furies tempt Prometheus), in *Adonais* we do not hear of this curse being recalled.
The conquest of Time has obscured the conquest of the Will.
Epimetheus has outrun Prometheus. The murderer-critic is hardly
even recalled in the last eighteen stanzas. (Stanzas forty-seven to
fifty-one, which K. N. Cameron calls "the final attack on the
critic," [10] are really addressed to the mourners.)

The Promethean world is invoked only to be replaced. Its stand-
ards of moral good and evil distinguish between the unregenerate
haters or self-concentrators and the regenerate lovers or self-tran-
scenders. The murderer is unregenerate and Adonais is regenerate.
The contrast is between two human wills, or, in the pronouns of
Adonais, between "thou" and "he." But in the Platonic world we
are all subject (in one degree or another) to the limitations of Time.
We are all decaying in our living death, the mourners as well as
the murderer. The Platonic contrast is between all men and the
Eternal (or any "portion" of it, once returned to the source). The
contrast is between the Many and the One, or, in terms of the pronouns of *Adonais,* "we" and "he."

Stanza thirty-seven ended its picture of the murderer's future as follows:

> Hot Shame shall burn upon thy secret brow,
> And like a beaten hound tremble thou shalt—as now.

The last movement of the poem then begins:

> Nor let us weep that our delight is fled
> Far from these carrion kites that scream below;
> He wakes or sleeps with the enduring dead;
> Thou canst not soar where he is sitting now.—
> Dust to the dust! but the pure spirit shall flow
> Back to the burning fountain whence it came,
>
> . . . .
>
> Through time and change, unquenchably the same,
> Whilst thy cold embers choke the sordid hearth of shame.
>
> . . . .
>
> He hath awakened from the dream of life—
> 'Tis we, who lost in stormy visions, keep
> With phantoms an unprofitable strife
>   *We* decay
> Like corpses in a charnel. . . .
>
> . . . .
>
> He has outsoared the shadow of our night.   (xxxviii, xxxix, xl)

In stanza thirty-eight Shelley wavers between the opposition of "thou" and "he" and that of "we" and "he." In the line, "Thou canst not soar where he is sitting now," although what the murderer is denied is a Platonic apotheosis, it is still implied that the murderer is in a special category; he is not a "pure spirit." The contrast is still between one man and another and not between men and the One. But by stanza thirty-nine the shortcomings of the murderer have faded before the universal shortcomings of the human lot. Adonais has returned home, but we are still lost. He remains, but we decay. In stanza forty we have a last resurgence of radical evil (from the point of view of the victim):

> Envy and calumny and hate and pain,
> And that unrest which men miscall delight,
> Can touch him not and torture not again.

But "hate" gives way to "unrest," and for the rest of the poem the enemy is Time.

Of Shelley's other long poems, *The Sensitive Plant* is perhaps closest to *Adonais*. It is even something of a pastoral elegy and mourns the passing of a garden and its attendant Lady. The consolation is a good deal slighter and simpler than that of *Adonais* (although comparable to it) and, as Donald Davie has pointed out, is stated in Shelley's most urbane and Caroline style: [11]

> but in this life
> Of error, ignorance, and strife,
> Where nothing is, but all things seem,
> And we the shadows of the dream,
>
> It is a modest creed, and yet
> Pleasant if one considers it,
> To own that death itself must be
> Like all the rest, a mockery.
>
> That garden sweet, that lady fair,
> And all sweet shapes and odours there,
> In truth have never passed away:
> 'Tis we, 'tis ours, are changed! not they.
>
> For love, and beauty, and delight,
> There is no death nor change; their might
> Exceeds our organs, which endure
> No light, being themselves obscure.   (III.122–37)

The far goal of each man in Shelley's radical framework is the regeneration of the will, and the far goal of Time is the millennium. We see here two related goals: one individual, the other social and historical. In Shelley's Platonic framework the far goal of each man is death and reunion with the One, and the far goal of Time should be the destruction of Time: the apocalypse. The clogs should finally disappear and the Pavilion of Thought shine out in stainless per-

fection. I say "should," because, whereas the conception of an individual conquest of Time is omnipresent in Shelley's poetry, the
conception of a final destruction of this enemy (more than simply
a series of individual victories) is much less apparent.

This is not to say that Shelley insisted on the Eternity of Time,
even if he did declare in one lyric, "Naught may endure but mutability." [12] In *Prometheus Unbound,* Asia's account of history begins before Time, although even then there is an essence called
Earth:

> There was the Heaven and Earth at first,
> And Light and Love; then Saturn, from whose throne
> Time fell, an envious shadow.   (II.iv.32–34)

Time emerges with the Saturnian age, just as radical evil emerges
with the Olympian. In a famous chorus of *Hellas* we learn of
"Time's tempestuous dawn" (52), and in Egypt the poet of *Alastor*
discovers "The thrilling secrets of the birth of Time" (128). Time
begins in an instant. But it seems never to end, although always
being defeated in single combat. Shelley's Platonic world, despite
its architectural imagery and its positive values of civilization, is a
good deal less social and political, a good deal less cooperative, than
his radical world. He is much less inclined to move from the
victory of a man to that of mankind, and his cyclical pessimism does
not easily rise to the conception of Time's finally leading to its own
destruction. Adonais and the Lady of *The Sensitive Plant* have survived and conquered the all-too-imaginable touch of Time, but the
many-colored glass is not shattered for once and for all.

This far goal of Time remains around the corner. When Adonais
beckons to the mourners from his seat in Eternity, Shelley fancies
himself embarking on the ocean, as "The massy earth and sphered
skies are riven!" The voyage is his own, but the splitting of earth
and sky is a foreshadowing of something beyond a private voyage,
something which Shelley invokes rather hopelessly after the cyclical
pessimism of *Hellas* has reached its climax:

> The world is weary of the past,
> O might it die or rest at last!   (1100–1)

But the death or rest of this world is never finally imagined in
Shelley's poetry, if indeed it is "imaginable" at all in his terms. In
Act Four of *Prometheus Unbound,* the Prometheans hack away at
the depredations of Chaos and Time, but again the victory is piece-
meal, and Demogorgon is still needed to warn as well as encourage.
Man, who was once "a decay, / A traveller from the cradle to the
grave" (iv. 550–51), has not said an irrevocable farewall to the
journey.

At the end of *Adonais* we can imagine the mourners, headed by
Shelley, waiting in single file for their own private apocalypses, but
we do not see anything like the giant Albion awakening in Blake's
Jerusalem when "Time was Finished," [13] or the "sundering ultimate
kingdom" into which the world of Dylan Thomas is consumed:

> Into the organpipes and steeples
> Of the luminous cathedrals,
> Into the weathercocks' molten mouths
> Rippling in twelve-winded circles,
> Into the dead clock burning the hour
> Over the urn of sabbaths
> Over the whirling ditch of daybreak
> Over the sun's hovel and the slum of fire
> And the golden pavements laid in requiems,
> Into the bread in a wheatfield of flames,
> Into the wine burning like brandy,
> The masses of the sea
> The masses of the sea under
> The masses of the infant-bearing sea
> Erupt, fountain, and enter to utter for ever
> Glory glory glory
> The sundering ultimate kingdom of genesis' thunder. [14]

X

THE DEVELOPMENT OF
PROMETHEUS UNBOUND

Unless the critic assumes the work of art to exist in a realm of pure being, self-contained and impossibly perfect, he is justified in committing the so-called "intentionalist fallacy." Between the intention and the product "falls the Shadow," the act of the human will, and it is the assumption of integration, of self-containment that is the fallacy. The work of art is an open society, a thoroughfare of crisscrossing entrances and exits. Things come from outside and return hence.

But to recognize that the work of art is intersected by the intention of the artist is not enough. In so time-ridden a thing as art, one needs to ask "when." When does the poet discover what he is doing? I have heard it said that the descriptive titles of Schumann's piano pieces are of no significance because he invented them after the pieces were written. But would they have been more significant if he had invented them before? Which is the author's intention: his first intuition of the whole or his last? Would Shelley's Preface to *Alastor* be more or less appropriate if he had written it before he started the poem? Would the letter to Raleigh be more or less useful if Spenser had written it in 1599? If writing a poem is a process of exploration moving from the first intuition to the last (and complicated by the process of revision), then neither intention is adequate, and, unless we look both before and after, the "intentionalist fallacy" is likely to return in another form.

The poet's discovery of what he wants to do is partly conditioned

at each stage by the aesthetic choices he has already made. Shelley's
choice of the Prometheus legend (like any aesthetic or moral choice)
was both an act of freedom and an act of servitude, a release and a
control. Moreover, it too looks before and after, and is fulfilled (if
ever) in the process of composition. In Act One of *Prometheus Unbound* we see Shelley discovering what he can make out of his
choice of the Prometheus legend. According to the Earth (early in
Act One) the birth of Prometheus from her bosom was an occasion for man to rejoice and Jupiter to grow pale.

> I am the Earth,
> Thy mother; she within whose stony veins,
> To the last fibre of the loftiest tree
> Whose thin leaves trembled in the frozen air,
> Joy ran, as blood within a living frame,
> When thou didst from her bosom, like a cloud
> Of glory, arise, a spirit of keen joy!
> And at thy voice her pining sons uplifted
> Their prostrate brows from the polluting dust,
> And our almighty Tyrant with fierce dread
> Grew pale, until his thunder chained thee here.   (I.152–62)

In other words, when Prometheus was born, the Olympian age and
the persecution of man were already under way. Prometheus re-
belled against the conditions he found on earth, was defeated by
Jupiter, and was bound to the Caucasian precipice. But when the
temptation scenes begin, Shelley forgets his oversimplification of
the legend and discovers that he can make use of other, earlier
aspects of it. Indeed, he begins to discover this when writing the
recalled curse:

> Thou art omnipotent.
> O'er all things but thyself I gave thee power,
> And my own will.   (I.272–74)

Prometheus' error in helping Jupiter to supremacy complicates his
position (and Jupiter's) in a way that just being born under a
tyranny could not. As Prometheus tells Mercury,

> Such is the tyrant's recompense. 'Tis just.
> He who is evil can receive no good;
> And for a world bestowed, or a friend lost,
> He can feel hate, fear, shame; not gratitude.
> He but requites me for his own misdeed.
> Kindness to such is keen reproach, which breaks
> With bitter stings the light sleep of Revenge.   (I.388–94)

In the temptation of Mercury Shelley chooses also to make use of Prometheus' fatal secret:

> there is a secret known
> To thee, and to none else of living things;
> Which may transfer the sceptre of wide Heaven,
> The fear of which perplexes the Supreme.
> Clothe it in words. . . .   (I.371–75)

Basically Prometheus is being tempted to be something, rather than to do something. But (as in the Gospel temptations) we need some act which will signal capitulation. Mercury, therefore, begins the temptation scene by asking Prometheus to reveal the fatal secret. Prometheus refuses, and, by the time the Furies have appeared, the secret has faded into the background and our attention is concentrated on their efforts to reduce Prometheus to self-contempt and despair.

But, once brought forward, the secret cannot easily be discarded. The secret in the legend is Prometheus' knowledge that Jupiter will be overthrown and replaced by his own child, fruit of his union with Thetis—in Shelleyan terms, he will breed his own overthrow. For Shelley, however, this natural law is represented by Demogorgon, who has to overthrow Jupiter at the same moment as Asia attends the unbinding of Prometheus. Thus Love, which regenerates the will, and "the secret strength of things" combine to assure that the overthrow of evil will usher in the millennium, and that the new age will not be like the old one. Strictly speaking, then, the child of Jupiter (unless Shelley is to scrap the legend completely at this point) must be Demogorgon. The logic is inescapable, and Shelley accepts what it demands. As Act Three opens, Jupiter, puffed up with pride, looks forward to consolidating his reign through the child he has begotten and trampling out the last sparks of human resistance:[1]

> Even now have I begotten a strange wonder,
> That fatal child, the terror of the earth,
> Who waits but till the destined hour arrive,
> Bearing from Demogorgon's vacant throne
> The dreadful might of ever-living limbs
> Which clothed that awful spirit unbeheld,
> To redescend, and trample out the spark.   (III.i.18–24)

Jupiter feels the chariot's approach and the imminent birth of the child, which unbodied hovers between him and Thetis. Finally Demogorgon arrives, and to Jupiter's cry, "Awful shape, what art thou?" he replies:

> Eternity. Demand no direr name.
> Descend, and follow me down the abyss.
> I am thy child, as thou wert Saturn's child;
> Mightier than thee; and we must dwell together
> Henceforth in darkness.   (III.i.51–56)

Almost all critics of Shelley have pointed out the absurdity of this. Demogorgon tries to remain as cryptic as usual. But he has to call himself Jupiter's child, and, by doing so, although he fulfills the requirements of the legend, he confuses some of the implications which Shelley has been drawing out of that legend. Demogorgon could legitimately call himself the birth of the child; the legend causes Shelley to equate him with the child itself, which may be why, although he descends to the abyss in this scene, he returns in Act Four to act as presiding genius at the latter part of the Promethean revels. That Demogorgon has already called himself Eternity (in the firmament of time he is Alpha and Omega, and may therefore claim the name by default at least) only adds to the confusion— whatever the "direr name" may be (presumably either Fate or Chaos, at the conjunction of which Demogorgon belongs).

These details of the plot are interesting symptoms. They can lead us to a more inclusive consideration of the main characters: how they are explored, what legendary pressures they undergo. Such a consideration should reveal a good deal about Shelley's developing aims in *Prometheus Unbound*.

We have skirted about Asia in this essay without ever coming to terms with her. After a brief glance at her in the song "Life of Life," we moved on to Shelley's conception of Love and the figures in which he expressed that conception. The works which sustained our conclusions were some prose essays and stories and *Epipsychidion*. Since then we have devoted some attention to Urania in *Adonais,* but have never returned to Asia, carrying whatever illumination we have acquired during the journey. It is time, certainly, to consider her role *in extenso.*

Since Shelley avoided the familiar distinction between them in *Adonais,* it will be as well not to use the terms Pandemos and Urania. Instead I shall speak of the Earthly Venus and the Heavenly Lady. In *Adonais* Urania is the former, in *Epipsychidion* Emily is the impossibly perfect image of the latter. Which (if either) is Asia? Before trying to answer the question, we may prepare the way by glancing at a related goddess, the Witch of Atlas.

The fanciful genealogy, provenance, and activity of the Witch ought not to be squeezed for the last drop of relevance. The detail of the poem is mainly decorative, not functional, and to scan it too closely would be futile as well as clumsy. The Witch comes from the age of Saturn and his Titans; her birthplace and home are Atlantis. At her birth Father Time already exists certainly, but "Incestuous Change" has not yet borne to him "those cruel Twins . . . Error and Truth" (1), who are responsible, Shelley tells us, for the death of the old mythology. Her father is the Sun and her mother "one of the Atlantides." Shelley describes their union of fire and water:

> He kissed her with his beams, and made all golden
> The chamber of gray rock in which she lay;
> She, in that dream of joy, dissolved away.   (11)

Ten lunar months later, the Witch is born:

> in that cave a dewy splendor hidden
> Took shape and motion; with the living form
> Of this embodied Power the cave grew warm.   (IV)

She is attended by the pastoral denizens of a Saturnian world, even by "universal Pan," who comes from "the quick heart of the great world" to touch her.

> And universal Pan, 'tis said, was there;
>
> .   .   .   .
>
> He passed out of his everlasting lair
>   Where the quick heart of the great world doth pant,
> And felt that wondrous Lady all alone,—
> And she felt him upon her emerald throne.
>
> And every nymph of stream and spreading tree,
>   And every shepherdess of Ocean's flocks,
> Who drives her white waves over the green sea,
>   And Ocean, with the brine on his gray locks,
> And quaint Priapus with his company,
>   All came, much wondering how the enwombed rocks
> Could have brought forth so beautiful a birth;
> Her love subdued their wonder and their mirth.
>
> The herdsman and the mountain maidens came,
>   And the rude kings of pastoral Garamant;
> Their spirits shook within them, as a flame
>   Stirred by the air under a cavern gaunt;
> Pygmies and Polyphemes by many a name,
>   Centaurs and Satyrs, and such shapes as haunt
> Wet clefts, and lumps neither alive nor dead,
> Dog-headed, bosom-eyed, and bird-footed.   (IX, X, XI)

Whereas at the Incarnation the representatives of both Nature and Civilization came to wonder, here Nature alone comes, and the kings are "the rude kings of pastoral Garamant." The Witch's relation to Pan and the character of her court suggest a minor Venus, a goddess of the creative processes of Nature.

But if, like Venus, she belongs to the family of the Atlantides,

unlike Venus, she has the Sun for a father. From her father she
inherits the excessive brilliance of her beauty, which must be veiled
to accommodate the limitations of men, or even of demi-gods.
Without such a veil, she must make the world fade into "the fleeting
image of a shade"; once having seen her plain, a "living spirit"
(XII) must forget any other object in the world.

> Which, when the Lady knew, she took her spindle
>   And twined three threads of fleecy mist, and three
> Long lines of light, such as the dawn may kindle
>   The clouds and waves and mountains with; and she
> As many star-beams, ere their lamps could dwindle
>   In the belated moon, wound skilfully;
> And with these threads, a subtle veil she wove—
> A shadow for the splendour of her love.   (XIII)

Here the Witch is obviously closer to Emily than to Venus Genetrix,
and Shelley presents her in a way that will surely remind us of
Epipsychidion, as well as the "Life of Life" lyric (note how Shelley
repeats the "kindle-dwindle" rhyme). Indeed, he almost makes her
as sexless as her charioteer, the Hermaphroditus, although the passage in question provides for a loss of innocence in the future:

> 'Tis said in after times her spirit free
>   Knew what love was, and felt itself alone;
> But holy Dian could not chaster be
>   Before she stooped to kiss Endymion,
> Than now this lady—like a sexless bee
>   Tasting all blossoms and confined to none.   (LXVIII)

This last simile of the bee would make her (among other things)
a sort of unmoved mover, causing fertility but infertile herself—at
least until "after times," when her spirit "felt itself alone." [2]

Although Saturnian, she survives into a later period, and her
cave is stored with the wisdom by which man might recover the
golden age. The two stanzas which summarize this wisdom are a
sort of brief abstract of *Prometheus Unbound.* The first applies to
the original three acts, and the second to Act Four (although we do
revert to "man's imperial will").

Her cave was stored with scrolls of strange device,
    The works of some Saturnian Archimage,
Which taught the expiations at whose price
    Men from the gods might win that happy age
Too lightly lost, redeeming native vice;
    And which might quench the earth-consuming rage
Of gold and blood, till men should live and move
Harmonious as the sacred stars above;

And how all things that seem untamable,
    Not to be checked and not to be confined,
Obey the spells of wisdom's wizard skill;
    Time, earth and fire, the ocean and the wind,
And all their shapes, and man's imperial will;
    And other scrolls whose writings did unbind
The inmost lore of Love—let the profane
Tremble to ask what secrets they contain.   (XVIII, XIX)

But the Witch herself is not entirely content to let man blunder
along on his way to the millennium. To her activities amid the
processes of nature (described with great gusto in stanzas forty-
three to fifty-eight) she adds occasional efforts on behalf of man
himself. In accordance with the playful spirit of the poem, these
are little more than merry pranks, although they are directed against
the usual enemies of Shelley's radicalism:

And she would write strange dreams upon the brain
    Of those who were less beautiful, and make
All harsh and crooked purposes more vain
    Than in the desert is the serpent's wake
Which the sand covers; all his evil gain
    The miser in such dreams would rise and shake
Into a beggar's lap; the lying scribe
Would his own lies betray without a bribe.

                    .   .   .   .

The soldiers dreamed that they were blacksmiths, and
    Walked out of quarters in somnambulism;
Round the red anvils you might see them stand,
    Like Cyclopses in Vulcan's sooty abysm,
Beating their swords to ploughshares. . . .   (LXXII, LXXV)

The Witch creates the illusion of regeneration, although, unfortunately, it is all just a joke and cannot last. Its victims are the unregenerate, "those who were less beautiful." For the benefit of
"those . . . most beautiful" (the distinction is similar to that between the murderer and the mourners in *Adonais*) she also tries
to thwart another enemy of man: Death.

> To those she saw most beautiful, she gave
>   Strange panacea in a crystal bowl;
> They drank in their deep sleep of that sweet wave,
>   And lived thenceforward as if some control,
> Mightier than life, were in them; and the grave
>   Of such, when death oppressed the weary soul,
> Was as a green and over-arching bower
> Lit by the gems of many a starry flower.
>
> For on the night when they were buried, she
>   Restored the embalmers' ruining and shook
> The light out of the funeral lamps, to be
>   A mimic day within that deathly nook;
> And she unwound the woven imagery
>   Of second childhood's swaddling bands, and took
> The coffin, its last cradle, from its niche,
> And threw it with contempt into a ditch.   (LXIX, LXX)

But this conquest of the grave is also something of an illusion; at
least, the conquest does not lead back to "the burning fountain."
The body remains asleep, in a sort of pleasantly suspended anima-
tion, visited by sweet dreams:

> And there the body lay, age after age,
>   Mute, breathing, beating, warm, and undecaying,
> Like one asleep in a green hermitage,
>   With gentle smiles about its eyelids playing,
> And living in its dreams beyond the rage
>   Of death or life, while they were still arraying
> In liveries ever new the rapid, blind,
> And fleeing generations of mankind.   (LXXI)

Sin and Death are here the enemies in a child's fairy tale, and the
Witch must be allowed to disperse them for the moment with

"strange panacea." We smile condescendingly at the illusion, even as we indulge it.

But, although the Witch has touched "universal Pan" and rejoices in the processes of Nature, although she likes to exert her magic on human vice and mortality, she is also detached from this world, almost unconcerned. At moments this Earthly Venus fades into the intense inane and resides among the Eternal Forms beyond Time. She sees human vice, "the strife / Which stirs the liquid surface of man's life."

> And little did the sight disturb her soul.
>   We, the weak mariners of that wide lake,
> Where'er its shores extend or billows roll,
>   Our course unpiloted and starless make
> O'er its wild surface to an unknown goal;
>   But she in the calm depths her way could take
> Where in bright bowers immortal forms abide,
> Beneath the weltering of the restless tide.　　(LXII, LXIII)

And earlier in the poem, when she leaves the pastoral demi-gods, friends of her youth, she has a vision of universal decay in which she herself is not involved:

> "The fountains where the Naiades bedew
> Their shining hair, at length are drained and dried;
>   The solid oaks forget their strength, and strew
> Their latest leaf upon the mountains wide;
>   The boundless ocean, like a drop of dew,
> Will be consumed—the stubborn centre must
> Be scattered, like a cloud of summer dust;

> "And ye with them will perish one by one.
>   If I must sigh to think that this shall be,
> If I must weep when the surviving Sun
>   Shall smile on your decay, oh, ask not me
> To love you till your little race is run;
>   I cannot die as ye must. . . ."　　(XXIII, XXIV)

This daughter of one of the Atlantides imagines the ocean being consumed and accepts its fate with resignation. She is also the radiant daughter of "the surviving Sun," and her allegiance is more to her father than to her mother. The original conception and gestation of the Witch suggested an actual union of fire and water ("dewy splendour" and "living form") but the Witch, in fact, is more of a mixture than a synthesis.

Asia is herself one of the Atlantides, or, more accurately, one of their cousins, the Oceanides. We meet her sisters, Panthea and Ione, in Act One, and learn of Asia's existence, but for any significant water imagery we have to wait for Panthea's visit to Asia in Act Two. As Panthea approaches, Asia hears

> The Aeolian music of her sea-green plumes
> Winnowing the crimson dawn,   (II.i.26–27)

and Panthea herself recalls the days before the fall of Prometheus when she

> slept
> Under the glaucous caverns of old Ocean
> Within dim bowers of green and purple moss.   (II.i.43–45)

Particularly striking, however, is the account of her first dream, in which she is dissolved and condensed like water vapor under the changing influence of the sun. The fire of Prometheus' love wraps her

> in its all-dissolving power
> As the warm ether of the morning sun
> Wraps e'er it drinks some cloud of morning dew. . . .
> And I was thus absorbed, until it passed,
> And like the vapors when the sun sinks down,
> Gathering again in drops upon the pines,
> And tremulous as they, in the deep night
> My being was condensed. . . .   (II.i.76–78, 82–86)

Asia herself uses imagery like Panthea's to describe the emergence of her sister. Not merely does she talk of Panthea's "sea-green plumes / Winnowing the crimson dawn," but also of her

> eyes which burn through smiles that fade in tears
> Like stars half-quenched in mists of silver dew.   (II.i.28–29)

The reader has already been made familiar with this image by Asia's immediately preceding description of the dawn;

> The point of one white star is quivering still
> Deep in the orange light of widening morn
> Beyond the purple mountains; through a chasm
> Of wind-divided mist the darker lake
> Reflects it; now it wanes; it gleams again
> As the waves fade, and as the burning threads
> Of woven cloud unravel in pale air;
> 'Tis lost! and through yon peaks of cloud-like snow
> The roseate sunlight quivers. . . .   (II.1.17–25)

The shifting emphases of Shelley's Platonic dialectic can be strikingly illustrated by the various relations of fire and water in his poems. Earl Wasserman has brilliantly examined these relations in *Adonais*.[3] At one extreme there is the abortive attempt of a "Splendor" to revivify the dead Adonais:

> the damp death
> Quenched its caress upon his icy lips;
> And, as a dying meteor stains a wreath
> Of moonlight vapor, which the cold night clips,
> It flushed through his pale limbs, and passed to its eclipse. (XII)

At the other extreme there is the injunction, "Thou young Dawn, / Turn all thy dew to splendor" (XLI), an injunction which, figuratively at least, we see being carried out in the last stanzas of the poem:

> The fire for which all thirst, now beams on me,
> Consuming the last clouds of cold mortality.   (LIV)

Somewhere between these two extremes, one the victory of water over fire and the other of fire over water, lies the marriage of fire and water, and the birth of that "dewy splendour," the Witch of Atlas.

According to Mary Shelley's note,

Asia, one of the Oceanides, is the wife of Prometheus—she was, according to other mythological interpretations, the same as Venus and

Nature. When the Benefactor of Mankind is liberated, Nature resumes the beauty of her prime, and is united to her husband, the emblem of the human race, in perfect and happy union.   (J.II.269)

There is a good deal in the poem to justify Mrs. Shelley's interpretation. At the end of Act One, Panthea sees her sister as the transforming presence which regenerates Nature, a presence which is sustained by the Love between her and Prometheus.

> Asia waits in that far Indian vale,
> The scene of her sad exile; rugged once
> And desolate and frozen, like this ravine;
> But now invested with fair flowers and herbs,
> And haunted by sweet airs and sounds, which flow
> Among the woods and waters, from the ether
> Of her transforming presence, which would fade
> If it were mingled not with thine.   (I.826–33)

Venus and Nature, or Venus Genetrix, would be an appropriate label for the Asia of this passage, and her identity as the "Child of Ocean" (II.I.170) (the name by which the Echoes address her) underlines her relation to fertility, as it does in classical myth. Moreover, when we first meet Asia, in the opening speech of Act Two, she is uttering a hymn of praise to the rebirth of Nature:

> From all the blasts of heaven thou hast descended;
>
>   . . . .
>
>   thou hast descended
> Cradled in tempests; thou dost wake, O Spring!
> O child of many winds;
>
>   . . . .
>
> Like genius, or like joy which riseth up
> As from the earth, clothing with golden clouds
> The desert of our life.   (II.i.1, 5–7, 10–12)

These clouds are life-giving more than quenching.

After Asia has descended to the cave of Demogorgon and ascended the chariot which will take her to the release of Prometheus, she undergoes something of an apotheosis. "The chariot passes within a cloud on the / Top of a snowy Mountain," and Panthea asks:

> O Spirit! pause, and tell whence is the light
> Which fills the cloud? the sun is yet unrisen.   (II.v.8–9)

The Spirit replies that the light comes from Asia herself. Panthea gazes at her sister, almost unable to bear "The radiance of thy beauty."

> The Nereids tell
> That on the day when the clear hyaline
> Was cloven at thy uprise, and thou didst stand
> Within a veined shell, which floated on
> Over the calm floor of the crystal sea,
> Among the Aegean isles, and by the shores
> Which bear thy name,—love, like the atmosphere
> Of the sun's fire filling the living world,
> Burst from thee, and illumined earth and heaven
> And the deep ocean and the sunless caves
> And all that dwells within them; till grief cast
> Eclipse upon the soul from which it came.
> Such art thou now.   (II.v.18, 20–32)

Here her identity as Venus is most specific. But it is also at this point that she shows signs of rising beyond the Earthly Venus and beyond Mary Shelley's Nature. She emerges out of the sea like Venus, but also like Apollo, and justifies the name which she shares with the continent of the rising sun. To be sure, sun and water are normally the two presiding genii of Nature's processes (see the dialogue of Apollo and Neptune which precedes the release of Prometheus), but by the time we reach the song "Life of Life," sung by a disembodied voice, Asia has surely become the Heavenly Lady, shrouded from the direct gaze of mortals, who, having once glimpsed her, joyously will their own destruction, "Dizzy, lost, yet unbewailing!" (II.v.71).

The song seems to go farther than the poem needs or, perhaps, can justify. Indeed, the erotic soaring and annihilation which the

"Voice in the air" describes is quite different from the love which Asia herself has just finished describing. According to Asia,

> all love is sweet,
> Given or returned. Common as light is love,
> And its familiar voice wearies not ever.
> Like the wide heaven, the all-sustaining air,
> It makes the reptile equal with the God. . . . (II.v.39–43)

But this "familiar voice" which "wearies not ever," this "light of common day" is not what the voice in the air sings of, it is not the radiance upon which, even when shrouded, "whoso gazes / Faints, entangled in their mazes" (II.v.52–53).

The Voice's song has its effect on Asia, and in her song, which concludes Act Two, she feels herself voyaging "Upon the silver waves of thy sweet singing" (II.v.74), led to a remote destination by the Voice itself.

> And we sail on, away, afar,
> Without a course, without a star,
> But, by the instinct of sweet music driven;
> Till through Elysian garden islets
> By thee most beautiful of pilots,
> Where never mortal pinnace glided,
> The boat of my desire is guided;
> Realms where the air we breathe is love,
> Which in the winds on the waves doth move,
> Harmonizing this earth with what we feel above.
>
> (II.v.88–97)

Wherever Asia is going, it is beyond the familiar voice of common love, where the reptile is equal to the god. She sails beyond the limits of any "mortal pinnace" to a world where the very air is love, and where the earth has become harmonized (the word means a good deal less than it might) "with what we feel above."

The final stanza of the song describes the route and the goal of Asia's voyage more definitely:

> We have passed Age's icy caves,
> And Manhood's dark and tossing waves,
> And Youth's smooth ocean, smiling to betray;
> Beyond the glassy gulfs we flee
> Of shadow-peopled Infancy,
> Through Death and Birth to a diviner day;
> A paradise of vaulted bowers
> Lit by downward-gazing flowers,
> And watery paths that wind between
> Wildernesses calm and green,
> Peopled by shapes too bright to see,
> And rest, having beheld; somewhat like thee;
> Which walk upon the sea, and chant melodiously!
>
> (II.v.98–110)

The route is through mortality and generation and out beyond it; in fact, Asia's bark is on the same voyage as Shelley's at the end of *Adonais,* except that it is moving in the opposite direction. From Age back to Manhood and Youth and Infancy, and finally to Birth, she sails, or, rather, to Death and Birth, since at this stage they are the same thing, and since it is neither Death nor Birth that is being left behind, but the process of which they are the two limits.

However, having reached the "diviner day," what is it like? On the one hand, it simply resembles the lush cosiness of an Earthly Paradise:

> A paradise of vaulted bowers
> Lit by downward-gazing flowers.

On the other hand, it resembles the beatific vision; the screens have been removed—and "now, face to face." This paradise is "peopled by shapes too bright to see," but she sees them, and rests "having beheld." The whole passage, from Asia's transfiguration to the end of the act, is further complicated because, whereas the Voice in its lyric addresses Asia as if she were the goal of Love, in her reply she becomes the motion of the soul toward that goal. She is presented at one time as a Platonic form and at another as a Platonic daemon: [4] as the form of the Good and also as Eros or Agape. The last two lines of Asia's song are a rather dismal anticlimax. The uncertainty of the comparison is underlined by Shelley himself ("somewhat like thee") and grammatically no comparison between "we" and "thee" is possible. The "thee" is apparently both part of "we" and also separate from it. Shelley's failure to define his grammar resembles his failure to define the nature and destiny of Asia herself.

Part of the difficulty (not merely with Asia, but with the Witch as well) arises from the nature of the classical goddesses whom Shelley is representing and from the Platonic and Christian associations which are likely to mix with and complicate them. The Venus of Olympus is eternal because the duration of her life has no limits, not because she belongs to a realm where Time has no meaning. Mythologically she is in Time, although not its servant. But Platonically she is out of Time, and the world's slow stain exists not in her but in the eye of the mortal beholder. Her home is, on the one hand, the order of Time stretched to its extremity and, on the other, a different order altogether. By using a similar terminology both for the Eternity of a mythological goddess and for the Eternity of a Platonic Form or a Beatrice in Paradise, Shelley assists as well as obscures his failure to distinguish between them adequately.

Similar tensions exist in the role of Prometheus. His legendary existence and his sort of timelessness are complicated by Shelley's making him, in Mary Shelley's words, "the emblem of the human race." As such, he shares its trials, its regeneration, and its release. Presumably he should also share its millennium. But Prometheus is not merely an emblem; he is also the chief figure in a legend. He is released as man and as god.[5] As man he would participate in the millennium, although feeling the limitations of his mortality. As god he would rejoice at man's new lot, although feeling his own separation from man and exemption from mutability. In Act Three Prometheus as god and culture hero overwhelms Prometheus as "the emblem of the human race." The consequence of Prometheus'

emblematic regeneration is the millennium; the mythological consequence is his reunion and retirement with Asia. These two consequences are not equivalent, but in partial contrast to one another.
When they have retired to their "simple dwelling," Prometheus
and Asia

> will sit and talk of time and change,
> As the world ebbs and flows, ourselves unchanged.
> What can hide man from mutability?   (III.iii.22, 23–25)

Indeed, Asia is not sure what death means, and asks the Earth to
enlighten her:

> O mother! wherefore speak the name of death?
> Cease they to love, and move, and breathe, and speak,
> Who die?   (III.iii.108–10)

But, although separate from human mortality and no longer emblematic, Prometheus remains a civilizing force, inventing "arts,
though unimagined, yet to be" (III.iii.56), and thus contributing to
man's advance in the Promethean age. If the separation of mortal
and god allowed him to be emblematic at all, it would be of
Thought or Art. The Promethean will recedes, its occupation gone.

But if the emblematic Prometheus gives way to the legendary
god, the god too shows signs of giving way to the Platonic Form.
The timefulness of the god merges with the timelessness of the
God. The winged child leads Prometheus and Asia (with their
attendant company) to the temple and the cave which await them.
The Earth describes the route and the goal:

>   Run, wayward,
> And guide this company beyond the peak
> Of Bacchic Nysa, Maenad-haunted mountain,
> And beyond Indus and its tribute rivers,
> Trampling the torrent streams and glassy lakes
> With feet unwet, unwearied, undelaying,
> And up the green ravine, across the vale,
> Beside the windless and crystalline pool,
> Where ever lies, on unerasing waves,

> The image of a temple, built above,
> Distinct with column, arch, and architrave,
> And palm-like capital, and overwrought,
> And populous with most living imagery,
> Praxitelean shapes, whose marble smiles
> Fill the hushed air with everlasting love.
> It is deserted now, but once it bore
> Thy name, Prometheus; there the emulous youths
> Bore to thy honour through the divine gloom
> The lamp which was thine emblem; even as those
> Who bear the untransmitted torch of hope
> Into the grave, across the night of life,
> As thou hast borne it most triumphantly
> To this far goal of Time. Depart, farewell!
> Beside that temple is the destined cave.   (III.iii.152–75)

The pool is "windless," and "unerasing." It does not "tremble" or "quiver" or "cleave . . . into chasms" like the Mediterranean of the *Ode to the West Wind;* it does not become the "watery bier" of "marble shrines,"

> Pointing with inconstant motion
> From the altar of dark ocean,   (120, 112, 108–9)

like the Adriatic of the *Lines Written among the Euganean Hills.* In the pool is an unchanging image of the temple "built above."

In the description which follows, the syntax at first does not make it clear whether we are still looking at the image or have turned to the temple, certain as we may ultimately be of the second alternative. Our uncertainty may make us pause over "living imagery" and its relation to the "image of a temple." Have we images in images or images of images? But the relation is probably infinitesimal, and we have to do with little more than an unconscious pun on two different meanings of "image." "Living imagery" may make us pause for another reason: it suggests the natural decoration of Pompeii, or the Coliseum, or the ruined temple in *Epipsychidion,* which would hardly suit this temple or its changeless image. But "Praxitelean shapes" are statues, and "living" apparently means human and lifelike, although the love with which they "Fill the hushed air" is "everlasting."

This temple suggests to the Earth three parallel scenes: (1) the "emulous youths" bearing the lamp (emblem of Prometheus) "through the divine gloom" of the temple, (2) men bearing

> the untransmitted torch of hope
> Into the grave, across the night of time,

and (3) Prometheus' own triumphant bearing of the torch of hope "To this far goal of Time." Now, the "torch of hope" (even if "untransmitted") suggests some of the Promethean virtues of Act One, his refusal to despair at man's lot or regard evil as "immedicable." But, in the main, the second analogy is talking neither of the victory of man's will over the temptations of evil, nor of the millennium reached by his regeneration. The goal is "across the night of life" and "into the grave." Logically, of course, it is not the goals which are being compared but the process of bearing the torch. We are not, therefore, asked to see Prometheus attaining the same end as the "emulous youths" who performed the original Promethean rites or as the torchbearers of the second analogy, who encounter death with undaunted hope. But the effect of the Earth's comparisons (and of the temple itself) is, nevertheless, to make Prometheus' victory seem less of an ethical and political revolution than of a Platonic quest against worldly clogs to an otherworldly goal. Prometheus, however, is not going to the temple at all. "Beside that temple is the destined cave": a more pastoral and Saturnian goal.

The dramatic characters of Prometheus and Asia may be static, but, as we have seen, their roles are fluid. Moreover, in a work whose pattern depends on the relation of three major figures, a shift in the position of one will affect both the other figures and the total pattern. In fact, the areas covered by Prometheus, Asia, and Demogorgon overlap one another, and too notable a shift can make one or another superfluous. In Act One Prometheus is an emblem of the human race; more narrowly, of the human will; more narrowly yet, of the human will's capacity for expansive love. But in Act Two, Asia is Love itself. Whatever is now of any significance in the Prometheus of Act One is comprehended in Asia. But, fortunately, the legendary Prometheus was also a pioneer of human civilization. In Act One his special gifts gave an edge to the temptations of the Furies. Now, with the regeneration of his will and the appearance of Asia, Prometheus' capacity for Thought can dominate his role; Asia can be Love (both the process and the goal), and Prometheus can attend to the arts and sciences. Love and Art are related, to be sure, in Shelley's concept of the sympathetic imagination, but Shelley is only beginning to explore this relationship when he writes *Prometheus Unbound*. At the same time, the less Prometheus' role overlaps Asia's, the more it overlaps Demogorgon's: the colonizer of Thought's empire over Chaos merges with the lawgiver of the dark abyss.

Equally interesting is the relation of Asia and Demogorgon. As the emergence of Asia affects the role of Prometheus, so the emergence of Demogorgon affects the role of Asia. Asia, in Mary Shelley's terminology, is Nature as well as Love. At the end of Act One and the beginning of Act Two, she is closer to the cyclical processes of Nature than at any other place in *Prometheus Unbound*. But obviously Asia as Nature trespasses on some of the territory soon to be assigned to Demogorgon. "Demogorgon's mighty law," the secret strength of things, the power of Necessity fertilizing the Womb of Chaos, Revolution itself—these are the masculine and harsher side of that Nature which (according to Panthea) Asia transforms with her presence. Asia and Demogorgon are both turning the same wheel.

But for the purposes of the crucial Hour Demogorgon and Asia need to be sharply differentiated. The moment, the milieu, and the power, which make revolution possible, must be separated from the ethical values which can make it a positive success. Necessity and free will must each play its independent part. "Demogorgon's mighty law" made a French Revolution inevitable; only the presence of Asia could have averted the Terror or Napoleon or the Restoration and made it a Promethean revolution. In *Prometheus Unbound* the possibility of failing to separate the two roles never becomes dangerous. It is only in retrospect that we see the problem. When Asia and Demogorgon meet, Demogorgon is careful not to blur the distinction between cyclic Nature and Love:

> For what would it avail to bid thee gaze
> On the revolving world? What to bid speak
> Fate, Time, Occasion, Chance and Change? To these
> All things are subject but eternal Love.   (II.iv.117–20)

Demogorgon's charioteer is "A Spirit with a dreadful countenance"; Asia's is a "young Spirit" with "soft smiles" and "the dove-like eyes of hope." Demogorgon, a "terrible Shadow," floats up to ascend his chariot like "the lurid smoke / Of earthquake-ruined cities" (II.v.142, 159, 161, 160, 150, 151–52). In her chariot Asia is transfigured, and comes as close to "eternal Love" in the Platonic sense as her role will allow. For the purposes of the crucial Hour Demogorgon exists at the verge of the subnatural and Asia of the supernatural. His task finished, Demogorgon sinks with Jupiter to "dwell together / Henceforth in darkness" (III.i.55–56). Her task finished, Asia is greeted by the released Prometheus as "thou light of life / Shadow of beauty unbeheld" (III.iii.6–7). But our last view of Asia is as the mother of the Spirit of the Earth and of his sister, the Spirit of the Moon; and our last view of Demogorgon is as the admonitory, but encouraging, speaker of the final speech of the play. Demogorgon's sentiments are Promethean in this speech, and we might have expected Prometheus himself to utter them. But, although Act Four (according to its stage direction) takes place "near the cave of Prometheus," neither Prometheus nor Asia makes an appearance. The last word is Demogorgon's.

And so it should be. Although one would be hard put to imagine him "dove-like brooding o'er the vast abyss," Demogorgon, with his form emerging out of chaos, and his imageless darkness at the point of meeting its visible image, is, nevertheless, an appropriate Muse for *Prometheus Unbound,* a profoundly transitional work, pavilioned on chaos, reassembling its parts as it moves, and reaching toward a far goal outside itself. In Romantic poetry (to some degree, in all poetry) the growth and formation of a human identity, the developing structure of a poem, and the process of history are likely to be obvious analogies. The poet's psychology, aesthetics, and theory of history trace the same path. The Shelleyan Poem is as unfulfilled as the Shelleyan Man or the Shelleyan Time.

But the kind of unfulfillment is more important than the fact itself. After all, poems are by nature unfulfilled. Like the improvisa-tions of Abt Vogler, a poem is a broken arc. Such is its glory as well as its limitation. It can be said less to be or to mean than to do—a transitive verb suspended between subject and object. But there are infinite gradations between such a suspension, strong with the thrust and pull of a real syntax (like the procession on Keats's urn, glimpsed for a moment in its journey from an emptied city to a green altar) and the flabby uncertainty of a poem which is simply spreading itself on the page, suspended in an artistic limbo because it has no place to go. As Arthur Barker describes them, Milton's poems belong near the first of my two poles:

They are works of poetic art, the pattern of their evolution in time be-ginning usually as a reminiscence of some pattern established in the past, and nearly always controlled by easily recognizable structural balance, but always in process of development through conflict and resolution towards a harmony which is dynamic because it is the result of tension released in a creative act. This harmony they by no means always per-fectly achieve, less frequently than Milton himself wished to believe. Nor need they so achieve it. They do not represent or express or entomb an unutterable perfection; they indicate a direction in which perfection may be achieved. At their best they pause, like Michael, betwixt a world destroyed and world restored; and the creative act for poet and reader often comes afterwards, while the poem is "thought . . . still speaking," like Raphael.[6]

It would be absurd to speak in this way of *Prometheus Unbound,* which is irresolute as well as unresolved. My second pole comes uncomfortably close. Nevertheless, the poem has more tension than muddle, more direction than aimlessness. It is a "bridge thrown over the stream of time" (C.289).

EPILOGUE

The Place of a Poet

We do not expect a critic of English poetry to defend Chaucer or Shakespeare or Milton. To justify reading them is to justify reading poetry at all. The idolater and the iconoclast, partisan in hand, seem equally irrelevant. To the critic who asks "Why read Shakespeare?" we can only reply: "That is not the question," as the poet stalks away in monumental mockery. Even considerably lesser figures like Donne or Pope or Wordsworth or Yeats, although they will suffer from vicissitudes of taste, refuse to abide our question; each obviously is his own excuse for being and might legitimately say to any committed reader of English poetry: "Not to know me argues yourself unknown."

But there are poets who come in a more questionable shape. I suppose that, by definition, a minor poet is one whose place can not be kept for him without persistent defense. We are told, rightly I believe, that the twentieth century is a golden age of minor poetry. Surely, if we wish to range abroad, the many excellent minor poets among our own contemporaries have more than enough to offer us and have special advantages over the minor poets of the past. Why read Herrick instead of R. S. Thomas, or Prior instead of Auden? Why, in particular, read *Epipsychidion* instead of W. J. Turner's *Hymn to Her Unknown?* [1] Since other nineteenth-century poets, like Keats, Hardy, and Hopkins, who are of approximately the same stature as Shelley, have been defended much more cogently than he, there is some excuse for asking ourselves: what are a few of the things that might be said to justify anyone's recommending this admittedly marginal poet to the reader of poetry? The things I intend to suggest will be a mixed lot; and people who like exclusively literary reasons for reading literature will not be impressed by some of them. But purity is not always a virtue in discussing the most impure of the arts, and the only reasons I would avoid on principle are the arbitrary or merely private.

First of all, in Shelley's poetry the two ancient strands of Western civilization, once united and transfigured under the influence of Christianity, step forth with a new innocence and prepare to meet in another and different marriage. Hebraism and Hellenism, deprived of the religion which united them, try what humanitarianism and transcendentalism can do as a substitute. In a sense, Shelley is trying singlehanded to remake the history of thought since the Incarnation. He begins again with the same components and tries to create a new synthesis. This effort is not quixotic; it can seem so only if we underestimate the post-Christian side of nineteenth-century English culture. Shelley is of special importance as almost the only English poet who had no desire to profess Christianity, but who did assume a comprehensive world view as the basis of his poetry. His only conceivable rivals (unless one wishes to take Swinburne seriously) are Hardy and Yeats, although the cosmology of these poets seems surprisingly detachable from their poetry, certainly far more than is that of Shelley.

I have spoken of Shelley's Hebraism, for (despite his immediate debt to French radicalism and Shaftesburian ethics) his prophetic and millennial strain, his ethical emphasis on the will, and his tirades against kings and priests are as indebted to the Bible as to the Enlightenment, as Bennett Weaver's *Toward the Understanding of Shelley* amply shows.[2] Up-to-date as Shelley's ethics and politics and his Platonic Hellenism no doubt were, he is far more archaic, or, let us say, he has more historical sweep than the typical philosophical radical of his time (say, Paine and Hazlitt before him and Mill and the Benthamites after). I am comparing poetry and prose, but the difference is more than just a difference in medium.

The historical range of Shelley's new and abortive synthesis, the effort and pressure and enthusiasm with which he tries to bring it together, and the surprising uniqueness of the poetic task he set himself—all these things recommend him to me. To them I would add his remarkable receptiveness to the poetry of other languages and cultures. Blake, Burns, Wordsworth, Keats, Hopkins, and Hardy are insular, even regional, poets, and the poetic cosmopolitanism of Byron and Browning is a good deal more superficial than Shelley's, which permeates his verse and makes him the most international of English poets since the Restoration. According to Medwin, Shelley

used to say that a good library consisted not of many books, but a few chosen ones; and asking him what he considered such, he said, "I'll give you my list—catalogue it can't be called:—The Greek Plays, Plato, Lord Bacon's Works, Shakespeare, The Old Dramatists, Milton, Goethe and Schiller, Dante, Petrarch and Boccacio, and Machiavelli and Guicciardini, —not forgetting Calderon; and last, yet first, the Bible." [3]

The Latin poets seem to have slipped out of this list, and Shelley would certainly have included Lucretius, if not Virgil. The omission of the French is probably intentional; Shelley seems to have read little outside the eighteenth century, and he regarded even his favorite Rousseau as a deeply flawed writer. The scope of Shelley's reading allowed him to be comparatively detached and unprovincial about his own medium. There is nothing striking about the following remarks (ascribed to him by Medwin), but I can think of few nineteenth-century English poets to whom one would think of ascribing anything like them:

Doubtless . . . there is no medium for poetry superior to our own. Its numerous monosyllables, for which we are indebted to the Saxons, enable us to squeeze into a line more matter than can be included in a German, Italian or French one. The Portuguese is perhaps an exception, as you [i.e., Medwin] found in the vain attempt of putting the octave stanza of the Lousiada into our own. I suspect also . . . that ours is the most musical of all languages, in spite of what Byron says, and the most sonorous, though it does not admit of so many poetical licenses as the Italian, and is poor in rhymes,—at least for serious poetry. *Hudibras* and *Don Juan* prove that for comic there is no want of such. German is indeed a mighty tongue, but harsh and consonantal. German hexameters I cannot, and never could endure. For rendering Greek it is unapproachable, admitting of a coinage of compound words on which we cannot venture,—that would be hostile to the spirit of our language, if carried to excess.[4]

But when anyone speaks of the international flavor of Shelley's poetry, he is mainly thinking of its absorption of Italian substance and technique. And, although Shelley read recent Italians like Alfieri and Manzoni, thought highly of Tasso and Ariosto, and included Boccaccio in his "good library," the substance and technique he absorbed were those of Dante and Petrarch (reinforced, as we have already observed by the impact of the Italian world itself). Discussing the *Paradiso,* T. S. Eliot has called Shelley "the one English poet of the nineteenth century who could even have begun to follow in those footsteps." [5] In *The Triumph of Life,* often regarded as his most Dantesque poem, when Shelley prepares for the mask scene, he refers specifically to Dante:

> Before the chariot had begun to climb
> The opposing steep of that mysterious dell,
> Behold a wonder worthy of the rhyme
>
> Of him who from the lowest depths of hell,
> Through every paradise and through all glory,
> Love led serene, and who returned to tell
>
> The words of hate and awe,—the wondrous story
> How all things are transfigured except Love.   (469–76)

Nevertheless, White and Roe are justified in emphasizing the strength of Petrarch's influence on Shelley.[6] *The Triumph of Life* is, in part at least, a successor to Petrarch's *Trionfi.* The stylistic qualities which Shelley most appreciated in Italian poetry—"the gentle seriousness, the delicate sensibility, the calm and sustained energy," and the absence of "an assumed and artificial style" (J.IX.312)—are not those which distinguish Dante from Petrarch or vice versa, but those which they have in common, or (to be more accurate) those which an English poet might be impressed by in both.

For what an English poet can learn from Dante or Petrarch is what his own culture allows him to learn. Just as the Poe of Baudelaire is not the Poe of Aldous Huxley, so (we may agree with Mario Praz) the Dante described by T. S. Eliot in his essay of 1929 is not the Dante which a cultivated Italian would be most likely to recognize as his own. In a more recent essay on his favorite, Eliot claims that the "style and soul" of Shelley's *The Triumph of Life* is a "supreme tribute" from one great poet to another which he himself could hardly hope to equal.[7] Nevertheless, he had already made his own tribute in the Dantesque passage of *Little Gidding,* where the footsteps he follows seem as much Shelley's as Dante's. The "familiar compound ghost" of Eliot's encounter, predicting a dismal descent into senility, is less the Virgil than the Rousseau of his poem.[8] The common occasion of the two poems is Dante, but *The Triumph of Life* and *Little Gidding* resemble one another more than the catalyst whose presence has brought them into being. If we set them side by side, we should acquire some insight into what the figure of Dante can represent for an English poet.[9]

Both poems show what Shelley has called "a delicate moral sensibility"; they seem to make careful distinctions in describing human conduct. And, in doing this, they include a good deal of statement, which, if not entirely imageless, suggests sharp abstraction rather than full embodiment:

> the shame
> Of motives late revealed, and the awareness
> Of things ill done and done to others harm
> Which once you took for exercise of virtue;
>
> Some flying from the thing they feared, and some
> Seeking the object of another's fear;

The action and the shape without the grace;

> I was overcome
> By my own heart alone, which neither age,
> Nor tears, nor infamy, nor now the tomb,
> Could temper to its object.

Even a paradox comes out an obvious statement of fact.

> Each like himself and like each other were;

> I was still the same,
> Knowing myself yet being someone other;

> The wonder that I feel is easy,
> Yet ease is cause of wonder.

And the wit is unobtrusive—an unexpected adjective here or there: "First, the cold friction of expiring sense"; "Half fainting in the affliction of vain breath"; "Obscure clouds, moulded by the casual air." Shelley's Rousseau, although unable to separate "the man who suffers from the mind which creates"[10] ("I / Have suffered what I wrote, or viler pain!") and "overcome" (like Eliot's *Hamlet*) by a heart always in excess of its object, is rhetorically akin to the more "impersonal" ghost of *Little Gidding*.[11] The last temptation of the Furies in *Prometheus Unbound* and some of Orsino's speeches in *The Cenci* are in a related vein, although perhaps the philosophical passages in *Epipsychidion* and *Adonais* are closer in style to *The Triumph of Life*.

This style is firm, continuous and transparent:

> and, long before the day

> Was old, the joy, which waked like heaven's glance
> The sleepers in the oblivious valley, died;
> And some grew weary of the ghastly dance,

> And fell, as I have fallen, by the wayside;—
> Those soonest from whose forms most shadows passed,
> And least of strength and beauty did abide.   (518-32, 537-43)

In his Dantesque or Petrarchan manner Shelley shows the "calm and sustained energy" which he missed in Ariosto and found in the

older Italian poets, the unobtrusive simplicity which he missed in
the "assumed and artificial style" of Tasso. When he translates
Dante directly, these qualities will be particularly obvious:

> My song, I fear that thou wilt find but few
>> Who fitly shall conceive thy reasoning,
>>> Of such hard matter dost thou entertain.
>> Whence, if by misadventure chance should bring
> Thee to base company, as chance may do,
>>> Quite unaware of what thou dost contain,
>> I prithee comfort thy sweet self again,
> My last delight; tell them that they are dull,
> And bid them own that thou art beautiful.

An imitator of Shakespeare or Milton would produce nothing like
this. Nor would he produce anything like Keats's vision of his
Muse in *The Fall of Hyperion* (his most Dantesque work):

> And yet I had a terror of her robes,
> And chiefly of the veils, that from her brow
> Hung pale, and curtained her in mysteries,
> That made my heart too small to hold its blood.
> This saw that Goddess, and with sacred hand
> Parted the veils. Then saw I a wan face,
> Not pined by human sorrows, but bright-blanch'd
> By an immortal sickness which kills not;
> It works a constant change, which happy death
> Can put no end to; deathwards progressing
> To no death was that visage; it had pass'd
> The lily and the snow; and beyond these
> I must not think now, though I saw that face.
> But for her eyes I should have fled away.
> They held me back with a benignant light.   (251–65)

Indeed, for an English poet, Dante will define himself as the
opposite pole to Shakespeare, the other limit of the European poetic
tradition. As Eliot claims, they "divide the modern world between
them. There is no third." What the English poet will emphasize in
Dante, therefore, is the qualities which are not characteristic of
Shakespeare; other qualities (like the grotesque vigor or the tedious

periphrasis) he will either overlook or at least minimize. Dante allows the English poet to envisage great poetry in a style more equable and effortless, more "sustained" in its energy (to use Shelley's word) than he could have conceived of before. Despite the exclamation marks, it is the sustained drive, the steady compulsion, that makes the last section of the *Ode to the West Wind* so impressive. Or, in a quieter vein and on a smaller scale, there is the level, firm movement and continuity of the famous fragment *To the Moon:*

> Art thou pale for weariness
> Of climbing heaven and gazing on the earth,
>   Wandering companionless
> Among the stars that have a different birth,—
> And ever changing, like a joyless eye
> That finds no object worth its constancy?

To poetry of this sort the appropriate response would be silent reading with held breath. It has what Shelley calls (speaking of a human form in *The Birth of Pleasure*) "the harmony divine / of an ever-lengthening line." This continuous line, impressive enough in *To the Moon* or *Ode to the West Wind* or in certain paragraphs of *Lines Written among the Euganean Hills,* begins to seem really "ever-lengthening" in such a passage as the opening of the dream in *The Triumph of Life* (ll.41–73).

The English poet (fresh from *Macbeth* or *Antony and Cleopatra*) will also be struck by the selective, unclotted presentation of Dante's images. We have already observed how profuse Shelley's figurative images can be. When he evokes the indescribable he does it by surrounding the target with a series of variously inadequate figures. What no single figure can do, the range and profusion of a series can; or, at least, they can reveal more adequately just what it is that can't be done. But natural description is something else again. When he represents our common world (for example, in *Lines Written among the Euganean Hills, The Invitation, Ode to the West Wind* or *The Cloud*), Shelley gives us a screen of process and

change, full of images fusing and unfusing, against a nature reduced, abstracted, geometrized—permanence fighting change, the
skeleton visible through the veil of flux, "Demogorgon's mighty
law" intersecting the abyss. It is the reduced, skeletal side of Shelley's
view of Nature that was stimulated by his appreciation of Italian
poetry:

> On the beach of a northern sea
> Which tempests shake eternally,
> As once the wretch there lay to sleep,
> Lies a solitary heap,
> One white skull and seven dry bones,
> On the margin of the stones,
> Where a few gray rushes stand,
> Boundaries of the sea and land.[12]

An English poet, recalling Cleopatra on her barge or the back-
grounds of Macbeth's castle, will find Dante touching a few significant points of stress, giving the essential scene without the packed
richness that we appreciate not merely in Shakespeare, but in
nineteenth-century poets like Keats, Tennyson, early Browning, and
Hopkins. Eliot expresses astonishment that so much can be created
with so few touches, and clearly he is trying to be equally selective
in the Dantesque passage of *Little Gidding,* as he reduces to its
essence this early morning after an air raid:

> While the dead leaves still rattled on like tin
>
> Over the asphalt where no other sound was
> Between three districts whence the smoke arose
> I met one walking, loitering and hurried
>
> As if blown toward me like the metal leaves
> Before the urban dawn wind unresisting.

Similarly, there is a selective, representative quality about the images
by which Shelley describes the public way with its hurrying stream
of people, or the waning victims of Life's Triumph:

> Numerous as gnats upon the evening gleam;

> borne amid the crowd, as through the sky
> One of the million leaves of summer's bier;
>
>   each one
> Of that great crowd sent forth incessantly
> These shadows, numerous as the dead leaves blown
> In autumn evening from a poplar tree.

Some of the family resemblance comes from Dante's familiar leaves ("numerous" suggests Milton's "leaves in Vallombroso" as well), but part from the lack of figurative compression. Eliot and Shelley are not, in these passages, struggling to load every rift with ore. The similes will not be crowded off the stage by their eager successors. A very effective example of the leisurely, representative image (not figurative this time) occurs in *Prometheus Unbound,* when the Spirit of the Earth describes the effect of the millennium on Nature or on man's perception of Nature:

>   and when the dawn
> Came, wouldst thou think that toads, and snakes, and efts
> Could e'er be beautiful? yet so they were,
> And that with little change of shape or hue;
> All things had put their evil nature off;
> I cannot tell my joy, when o'er a lake,
> Upon a drooping bough with nightshade twined,
> I saw two azure halcyons clinging downward
> And thinning one bright bunch of amber berries
> With quick long beaks, and in the deep there lay
> Those lovely forms imaged as in a sky. . . .   (III.IV.73–83)

I have drawn attention to the similes in *The Triumph of Life.* Italian poetry no doubt contributed to Shelley's increasing fondness for them, although we must not underestimate the influence of Milton and Homer. If in the Shakespeare pole of modern poetry the key figure is the metaphor, in the Dante pole it is the simile, which is more continuous and exhaustive than the metaphor with its sudden, glancing blows, and which is much less uncompromising in the assertion of figurative identity:

> As sheep come from the fold where they were penned
> By one, by two, by three; and, eye and nose
> Keeping to earth, timid the others stand;
>
> And what the first one does the other does,
> All simple and quiet in their ignorance,
> And, if she stand still, huddle to her close;
>
> So I beheld now moving to advance
> Toward us, the leader of that happy flock,
> With stately gait and modest countenance.[13]

Even when Dante uses more than one, as in the starling and crane
figures of the *Inferno,* canto five, they do not rush or dart. The following similes from *The Triumph of Life,* though more successive
than is characteristic of Dante, have a similar even tone:

> And, as I gazed, methought that in the way
> The throng grew wilder, as the woods of June
> When the south wind shakes the extinguished day;
>
> And a cold glare, intenser than the noon
> But icy cold, obscured with blinding light
> The sun, as he the stars. Like the young moon,
>
> When on the sunlit limits of the night
> Her white shell trembles amid crimson air,
> And, whilst the sleeping tempest gathers might,
>
> Doth, as the herald of its coming, bear
> The ghost of its dead mother, whose dim form
> Bends in dark ether from her mother's chair;—
>
> So came a chariot on the silent storm
> Of its own rushing splendour; and a Shape
> . . . sat within. . . .   (74–88)

Sustained in a different way is one of the most remarkable similes
in *Prometheus Unbound.* Here the comparison is made to move
both ways. The first part of *A* is compared to the first part of *B,*
which continues to its second part and is then compared back to
the second part of *A:*

> Hark! the rushing snow!
> The sun-awakened avalanche! whose mass,
> Thrice sifted by the storm, had gathered there
> Flake after flake, in heaven-defying minds
> As thought by thought is piled, till some great truth
> Is loosened, and the nations echo round,
> Shaken to their roots, as do the mountains now.   (II.iii.36–42)

One of Shelley's claims to our attention, then, is his reflection in English of the Dante pole of modern poetry, as the "one English poet of the nineteenth century who could even have begun to follow in those footsteps." What Shakespeare's stature and influence obscure for the modern reader of English poetry, Shelley at least partly preserves, as an Italianate Englishman like Rossetti hardly does. But, although this preservation is the most obvious result of Shelley's cosmopolitanism, that cosmopolitanism extends well beyond it and is itself only one facet of his enterprising and experimental approach to his craft, his awareness of the possible virtues of a wide variety of styles. He is not an easy poet to identify in casual quotations. From "the tender and solemn enthusiasm" which Shelley saw in Petrarch and reproduced in the last section of *Adonais,* he can move to such things as the urbane melancholy of *Lines Written in the Bay of Lerici:*

> And the fisher with his lamp
> And spear about the low rocks damp
> Crept, and struck the fish which came
> To worship the delusive flame.
> Too happy they, whose pleasure sought
> Extinguishes all sense and thought
> Of the regret that pleasure leaves,
> Destroying life alone, not peace!

or the arbitrary fancy of the *Letter to Maria Gisborne,* with its many quotable *aperçus:*

> As water does a sponge, so the moonlight
> Fills the void, hollow, universal air;

>   his fine wit
>   Makes such a wound, the knife is lost in it;
>
>   The self-impelling steam-wheels of the mind;
>
>   Coleridge—he who sits obscure
>   In the exceeding lustre and the pure
>   Intense irradiation of a mind,
>   Which, with its own internal lightning blind,
>   Flags wearily through darkness and despair;

or the mingled architecture and nature (discussed in Chapter Four)
of a passage like this from the *Ode to Naples:*

>   Through white columns glowed
>   The isle-sustaining Ocean-flood,
>   A plane of light between two Heavens of azure:
>   Around me gleamed many a bright sepulchre
>   Of whose pure beauty, Time, as if his pleasure
>   Were to spare Death, had never made erasure;
>   But every living lineament was clear
>   As in the sculptor's thought; and there
>   The wreaths of stony myrtle, ivy and pine,
>   Like winter leaves o'ergrown by moulded snow,
>   Seemed only not to move and grow
>   Because the crystal silence of the air
>   Weighed on their life;

or his perceptive criticism of Wordsworth in *Peter Bell the Third,*
which Arnold diluted in his *Memorial Verses:*

>   But Peter's verse was clear, and came
>   Announcing from the frozen hearth
>   Of a cold age, that none might tame
>   The soul of that diviner flame
>   It augured to the Earth;
>
>   Like gentle rains, on the dry plains,
>   Making that green which late was grey,
>   Or like the sudden moon, that stains
>   Some gloomy chamber's window panes
>   With a broad light like day;   (V.xiii, xiv)

or a stanza which alone could have made the reputation of Walter de la Mare, and seems to me worth the whole of *Alastor:*

> Some say when nights are dry and clear,
>   And the death-dews sleep on the morass,
> Sweet whispers are heard by the traveler
>   Which make night day;
> And a silver shape like his early love doth pass,
>   Upborne by her wild and glittering hair,
> And, when he wakes on the fragrant grass,
>   He finds night day;

or the firm, vigorous rhetoric (Biblical and Miltonic) of this passage from the *Ode to Naples:*

> Hear ye the march as of the Earth-born Forms
>   Arrayed against the ever-living Gods? . . .
> Dissonant threats kill Silence far away,
>   The serene Heaven which wraps our Eden wide
>   With iron light is dyed,
> The Anarchs of the North lead forth their legions
>   Like Chaos o'er creation, uncreating;
> An hundred tribes nourished on strange religions
> And lawless slaveries,—down the aerial regions
>   Of the white Alps, desolating,
>   Famished wolves that bide no waiting,
> Blotting the glowing footsteps of old glory,
> Trampling our columned cities into dust,
>   Their dull and savage lust
>   On Beauty's corse to sickness satiating—
> They come!

Although Shelley is a minor poet, one of the things he shares with most major poets is the range of his available styles, the many sorts of poem he is capable of writing.

Shelley also claims our attention because he exemplifies with such thoroughness a significant theory of poetry. His later poetry takes the Platonic side of his aesthetics seriously. There have been many poets who admired Plato or the Platonists, but in most of them

Christianity has obscured the problems of a Platonic aesthetic, and
in none have its practical implications been exemplified so clearly.
If, like John Crowe Ransom, you believe a Platonic aesthetic to be
self-defeating and futile,[14] you can watch it defeating itself in the
substance and technique of Shelley's poetry, as the unknown is
defined in terms of the inadequate:

> What thou art we know not;
>   What is most like thee?
> From rainbow clouds there flow not
>   Drops so bright to see
> As from thy presence showers forth a rain of melody.

From this point of view, Shelley's finest poetry becomes its own
reductio ad absurdum and makes it unnecessary for anyone to make
the demonstration again—a brilliant and perverse *tour de force,* with
its special, if negative, interest for the regenerate. We have already
looked at some of Shelley's similes from *The Triumph of Life.*
From the same poem here is an extreme example of imageless truth
calling to its aid a series of similes, each pulling another in its
wake:

> I rose; and, bending at her sweet command,
> Touched with faint lips the cup she raised,
> And suddenly my brain became as sand
>
> Where the first wave had more than half erased
> The track of deer on desert Labrador,
> Whilst the wolf, from which they fled amazed,
>
> Leaves his stamp visibly upon the shore
> Until the second bursts;—so on my sight
> Burst a new Vision, never seen before,
>
> And the fair Shape waned in the coming light,
> As veil by veil the silent splendour drops
> From Lucifer, amid the chrysolite
>
> Of sunrise, ere it tinge the mountain tops;
> And as the presence of that fairest planet,
> Although unseen, is felt by one who hopes

That his day's path may end, as he began it,
In that star's smile whose light is like the scent
Of a jonquil when evening breezes fan it,

Or the soft note in which his dear lament
The Brescian shepherd breathes, or the caress
That turned his weary slumber to content,—

So knew I in that light's severe excess
The presence of that Shape which on the stream
Moved, as I moved along the wilderness,

More dimly than a day-appearing dream,
The ghost of a forgotten form of sleep,
A light of heaven whose half-extinguished beam

Through the sick day in which we wake to weep,
Glimmers, forever sought, forever lost;
So did that Shape its obscure tenor keep

Beside my path, as silent as a ghost.   (403–33)

In this passage Shelley is trying to represent the relation between
two visions; more specifically, between two kinds of light, one
whose source is beyond the world of generation, and one whose
source is the chariot of life itself. The "Shape all light" who offers
him the cup competes with the "severe excess" of the light which
succeeds it. The similes show us what in Wordsworth's terms would
be the relation between the "glory" and the "light of common day."
The moment when the cup touches the speaker's lips is the moment
when this relation begins, perhaps the moment of birth itself.

The first simile sees the visions as footprints on the sand of
consciousness. Shelley liked this sand figure, and uses it effectively
in *The Sensitive Plant* to describe the sleep of an unfallen garden:

an ocean of dreams without a sound,
Whose waves never mark, though they ever impress
The light sand which paves it, consciousness.   (I.103–5)

In a fragment first printed by W. M. Rossetti, we have fierce beasts,
tracks in the sand and a magic drink:

> The fierce beasts of the woods and wildernesses
> Track not the steps of him who drinks of it;
> For the light breezes, which forever fleet
> Around its margin, heap the sand thereon;

but here the erasing agent is the wind, and, in any case, this rude sketch could hardly prepare us for the full-blown simile when it finally comes, with its half-erased deer-prints and new-pressed wolf-prints on the sand of the brain.

The second simile stresses the object rather than the subject, the visions themselves rather than the mind which receives their impress. The figure by which Shelley represents the relation of the two lights is again a favorite of his. He was fascinated by the balance of the dawn and its mingling of sunlight and moonlight, by the moment at which a light still felt to be there becomes in fact invisible, extinguished by the light that has succeeded it.

> The point of one white star is quivering still
> Deep in the orange light of widening morn;
>
>   .   .   .   .
>
> now it wanes; it gleams again;
>
>   .   .   .   .
>
> 'Tis lost!   (II.1.17–18, 21, 24)

Even more familiar than these lines from *Prometheus Unbound* is the stanza from *To a Skylark* which T. S. Eliot found so difficult to visualize. He might have had even more trouble if he had quoted the previous line and recognized that Shelley is trying to express the supersonic in terms of the superluminous:

> Thou art unseen,—but yet I hear thy shrill delight,
>
>   Keen as are the arrows
>   Of that silver sphere
>   Whose intense lamp narrows
>   In the white dawn clear
> Until we hardly see—we feel that it is there.

In *The Triumph of Life* this figure begins well—

> As veil by veil the silent splendour drops
> From Lucifer, amid the chrysolite
> Of sunrise

—but continues with gradually decreasing vitality until with the Brescian shepherd it has reached bottom. But when the principal clause appears, the vitality returns with it and continues to the end of the sentence.

Whereas the first part of the sentence mainly consists of two long similes, the last part consists of a series of short ones, each intended to define the indefinable presence of the "Shape all light." Whereas the first long simile defines it in terms of footprints in the sand and the second in terms of competing lights, this next series defines it mainly in terms of dream-memory, obscure survivals in the mind. The figurative process gains momentum as it moves; the rhythm of its syntax speeds up. The first simile is single and interwoven. The second breaks up into four parts joined by "or." The third simile is a series of figures, reinforced by the neat parallel structure of its syntax and the equivalent regularity of its versification. The final principal clause carries in its wake a single, brief, commonplace simile, "as silent as a ghost," and the sentence is over. Shelley did not live to revise this passage, and I, for one, would be happier without a number of things: the Brescian shepherd, whose "soft note" and puzzling "caress" break down the order of Shelley's second simile; the weak repetition of "ghost"; and the "light of heaven," which is made superfluous by the planetary simile which has preceded it; but the breadth and richness of the passage make it a forceful illustration of my point. Thus (for the anti-Platonist) we observe the self-defeating struggles of a Platonic aesthetic.

On the other hand, even if you are not a Platonist (as I certainly am not) you may still find the consequences of the Platonic aesthetic something less than absurd. To be sure, if a poem is by nature integral and self-contained, if a poem is indivisible, then there is very little to be said for the Platonic ills which *Epipsychidion* or *The Triumph of Life* or the *Skylark* have let themselves fall heir to. But, if we assume anything less than such integration, we also assume that at some point in the poetic process and in the poem itself "falls the Shadow." "The mind in creation is as a fading coal which some invisible influence, like an inconstant wind, awakens to transitory brightness" (C.294), says Shelley, giving us an aesthetic equivalent to the doctrine of preexistence. But the presence of "the Shadow" may be explained in terms less Platonic and more secular, even more Christian. If a poem is a symbol of an act of will, its incomplete integration is assured both by the unfinality of the private will or its acts and by the partial unfitness of any symbol for the thing symbolized. After all, the poet is not a priest; the marriage of form and content, although not just a marriage of convenience, is not a sacrament, and the critic must be as careful to avoid the one conception as the other. Here the Christian (who will, however, see the poem as capable of serving a unity which it cannot possess) and the secularist can come to a working agreement. In Shelley's poetry the struggle of form and content, which is as important as their cooperation, stands out in relief, as it does in no other poet of comparable talents.

At the same time, I am far from contending that Shelley's Platonism was an unmixed blessing. Although his voluntaristic radicalism, his belief in the two-way relation between individual degeneration or regeneration and social action or institutions, is never wholly obscured, it is somewhat devitalized by the passivity which follows from an increasing emphasis on the temporal cycle and on an otherworldly goal attainable only through death. Shelley's development was not entirely from folly to wisdom, as those who equate wisdom with a pessimistic awareness of inescapable human limitations might lead us to believe. Indeed, more "highly wrought" (J.X.270) as it undoubtedly is, *Adonais* seems to me in some ways less mature than *Prometheus Unbound*. In *Prometheus Unbound* there was something to do; and I mean not only to perfect the will by casting out hate, self-contempt, and despair, by returning good for evil, and by maintaining an independent and resolute will in the face of persecution; but also (it is surely implied) by such political action as time, power, and opportunity permit. In *Adonais* there is nothing for the mourners to do but wait until death shatters the many-colored dome. The ethical will has shrunk to insignificance. Keats did not slay the unpastured dragon, and the mourners are not being prepared for the role of St. George. Nor are they asked to prepare themselves for the burning fountain by slaying the old Adam (or perhaps the self-love of the *philosophes*) in themselves. Shelley had written of the Spaniards,

> Glory, glory, glory,
> To those who have greatly suffered and done!
> Never name in story
> Was greater than that which ye shall have won.
> Conquerors have conquered their foes alone,
> Whose revenge, pride, and power, they have overthrown.
> Ride ye, more victorious, over your own.[15]

No such ethical imperative is given the mourners, the elect of a Platonic heaven.

But *Adonais,* as a poem about death, is an extreme case. In *Ode to the West Wind* and *To a Skylark* the seasonal determinism or the Platonic idealism does not dehumanize the poem. The *Ode* gives an equally powerful impression of both free will and determinism, Prometheus and Demogorgon. Nature, history, art, and the human will work together under the influence of prophetic inspiration. Although the West Wind is to carry the poet's words as it carries a leaf, a cloud, and a wave, the poet, unlike these natural objects, wills his own passivity in a series of active imperatives, and so wills the cycle which absorbs him:

> Be thou, Spirit fierce,
> My spirit! Be thou me, impetuous one!

> Drive my dead thoughts over the universe
> Like withered leaves to quicken a new birth!
> And, by the incantation of this verse,
>
> Scatter, as from an unextinguished hearth
> Ashes and sparks, my words among mankind!
> Be through my lips to unawakened earth
>
> The trumpet of a prophecy! O wind,
> If Winter comes, can Spring be far behind?

In the end the natural cycle itself seems to hinge on the answer to a question.

But Shelley's Platonism combines with his radicalism to cause what many will regard as an even more serious flaw than his Platonic aesthetics or than the negative ethics of *Adonais* (although it is related to both). What Keats would have missed (and the Christian apologist of today does miss) is any sense of the function of evil. Although Prometheus tells us at the moment of regeneration that misery has made him wise, Shelley does not stress the point. He believed that such "acceptance" could cause, at its best, complacence ("And yet they know not that they do not dare" [16]) and, at its worst, the love of evil (as in Count Cenci). Moreover, he was closer than we to the theodicies of the eighteenth century, continually educing real good out of apparent evil. "The uses of adversity" would have a familiar, hollow ring, particularly after Malthus. Shelley counteracted what seemed to him a pernicious trend by insisting that "Suffering makes suffering, ill must follow ill," [17] or "force from force must ever flow." [18] Demogorgon is not Providence. In the natural realm, winter can not produce spring, it can only delay it; like Proserpina, spring simply departs and returns, in a cycle that is more a mechanical arrangement than an organic process. Within the destroyed world are preserved the indestructible seeds of a future new birth. But the destruction does not generate the new birth. At best it provides a winter covering and some quickening fertilizer. The Destroyer may clear away the dead rubbish, it may preserve the living seeds; but Destroyer and

Preserver do not become Creator. In the political realm, despotism leads to revolution, which in turn leads to counterrevolution and more despotism. In the moral realm, Cenci's violation of Beatrice does not refine her soul. Shelley's natural, moral, and political universe contains, therefore, a Heaven and Hell, but no Purgatory. I restrict the statement to "natural, moral, and political" because what Shelley thought it salutary to deny as moralist he allowed some entry as aesthetician. Pan (although not Apollo) can sing songs whose "secret alchemy turns to potable gold the poisonous waters which flow from death through life" (C.295). The poet (although not the moralist) can say:

> Make me thy lyre, even as the forest is:
> What if my leaves are falling like its own!
> The tumult of thy mighty harmonies
>
> Will take from both a deep, autumnal tone
> Sweet though in sadness.

In the Preface to *The Cenci* Shelley says, "Imagination is as the immortal God which should assume flesh for the redemption of mortal passion." In context the statement does not seem significant, and Shelley did not take the idea of "Incarnation" very seriously. But it suggests a position that Shelley approaches at moments and which the critic might well approach if he wishes to understand what Shelley has to offer: that the created poem is the purgatory of the imagination.[19]

It is the *Ode to the West Wind* which seems best able to throw "a bridge over the stream of time" which separates us from Shelley's Regency verse. And it is in terms of this poem that R. S. Thomas has written his fine *Song at the Year's Turning,* exemplifying for me the kind of sympathetic yet exacting consideration with which Shelley deserves to be recalled by the modern reader:

> Shelley dreamed it. Now the dream decays.
> The props crumble. The familiar ways
> Are stale with tears trodden underfoot.

The heart's flower withers at the root.
Bury it, then, in history's sterile dust.
The slow years shall tame your tawny lust.

Love deceived him; what is there to say
The mind brought you by a better way
To this despair? Lost in the world's wood
You cannot stanch the bright menstrual blood.
The earth sickens; under naked boughs
The frost comes to barb your broken vows.

Is there blessing? Light's peculiar grace
In cold splendour robes this tortured place
For strange marriage. Voices in the wind
Weave a garland where a mortal sinned.
Winter rots you; who is there to blame?
The new grass shall purge you in its flame.[20]

NOTES

Notes to Prologue

1. See the forum entitled "Reading Shelley" in *Essays in Criticism*, IV (1954), 87-103, for conflicting opinions on this supposed deficiency.
2. Roe, *Shelley: the Last Phase*, p. 16. Shelley's remarks are quoted by Roe on p. 15.
3. *Ibid.*, p. 37.
4. See White, *Shelley*, II, 55.
5. Elton, *Shelley*, pp. 11, 65. It should be emphasized, in fairness, that Elton is explicitly restricting these last generalizations to Shelley's lyricism. On his narrative and dramatic talents Elton has different things to say.
6. Norman, *Flight of the Skylark*, p. 98.
7. Morpurgo, ed., *The Last Days of Shelley and Byron*, p. 52.
8. The reference for all quotations in this paragraph is C.304.
9. See, for example, Rogers, *Shelley at Work*, which appeared too late for me to make any appropriate use of it in this study.
10. Shelley-Rolls and Ingpen, eds., *Verse and Prose*, pp. xi, xii.
11. Morpurgo, ed., *The Last Days of Byron and Shelley*, p. 50.
12. On such differences of opinion, see Shelley's remarks to his wife: "We talked a great deal of poetry and such matters last night; and as usual differed and I think more than ever. He affects to patronise a system of criticism fit for the production of mediocrity" (J.X.297).
13. Peck, *Shelley: His Life and Work*, II, 423-24.
14. *Ibid.*, II, 424.
15. *Ibid.*, pp. 424-25.
16. Farrer, *A Rebirth of Images*, p. 304.

E. C. Pettet, in *On the Poetry of Keats*, p. 291, also supposes that Keats is the exception to a Romantic rule that poets, although "they occasionally philosophized generally about poetry, by and large . . .

did not think much about its technique, nor, rating inspiration and rapture so highly, were they fond of the arduous labour of revision." Wordsworth certainly was not fond of revision (who is? although, if you are a Thomas Gray, you may prefer the labor of revising an old poem to the greater labor of writing a new one), but he still took forty-five years to revise *The Prelude*, for better and for worse. And Keats's self-criticism can hardly be documented any better than Shelley's. I suspect that persistent revision (which is not necessarily a virtue) is, if anything, more characteristic of English Romanticism than of English neoclassicism. The Romantic poet who best fills Mr. Pettet's generalization is Byron (although the variorum edition of *Don Juan* may make even him seem a doubtful candidate). But, of all the Romantics, Byron was most fond of separating himself from his great contemporaries.

17. Ridley, *Keats' Craftsmanship*, pp. 13–14.

18. Rogers uses this statement as a text to begin his enquiry in *Shelley at Work*, p. 1.

19. I am not, of course, forgetting that Keats's manuscripts give evidence of a good deal of substitution. But these seem to indicate not so much a careful revision, after the fervors of imagination had subsided, as a renewal of the original creative act brought on by the process of copying or proofreading. Keats recreated rather than revised, and in his remark to Woodhouse refuses to divide the poetic act into a series of acts performed by separable faculties. See also Ridley's remarks in *Keats' Craftsmanship*, pp. 14–16.

20. Coleridge, *Biographia Literaria and Two Lay Sermons*, pp. 177, 150.

21. Greene, " 'Logical Structure' in Eighteenth-Century Poetry," *Philological Quarterly*, XXXI (1952), 315–36.

22. *Ibid.*, p. 336.

23. Eliot, *Selected Essays*, p. 283.

24. In 1817, for example, describing the dangers of an open franchise, Shelley speaks of "men who have been rendered brutal and torpid and ferocious by ages of slavery" (Clark, *Shelley's Prose*, p. 162).

25. Jones, *The Letters of Mary W. Shelley*, I, p. 50.

26. See Pottle, "The Case of Shelley," *PMLA*, LXVII (1952), 606–7.

27. See Chapter Six, pp. 218–230.

28. See Fogle, *The Imagery of Keats and Shelley*, pp. 258–64. I disagree with Mr. Fogle on a few details, but his account of the poem is the best I have come across.

29. See Pottle's footnote in "The Case of Shelley," pp. 607–8, for an effective rejoinder to Tate's criticism of the last stanza.

30. *Proserpine and Midas,* ed. by Koszul, p. 50.

31. *Ibid.,* p. 56.

32. Fogle, *The Imagery of Keats and Shelley,* p. 59.

Notes to I: Lyrical Drama

1. Tovey, *Essays in Musical Analysis,* III, 93.

2. Kitto, *Greek Tragedy,* pp. 66–67.

3. Sophocles, *Oedipus at Colonus,* I.45. My quotation is from Jebb's translation.

4. Adams, "Unity of Plot in the *Oedipus Coloneus,*" *Phoenix,* VII (1953), 139.

5. Tillyard, *Shakespeare's History Plays,* pp. 268–69. Tillyard's comparison of *Henry IV* to *The Tempest* is relevant to my next paragraph.

6. In *Henry IV, Part Two,* the dialogue between Hal and Poins (II.ii) has a similar function.

7. "The dramatic life of the poem is secondary, and . . . at any moment the lyrical and musical life may take charge and impose a logic of its own. . . . Neither Faust nor any of the characters in this work are sufficiently individualized to admit of real development. . . . Faust . . . is an instrument in Goethe's orchestra. . . . He must go on voicing the invincible aspiration of the human spirit to master the universe, much as the trombone player goes on playing his trombone. He does this from first to last; there is no change, and no change of this sort should be looked for." Fairley, *Goethe as Revealed in His Poetry,* pp. 94–95.

8. Pulos, *The Deep Truth, passim.*

9. His treatment of immortality provides the most obvious example. But see also Shelley's comment on the myth of a Saturnian age in his *Essay on Christianity* (Clark, *Shelley's Prose,* p. 211) and compare it with his treatment of the same myth in *Prometheus Unbound,* II.iv.32–38.

10. Clark, *Shelley's Prose,* p. 33.

11. I am open to legitimate criticism for using the word "Platonic" to identify this particular world of Shelley's, and I have considered "Orphic" or even "Pythagorean" as an alternative. We should, no doubt, deplore the indiscriminate use of "Platonic" as a synonym for "sharply

dualistic," and an essay like F. H. Anderson's "Plato's Aesthetics Reconsidered" is a salutary corrective. According to Anderson's account, "beauty . . . as an object of perception and desire . . . is attained by man through a love which ranges unbroken from the human to the divine. When Plato in his "myths" describes this love as the operation of the semi-divinity Eros and depicts the life of beauty as a choral ritual in which the gods do and men may, on joining this, festively behold and feed upon realities, he is not introducing discontinuity between divine things and those of nature and art but—after the fashion of his contemporaries—bringing the two into co-ordination." *University of Toronto Quarterly,* XXV (1956), 426.

But I am retaining the term. Shelley himself, whatever our own reservations may be, would, I think, have found "Platonic" (more than any conceivable alternative) appropriate to the world described above, although he would hardly have supposed that world an adequate representation of Plato's own. Shelley's favorite Platonic dialogues were the *Republic, Symposium,* and *Phaedo;* if my term "Platonic" is to apply to any particular Plato, it is surely to that of the *Phaedo.*

Notes to II: Regeneration

1. *Julian and Maddalo,* 11.210–11.
2. For Shelley it is possible to know the truth and not act accordingly. But Godwin never allows the operation of a separable will, undetermined by the opinions of its possessor. In Book I of *Political Justice* he spends all of Chapter Five proving that "the Voluntary Actions of Men Originate in their Opinions":

"If we entertain false views and be involved in pernicious mistakes, this disadvantage is not the offspring of an irresistible destiny. We have been ignorant, we have been hasty, or we have been misled. Remove the causes of this ignorance or this miscalculation, and the effects will cease. . . .

"It would . . . be absurd, if we regard truth in relation to its empire over our conduct, to suppose that it is not limited in its operation by the faculties of our frame. . . . But, within these limits, the deduction which forms the principal substance of this chapter, proves to us, that whatever is brought home to the conviction of the understanding, so long as it is present to the mind, possesses an undisputed empire over the conduct." *Enquiry concerning Political Justice,* ed. by Priestley, I, 45, 91–92.

The Socrates of the *Gorgias* would have recognized the arguments by which Godwin shows that the nature of our conduct follows from the nature of our opinions. But both Plato and Godwin include so much of man in his mind that their difference from Shelley is, in part, only an apparent difference. Since for Plato true knowledge is the goal of an erotic pursuit (see Anderson, "Plato's Aesthetics Reconsidered," pp. 433–35), and since for Godwin to grasp truth is to be passionately convinced that it must prevail, they would hardly have found in Shelley's "knowledge" all that the term includes for them. Nevertheless, by allowing a separable will, capable of corruption and in need of stimulation by the imagination, Shelley does differ from Plato and Godwin. Unlike them, Shelley would have recognized what Shaw has John Tanner say in the *Revolutionist's Handbook:*

"Men like Ruskin and Carlyle will preach to Smith and Brown for the sake of preaching, just as St. Francis preached to the birds and St. Anthony to the fishes. But Smith and Brown, like the fishes and birds, remain as they are; and poets who plan Utopias and prove that Man should will them, perceive at last, like Richard Wagner, that the fact to be faced is that Man does not effectively will them. . . . What can be said as yet except that where there is a will, there is a way? If there be no will, we are lost." *Man and Superman,* pp. 264–65.

Indeed, the dialogue between Don Juan and the Devil in this same play is simply *Julian and Maddalo* writ large, and we do not have to be over-subtle to be struck by the fact that the whole play is about discovering the meaning of a will. Shelley and Shaw, although not Christians, are a part of the Pauline-Augustinian tradition, as Plato and Godwin are not. Theologically, they would be called voluntarists not intellectualists.

Of course, any discussion of Shelley's relation to Plato and Godwin is complicated by the still prevalent habit of setting up the two of them as opposite poles and depicting Shelley as faced with a sort of morality-play choice between them. For a spectator of this play, since the influence of Plato apparently increases as Shelley grows older, the influence of Godwin must inevitably decline. But, in fact, Godwin's influence remains strong to the end. Even Godwinian Necessity, despite some unlikely companions, reappears in *The Triumph of Life.* But there is no need to go to the other extreme and deny the reality of Shelley's Platonism itself. Priestley's insistence on Godwin's own Platonism should, if noted, prevent Shelley's critics from providing him with imaginary dilemmas (see Priestley, "Platonism and Godwin's *Political Justice*," *Modern Language Quarterly*, IV (1943), 63–69, and the discussion of Shelley and Godwin in the introduction to his edition of the *Enquiry concerning Political Justice*, III, 108–12).

3. Baker, *Shelley's Major Poetry*, p. 97.

4. Cunningham, *Woe or Wonder*, pp. 121–23.

5. Eliot, *The Waste Land*, ll. 403–5.

6. The millennium itself, while its appearance is instantaneous, also allows some gradual moral (as well as intellectual) development. After his release from the Caucasian mountains, Prometheus imagines the arts which he contributes to man growing

> More fair and soft as man grows wise and kind,
> And, veil by veil, evil and error fall.   (III.iii.61–62)

7. My discussion of conversion and the millennium is made from a very restricted historical perspective. No doubt the tension between a momentary and a gradual view of the millennium is perennial, and the Jews of the Old Testament or the Fathers of the Church bear witness to it as much as do the Puritans of the seventeenth century or the prophets of the nineteenth. The nature of the tension depends on how close to the "end" of the world your historical predicament allows you to imagine yourself. See Tuveson, *Millennium and Utopia*, and, for the Puritan Millennarians, Barker, *Milton and the Puritan Dilemma*, *passim*.

8. Woodberry, *The Complete Poetical Works of Shelley*, p. 622.

9. "I believe we have here a deliberate throwback to a magic ritual out of which tragedy grew, a ritual in which words are potent—helpful or injurious or capable of different meanings. . . . It seems hardly necessary to remark that every Greek knew, or had heard, that words could *do* things; and even if by the time of Aeschylus this belief in the magic power of words had lost some of its savor as one of the practical features of life, it had an honorable tradition, and might well be material for a poet who proposed to treat of the mystic early warfare of gods." Adams, "The Four Elements in the *Prometheus Vinctus*," *Classical Philology*, XXVIII (1933), 100.

10. Baker, *Shelley's Major Poetry*, p. 97.

11. Clark's footnote points out the derivation from Paine. The word "depravity," however, is Shelley's contribution.

12. *Ode to Liberty*, ll. 241–45.

13. *Paradise Lost,* I.157–58.

14. See the discussion of *The Tower of Famine* above.

15. *Lines Written among the Euganean Hills,* ll. 231–35.

16. See also Cythna's description of

> Necessity, whose sightless strength forever
> Evil with evil, good with good, must wind
> In bands of union, which no power may sever,
> They must bring forth their kind, and be divided never!

(IX.xxvii)

17. The full title of the poem is *An Ode Written October, 1819, before the Spaniards Had Recovered Their Liberty.*

18. According to Shelley, "man in his wildest state is a social being" (C.219).

Notes to III: Temptations

1. Eliot, *Murder in the Cathedral,* p. 24.

2. In *The Platonism of Shelley,* p. 227. Notopoulos points out that the most likely Platonic source for this conception is Book III of the *Republic:*
"For we would not have our guardians reared among images of evil as in a foul pasture, and there day by day and little by little gather many impressions from all that surrounds them, taking them all in until at last a great mass of evil gathers in their inmost souls, and they know it not. . . . Is it not a further reason for musical education that he who has been rightly trained in music would be quick to observe all works of art that were defective and ugly, and all natural objects that failed in beauty? They would displease him, and rightly; but beautiful things he would praise, and receiving them with joy into his soul, would be nourished by them and become noble and good." *Republic,* trans. by Lindsay, pp. 84–85.

But Notopoulos also relates Shelley's phrasing to a sentence in Paine's *Rights of Man:* "It is the faculty of the human mind to become what it contemplates, and to act in accordance with its object." Readers of Blake will recall his especial fondness for figures who become what they behold. Indeed, in Plate 36 of *Jerusalem,* the phrase "became what they beheld" occurs four times. At the end of Night the Fourth of *The Four Zoas,* Los himself,

> terrified at the shapes
> Enslaved humanity put on, . . . became what he beheld:

He became what he was doing: he was himself transformed.

> *Poetry and Prose of William Blake,* ed. by Keynes, p. 293

Prometheus would certainly have understood what is happening to Los. So, I suspect would Coleridge. In the note on Entry 189 in the first volume of her edition of *The Notebooks of Samuel Taylor Coleridge,* Miss Kathleen Coburn mentions Coleridge's interest in this process and quotes from the *Statesman's Manual:* "That which intuitively it [the Soul] at once beholds and adores, praying always, and rejoicing always— *that* doth it tend to become." As Miss Jay Macpherson has pointed out to me, the most important poetic model for degradation by such a process would be the transformation of the fallen angels in *Paradise Lost:*

> horror on them fell,
> And horrid sympathy; for what they saw,
> They felt themselves now changing. (X.539–41)

However, in Milton it is by no means clear that the beholding leads to the becoming.

3. Clutton-Brock, *Shelley the Man and the Poet,* p. 203.

4. Notopoulos, "Shelley's 'Disinterested Love' and Aristotle," *Philological Quarterly,* xxxii (1953), 216–17.

5. Hoffman, in *An Odyssey of the Soul: Shelley's Alastor,* interprets the poem as a study of self-destructive narcissism. For further comments on *Alastor,* particularly its Preface, see Chapter Six.

6. According to Notopoulos, *The Platonism of Shelley,* p. 263, "unremembered world" is "an allusion to Plato's doctrine of the pre-existence of the soul." But Cenci is not a Platonist.

7. Eliot, *Selected Essays,* p. 377.

8. Bates, *A Study of Shelley's Drama The Cenci,* p. 55.

9. Medwin, *The Life of Percy Bysshe Shelley,* p. 256.

10. Baker, *Shelley's Major Poetry,* p. 150.

11. See Baker, *Shelley's Major Poetry,* p. 150.

12. See Shelley's comment to Peacock on a Crucifixion by Guido which he saw at Bologna in November, 1818: "There was a Xt Crucified by the same very fine. One gets tired indeed whatever may be the conception and execution of it of seeing that monotonous and agonized form for ever exhibited in one prescriptive attitude of torture" (J. IX.343–44).

13. See Cameron, "The Political Symbolism of *Prometheus Unbound,*" *PMLA,* LVIII (1943), 734–35.

14. The former quotation is Godwinian in its minimizing of the

separable will (and in its use of the word "opinions"), while the latter is more characteristically Shelleyan. See Chapter Two, note 2.

15. This refrain occurs here for the first time since before Prometheus' conversion.

Notes to IV: Imagery

1. Spender, *Shelley*, p. 46.

2. Some of my remarks in this paragraph (including the example from Shakespeare) were suggested by Elder Olson's review of W. J. Bates's *The Stylistic Development of Keats* in *Modern Philology*, XLIV (1946), 196–200. See esp. p. 199.

3. Fogle, *The Imagery of Keats and Shelley*, p. 36.

4. Lehmann, ed., *Shelley in Italy*, p. 8.

5. *Stanzas, Written in Dejection, near Naples*, and *Ode to Naples*.

6. These particular words are actually addressed to Hogg.

7. An earlier version of this passage is addressed to the Gisbornes: "I take great delight in watching the changes of the atmosphere here, and the growth of the thunder showers with which the morn is often overshadowed, and which break and fade away towards evening into flocks of delicate clouds" (J.IX.312).

8. "The rapid flow of his swift-moving forms and essences is usually set in a motionless and solid frame. In that poem of his which most vividly conveys the feeling of fierce and breathless speed, the *Ode to the West Wind*, it is too seldom noticed that the wind moves beneath a solid dome within which the scene is enclosed." Fogle, *The Imagery of Keats and Shelley*, p. 55.

9. Fogle, *The Imagery of Keats and Shelley*, p. 47.

10. *Ibid.*, p. 48.

11. Such susceptibility is by no means unusual. Shelley shares the fondness of Romantics and Victorians for architecture in poetry. A good thesis (using such documents as *Jerusalem, Kubla Khan, Gebir, Thalaba, The Palace of Art*, and *Abt Vogler*) could be written under the title "From Golgonooza to Byzantium: the Palace of Art and the City of God in Nineteenth-Century Poetry."

12. Fogle, *The Imagery of Keats and Shelley*, p. 59.

13. See Oras, "The Multitudinous Orb: Some Miltonic Elements in Shelley," *Modern Language Quarterly*, XVI (1955), 247–57.

14. Grabo, *A Newton among Poets*, pp. 142–43.

15. By providing a new context for l. 482 of *Epipsychidion*, I distort its meaning somewhat.

16. *Among School Children.*

17. Spender, *Shelley*, p. 39.

18. See Priestley, "Newton and the Romantic Concept of Nature," *University of Toronto Quarterly*, XVII (1948), 323–36.

Notes to V: Demogorgon

1. See Grabo, *Prometheus Unbound, an Interpretation.*

2. See Cameron, "The Political Symbolism of *Prometheus Unbound*," *PMLA*, LVIII (1943), pp. 728–53.

3. Grabo, *Prometheus Unbound: an Interpretation*, p. 52.

4. Cameron, "The Political Symbolism of *Prometheus Unbound*," p. 740.

5. Todhunter, *A Study of Shelley*, pp. 138–39.

6. Baker, *Shelley's Major Poetry*, p. 103.

7. *Selected Poetry and Prose*, ed. by Cameron, p. 525.

8. Grabo, *Prometheus Unbound: an Interpretation*, p. 66.

9. *Prometheus Unbound*, ed. by Scudder, p. 151.

10. See Baker, *Shelley's Major Poetry*, p. 116 f. It would be pleasant to suppose that Shelley had seen Coleridge's lines,

> and shall some fated hour
> Be pulveriz'd by Demogorgon's power,

which were later included in the poem *Limbo*, but were first published in *The Friend* (collected edition, 1818).

11. Milton's phrase in *Paradise Lost* is "unessential Night" (II.439).

12. Pulos, *The Deep Truth*, p. 63.

13. *Ibid.*, pp. 65–66.

14. The last lines of Scene 3 might seem to assert the complete supremacy of Love.

> Such strength is in meekness
> That the Eternal, the Immortal,
> Must unloose through life's portal
> The snake-like Doom curled underneath his throne
> By that alone.

Here "meekness" is presented as capable of forcing Demogorgon to release "the snake-like Doom." This "Doom," however, is not the downfall of Jupiter, but the millennium which that downfall may lead to under the right auspices. When Demogorgon's law overthrows Jupiter, Love's strength is the only thing that can then force him also to release the millennium. This "strength" makes a brief appearance as Hercules in the next act.

15. Eliot, *Murder in the Cathedral,* p. 24.

16. This paragraph is indebted to Cameron, "The Political Symbolism of *Prometheus Unbound,*" pp. 746–47.

17. For Mary Shelley's interpretation see J.II.269.

Notes to VI: Sorrow

1. *The Letters of John Keats,* ed. by Forman, p. 336.

2. *Poets of the English Language,* ed. by Auden and Pearson, IV, xiii, xiv, xvi.

3. See note 2 on p. 306 above.

4. However, what Clark calls *A Treatise on Morals* may possibly be dated as early as 1815. Its statements on the function of the imagination (quoted above and below) certainly anticipate, if somewhat crudely, some of the pronouncements in *A Defence of Poetry.*

5. When Keats speaks of "the ballance of good and evil" (*The Letters of John Keats,* ed. by Forman, p. 144), he simply means "the balance of pleasure and pain."

6. Wordsworth, *The Excursion,* iv.1146–47.

7. *Martin Chuzzlewit,* Chapter xxviii.

8. Weeks, "Image and Idea in Yeats' *The Second Coming,*" PMLA LXIII (1948), 289–90. Weeks is thinking of the Fury's speech (I.625–29), not of Shelley's use of the opposition between center and circumference in Act Four. See Chapter Eight.

9. The best discussion of *Alastor* that I have seen is Hildebrand's *A Study of Alastor.* His emphasis on the Poet as "luminary" has left its traces on the foregoing pages.

10. The reference for all quotations from *On Love* is C.170.

11. See Gibson, *"Alastor:* a Reinterpretation," PMLA, XLII (1947), 1028–29.

12. Dowden, *The Life of Percy Bysshe Shelley,* II, p. 128.

Notes to VII: Chaos

1. For a commentary on this aspect of Act Three, made from a somewhat different point of view, see Kurtz, *The Pursuit of Death*, pp. 178–84.

2. I quote *Adonais*, XLIX, L, *The Sensitive Plant*, 220–23, and *Time*.

3. *Selected Poetry and Prose*, ed. by Cameron, p. 504.

4. *The Complete Poetical Works of Shelley*, ed. by Woodberry, p. 639.

5. The remaining quotations from *Hellas* are all from the final chorus.

6. See Medwin, *A Life of Percy Bysshe Shelley*, p. 251: "of all the Odes in our language, he most preferred Coleridge's on the French Revolution . . . , which he used to thunder out with marvellous energy."

7. Hungerford, *Shores of Darkness*, p. 197.

Notes to VIII: Time

1. Strictly speaking I should say the millennium and the new Jerusalem (or new heaven and earth), since St. John's Apocalypse includes the millennium as well as the new Jerusalem which succeeds it. But I use the word "apocalypse" in a semipopular sense to mean just the last stages in the apocalyptic sequence: the conquest of death (the second death, in St. John's terms), the advent of the new Jerusalem, and the revelation of its eternal forms.

2. Hungerford, *Shores of Darkness*, p. 192.

3. See Frye, *Fearful Symmetry*, p. 248.

4. See Grabo, *A Newton among Poets*, p. 160.

5. *Hellas*, ll. 746–47.

6. Yeats, *The Second Coming*.

7. As Miss Jay Macpherson has pointed out to me, there is a good deal of difference between a Time which contains Eternity and an Eternity which contains Time. The latter is apocalyptic and irrevocable, the former is millennial and fragile—an "infirm" Eternity.

8. For Strong's discussion of the veil figure, see *Three Studies in Shelley*, pp. 70–79.

9. *Milton*, Plate 26.

10. Wordsworth, *The Prelude* (1850), VI, ll. 600–2.

11. Eliot, *The Use of Poetry and the Use of Criticism*, pp. 92–93.

12. The italics are mine.

13. Baker, *Shelley's Major Poetry*, p. 234.

14. See also the conquest of Death by Love in ll. 405–7.

Notes to IX: Heaven

1. Wasserman, *"Adonais:* Progressive Revelation as a Poetic Mode," *Journal of English Literary History,* XXI (1954), 274–326.

2. See L. B. Campbell, "The Christian Muse," *Huntington Library Bulletin,* VIII (1935), 29–70, for Urania's Christian history.

3. Wasserman, *"Adonais,"* p. 318.

4. Norlin, "The Conventions of Pastoral Elegy," *American Journal of Philology,* XXXII (1911), 307–9. Mr. Norlin provides some of my examples, below.

5. *The Pastoral Elegy,* ed. by Harrison, p. 39.

6. *The Correspondence of William Cowper,* ed. by Wright, II, 146–47. I have corrected "when" to "were" in my fifth line.

7. Job 14.7–10.

8. *Correspondence of Cowper,* II, 146.

9. Nemesian, *Eclogue I,* in *The Pastoral Elegy,* ed. by Harrison, p. 54.

10. *Selected Poetry and Prose,* ed. by Cameron, p. 520.

11. Davie, "Shelley's Urbanity," in *Purity of Diction in English Verse.*

12. *Mutability* (1821).

13. *Jerusalem,* Plate 94.

14. "Ceremony after a Fire Raid," in *Collected Poems, 1934–1952,* p. 131.

Notes to X: Development

1. For the interesting suggestion that, from Jupiter's point of view, his child is the consolidation of tyranny by Malthusianism, see Pulos, "Shelley and Malthus," *PMLA,* LXVII (1952), 120–23.

2. The phrase is not entirely clear. Presumably Shelley is thinking of the feeling of vacancy which precedes the quest for love in the Preface to *Alastor* or in the essay *On Love.* But what the Witch's knowledge of love consists of and whether it causes or diminishes her loneliness is not obvious to me.

3. Wasserman, *"Adonais:* Progressive Revelation as a Poetic Mode," *Journal of English Literary History,* XXI (1954), 274–326.

4. See Rogers, *Shelley at Work,* pp. 58–63.

5. This is perhaps the place to comment on Shelley's handling of the release itself. Hercules is permitted to fulfill his traditional role as deliverer; but, stripped of its mythological details, the method of release simply demonstrates in a bare figure the "strength . . . in weakness" (II.III.94) of which we have had intimations earlier, and of which Hercules' speech reminds us bluntly now. Shelley undoubtedly recalled how his favorite Bacon uses the incident in the essay *Of Adversity* to illustrate the union of human frailty and divine certainty:

". . . it is in effect the thing which is figured in that strange fiction of the ancient poets, which seemeth not to be without mystery; nay, and to have some approach to the state of a Christian: that 'Hercules, when he went to unbind Prometheus' (by whom human nature is represented), 'sailed the length of the great ocean in an earthen pot or pitcher'; lively describing Christian resolution, that saileth in the frail bark of the flesh through the waves of this world."

But Shelley's Hercules does none of the peculiar acts expected of him: he shoots no eagle and sails in no pitcher. Although in *Prometheus Unbound* the moment of Prometheus' release represents in some degree the point of intersection between man and god, or the point when passion and action are at one, Shelley has not enriched the representation by his treatment of Hercules.

6. Barker, "Structural Pattern in *Paradise Lost,*" *Philological Quarterly,* XXVIII (1949), 29–30.

Notes to Epilogue

1. Turner, *Songs and Incantations,* pp. 54–56.

2. See Weaver, *Toward the Understanding of Shelley,* pp. 57–74 and *passim.*

3. Medwin, *The Life of Percy Bysshe Shelley,* p. 255.

4. *Ibid.,* pp. 348–49.

5. Eliot, *Selected Essays,* p. 250.

6. White, *Shelley,* II, 630–31; and Roe, *Shelley: the Last Phase,* pp. 194–210.

7. Eliot, "A Talk on Dante," *Kenyon Review,* XIV (1952), 185.

8. In its last lines Eliot's ghost moves, of course, from the cycle of nature to the divine pattern:

> From wrong to wrong the exasperated spirit
> Proceeds, unless restored by that refining fire
> Where you must move in measure, like a dancer.

Thereby Rousseau's "ghastly dance" is transfigured; but the poet himself is left "in the disfigured street"—where the adjective is perhaps the most complex pun in Eliot's entire work.

9. To complete the comparison, *Epipsychidion* should be set beside *Ash Wednesday*.

10. Eliot, *Selected Essays*, p. 18.

11. I leave it to the reader to apportion the above quotations to Shelley or Eliot.

12. *Lines Written among the Euganean Hills*, ll. 45–52.

13. *Purgatorio*, trans. by Binyon, III.79–87.

14. Ransom, *The World's Body*, pp. 120–28.

15. *An Ode Written October, 1819, before the Spaniards Had Recovered their Liberty*.

16. *Prometheus Unbound*, I.624.

17. *A Satire on Satire*.

18. *Lines Written among the Euganean Hills*, l. 232.

19. Writing to his publishers (J.X.232), Shelley, rather wearily, sees himself tormented in the purgatory of poetry. "I doubt whether I *shall* write more. I could be content either with the Hell or the Paradise of poetry; but the torments of its purgatory vex me, without exciting my power sufficiently to put an end to the vexation."

20. R. S. Thomas, *Song at the Year's Turning: Poems 1942–1954*, p. 101.

BIBLIOGRAPHY

Note. In quoting Shelley's letters I have followed the Julian Edition of his *Complete Works,* although, for the Hogg correspondence, I have also consulted Scott's *New Shelley Letters.* Prose quotations follow Clark's edition throughout. The texts of Shelley's poetry are by no means fixed; there is still much to be done by future editors, particularly in matters of punctuation. Therefore, although I have for the most part followed Woodberry's edition for poetry quotations, I have in a fair number of instances modified his text. For those works not included by Woodberry, I have used the Julian Edition. In all abbreviated references in this book C = Clark and J = Julian.

The bibliography includes all works referred to in footnotes and any additional works which may have tangibly (even if not verbally) influenced my criticism of Shelley. It is not intended to be an exhaustive bibliography of my subject or a list of the relevant works read or consulted.

Adams, S. M., "The Four Elements in the *Prometheus Vinctus*," *Classical Philology,* XXVIII (1933), 97–103.
———— "Unity of Plot in the *Oedipus Coloneus*," *Phoenix,* VII (1953), 136–47.
Anderson, F. H., "Plato's Aesthetics Reconsidered," *University of Toronto Quarterly,* XXV (1956), 425–36.
Auden, W. H., and N. H. Pearson, eds. Poets of the English Language. 5 vols. New York: Viking Press, 1950.
Baker, Carlos. Shelley's Major Poetry. Princeton: Princeton University Press, 1948.
Baldwin, D. L. A Concordance to the Poems of John Keats. Washington, D.C.: The Carnegie Institution of Washington, 1917.

320   BIBLIOGRAPHY

Barker, Arthur. Milton and the Puritan Dilemma. Toronto: University of Toronto Press, 1942.

—— "Structural Pattern in *Paradise Lost*," *Philological Quarterly*, XXVIII (1949), 17–30.

Barnard, Ellsworth. Shelley's Religion. Minneapolis: University of Minnesota Press, 1937.

Bates, E. S. A Study of Shelley's Drama *The Cenci*. New York: Columbia University Press, 1908.

Blake, William. Poetry and Prose of William Blake, ed. by Geoffrey Keynes. London: Nonesuch Press, 1927.

Butter, Peter. Shelley's Idols of the Cave. Edinburgh: Edinburgh University Press, 1954.

Cameron, K. N., "The Planet-Tempest Passage in *Epipsychidion*," *PMLA*, XLIII (1948), 950–72.

—— "The Political Symbolism of *Prometheus Unbound*," *PMLA*, LVIII (1943), 728–53.

—— "Shelley *versus* Southey: New Light on an Old Quarrel," *PMLA*, LVII (1942), 489–512.

—— "The Social Philosophy of Shelley," *Sewanee Review*, L (1942), 457–66.

—— The Young Shelley. New York: Macmillan, 1950.

Campbell, L. B., "The Christian Muse," *Huntington Library Bulletin*, VIII (1935), 29–70.

Campbell, O. W. Shelley and the Unromantics. London: Methuen, 1924.

Clutton-Brock, A. Shelley, the Man and the Poet. London: Methuen, 1910.

Coleridge, S. T. Biographia Literaria and Two Lay Sermons. London: George Bell & Sons, 1905.

—— The Notebooks of Samuel Taylor Coleridge, ed. by Kathleen Coburn. Vol. I. New York: Pantheon Books for the Bollingen Foundation, 1957.

Cowper, William. The Correspondence of William Cowper, ed. by Thomas Wright. 4 vols. London: Hodder and Stoughton, 1904.

Cunningham, J. V. Woe or Wonder. Denver: University of Denver Press, 1951.

Davie, Donald. Purity of Diction in English Verse. London: Chatto and Windus, 1952.

Dowden, Edward. The Life of Percy Bysshe Shelley. 2 vols. London: Kegan Paul, Trench, 1886.

Eliot, T. S. Murder in the Cathedral. New York: Harcourt, Brace, 1935.

——— Selected Essays, 1917–1932. New York: Harcourt, Brace, 1932.

——— "A Talk on Dante," Kenyon Review, XIV (1952), 178–88.

——— The Use of Poetry and the Use of Criticism. London: Faber and Faber, 1933.

Ellis, F. S. A Lexical Concordance to the Poetical Works of Percy Bysshe Shelley. London: Quaritch, 1892.

Elton, Oliver. Shelley. London: Edward Arnold, 1924.

Fairley, Barker. Goethe as Revealed in His Poetry. London: Dent, 1932.

Farrer, Austin. A Rebirth of Images. London: The Dacre Press, 1949.

Fogle, R. H. The Imagery of Keats and Shelley. Chapel Hill: University of North Carolina Press, 1949.

Frye, H. N. Anatomy of Criticism. Princeton: Princeton University Press, 1957.

——— Fearful Symmetry. Princeton: Princeton University Press, 1947.

Gibson, E. K., "Alastor: a Reinterpretation," PMLA, XLII (1947), 1022–45.

Godwin, William. Enquiry concerning Political Justice and Its Influence on Morals and Happiness, ed. by F. E. L. Priestly. 3 vols. Toronto: University of Toronto Press, 1946.

Grabo, Carl. A Newton among Poets. Chapel Hill: University of North Carolina Press, 1930.

——— Prometheus Unbound: an Interpretation. Chapel Hill: University of North Carolina Press, 1935.

Greene, D. J., " 'Logical Structure' in Eighteenth-Century Poetry," Philological Quarterly, XXXI (1952), 315–36.

Grube, G. M. A. Plato's Thought. London: Methuen, 1935.

Harrison, T. P., ed. The Pastoral Elegy: an Anthology. Austin: University of Texas Press, 1939.

Havens, R. D., "Shelley's Alastor," PMLA, XLV (1930), 1098–1115.

Hildebrand, W. H. A Study of Alastor. Kent State University Bulletin, Research Series II. Kent, Ohio, 1954.

Hoffman, H. L. An Odyssey of the Soul: Shelley's Alastor. New York: Columbia University Press, 1933.

Hughes, A. M. D. The Nascent Mind of Shelley. London: Oxford University Press, 1947.

Hungerford, E. B. Shores of Darkness. New York: Columbia University Press, 1941.

Jones, F. L., "Shelley and Milton," *Studies in Philology*, XLIX (1952), 488–519.

Kapstein, I. J., "The Meaning of Shelley's 'Mont Blanc'," *PMLA*, LXII (1947), 1046–60.

Keats, John. The Letters of John Keats, ed. by M. B. Forman. London: Oxford University Press, 3d ed., 1947.

Kitto, H. D. F. Greek Tragedy. New York: Doubleday, 1954.

Kurtz, B. P. The Pursuit of Death. New York: Oxford, 1933.

Langston, Beach, "Shelley's Use of Shakespeare," *Huntington Library Quarterly*, XII (1949), 163–90.

Lotspeich, H. G., "Shelley's 'Eternity' and Demogorgon," *Philological Quarterly*, XIII (1934), 309–11.

Medwin, Thomas. The Life of Percy Bysshe Shelley. London: Oxford University Press, 1913.

Norlin, George, "The Conventions of Pastoral Elegy," *American Journal of Philology*, XXXII (1911), 294–312.

Norman, Sylva. Flight of the Skylark. Norman: University of Oklahoma Press, 1954.

Notopoulos, J. A., "The Dating of Shelley's Prose," *PMLA*, LVIII (1943), 477–98.

—— The Platonism of Shelley. Durham, N.C.: Duke University Press, 1949.

—— "Shelley's 'Disinterested Love' and Aristotle," *Philological Quarterly*, XXXII (1953), 214–17.

Oates, W. J., and Eugene O'Neill, Jr., eds. The Complete Greek Drama. 2 vols. New York: Random House, 1938.

Oras, Ants, "The Multitudinous Orb: Some Miltonic Elements in Shelley," *Modern Language Quarterly*, XVI (1955), 247–57.

Peck, W. E. Shelley: His Life and Work. 2 vols. Boston: Houghton, Mifflin, 1927.

Pettet, E. C. On the Poetry of Keats. Cambridge: The University Press, 1957.

Plato's *Republic*, trans. by A. D. Lindsay. London: Dent, 1935.

Pottle, F. A. "The Case of Shelley," *PMLA*, LXVII (1952), 589–608.

Priestley, F. E. L., "Newton and the Romantic Concept of Nature," *University of Toronto Quarterly*, XVII (1948), 323–36.

—— "Platonism in Godwin's *Political Justice,*" *Modern Language Quarterly*, IV (1943), 63–69.

Pulos, C. E. The Deep Truth. Lincoln: University of Nebraska Press, 1954.

—— "Shelley and Malthus," *PMLA*, LXVII (1952), 113–24.

Ransom, J. C. The World's Body. London: Charles Scribner's Sons, 1938.

Ridley, M. R. Keats' Craftsmanship. Oxford: Clarendon Press, 1933.

Roe, Ivan. Shelley: the Last Phase. London: Hutchinson, 1955.

Rogers, Neville. Shelley at Work. Oxford: Clarendon Press, 1956.

Shelley, Mary. The Letters of Mary W. Shelley, ed. by F. L. Jones. 2 vols. Norman: University of Oklahoma Press, 1944.

—— Mary Shelley's Journal, ed. by F. L. Jones. Norman: University of Oklahoma Press, 1947.

—— Proserpine and Midas, ed. by A. Koszul. London: Oxford University Press, 1922.

Shelley, Percy Bysshe. The Complete Poetical Works of Shelley, ed. by G. E. Woodberry. Cambridge, Mass.: Houghton, Mifflin, 1901.

—— The Complete Works of Percy Bysshe Shelley, ed. by Roger Ingpen and W. E. Peck. Julian Editions. 10 vols. New York: Scribners, 1926–30.

—— The Last Days of Shelley and Byron, ed. by J. E. Morpurgo. Westminster: Folio Society, 1952.

—— New Shelley Letters, ed. by W. S. Scott. London: The Bodley Head, 1948.

—— Prometheus Unbound, ed. by V. D. Scudder. Boston: Heath, 1910.

—— Selected Poetry and Prose of Percy Bysshe Shelley, ed. by K. N. Cameron. New York: Rinehart, 1951.

—— Shelley in Italy, ed. by John Lehmann. London: John Lehmann, 1947.

—— Shelley's Prose, ed. by D. L. Clark. Albuquerque: University of New Mexico Press, 1954.

—— Verse and Prose from the Manuscripts of Percy Bysshe Shelley, ed. by Sir John C. E. Shelley-Rolls and Roger Ingpen. London: privately printed, 1934.

Spender, Stephen. Shelley. London: Longmans, Green, 1952.

Strong, A. T. Three Studies in Shelley. London: Oxford University Press, 1921.

Thomas, Dylan. Collected Poems, 1934–1952. London: Dent, 1952.

Thomas, R. S. Song at the Year's Turning: Poems 1942–1954. London: Rupert Hart-Davis, 1955.

Tillyard, E. M. W. Shakespeare's History Plays. London: Chatto and Windus, 1948.

Todhunter, John. A Study of Shelley. London: C. Kegan Paul, 1880.

Tovey, D. F. Essays in Musical Analysis. 6 vols. London: Oxford University Press, 1935–39.

Turner, W. J. Songs and Incantations. London: Dent, 1931.

Tuveson, E. L. Millennium and Utopia. Berkeley: University of California Press, 1949.

Walker, A. S., "Peterloo, Shelley and Reform," *PMLA*, XL (1925), 128–64.

Wasserman, Earl, *"Adonais:* Progressive Revelation as a Poetic Mode," *English Literary History*, XXI (1954), 274–326.

Weaver, Bennett. Toward the Understanding of Shelley. University of Michigan Publications in Language and Literature, Vol. IX. Ann Arbor, 1932.

Weeks, Donald, "Image and Idea in Yeats' *The Second Coming*," *PMLA*, LXIII (1948), 281–92.

White, N. I. Shelley. 2 vols. New York: Knopf, 1940.

——— "Shelley's *Prometheus Unbound* or Every Man His Own Allegorist," *PMLA*, XL (1925), 172–84.

Wilcox, S. C., "Imagery, Ideas and Design in Shelley's 'Ode to the West Wind'," *Studies in Philology*, XLVII (1950), 634–49.

INDEX

Abstract, in Shelley's poetry, 103, 104-5, 124-26
Adams, S. M., 44, 308
Addison, Joseph, 123
Adonais (Shelley): self-portrait in, 2, 5; and Shelley's versatility, 9; and The Revolt of Islam, 10; revisions of, 14; Italian imagery in, 109; creation in, 123; self in, 157; circle figure in, 157-58; Platonism in, 180, 236-37, 243-44, 246, 248-53; analysis of, 236-55; time in, 246-55; will in, 251, 298-99; criticism of, 298-300
Aeschylus, 43-44, 68
Alastor (Shelley): poetic style of, 7-8; and Shelley's versatility, 9; Preface to, 13; and self, 76-78; mirror figure in, 77, 159-60, 162, 167; Shelley's criticism of main character in, 87; love in, 148, 161-65, 169, 170, 180; self-love in, 159-60; as tragic poem, 164-65; veil figure in, 220
Alfieri, Vittorio, Conte, 283
Allegory, 129-30, 133-34, 145
Anderson, F. H., 306
Apocalypse, 51, 207, 236-37, 253
Apocalypse, of St. John, 17, 314
Architectural images: in Shelley's poetry, 116-24, 177-81, 292; in Romantic and Victorian poetry, 311
Ariosto, 10, 283
Aristotle, 76
Arnold, Matthew, 152, 244
Athens, 120
Auden, W. H., 17, 151-52

Bacon, Francis, 155, 316
Baiae, 108, 109
Baker, Carlos, 57, 86; quoted, 57, 229
Barker, Arthur, 278

Bates, E. S., 86
Baths of Caracalla, 120-22
Baudelaire, Charles, 82, 284
Beethoven, Ludwig van, 42-43
Berkeley, George, 128
Bible, 281
Birth of Pleasure, The (Shelley), 287
Blake, William, 5, 211, 255, 282; quoted, 220, 309-10
Blank verse, 6-8
Boccaccio, Giovanni, 135, 283
Bologna, 310
Browning, Robert: on Shelley, 1-2; and rhythm, 32; and conversion, 58; and self, 152; cosmopolitanism of, 282; poetic style of, 288
Buried Life, The (Arnold), 152
Burns, Robert, 282
Byron, Lord: and Shelley, 4; and precocity, 6; and Shelley's ottava rima, 10; dialogue with Shelley of, 15-16; on Shakespeare, 15-16; and rhythm, 31; Shelley on, 167, 303; cosmopolitanism of, 282; and revision, 304

Calderón de la Barca, Pedro, 10
Calvinism, 239
Cameron, K. N., 95, 129, 131; quoted, 192-93, 251
Caracalla, Baths of, 120-22
Casi Magni, 5
Causality, 49, 138; see also Necessity
Cenci, The (Shelley): and revenge, 67-68; and self-love, 74, 78-92; mirror figure in, 83-85; Shelley and, 90-91
Ceremony after a Fire Raid (Dylan Thomas), 255
Cézanne, Paul, 124
Chance, 138, 144, 174; see also Chaos
Change, 144, 175

DATE DUE

MR 14 '66	NO 12 '71		
Mr. 28	MY 4 '72		
OC 14 '66	MY 8 '73		
MR 7 '67	NO 13 '73		
AP 27	SE 12 '74		
MY 24	RESERVE		
NO 10 '67	JA 15 '75		
NO 21 '67	MY 10 '83		
JA 3 '68	6/5/84		
JA 25 '68	JA 5 '94		
MR 18 '68			
FE 24 '69			
RESERVE			
AP 24 '69			
FE 19 '70			
MR 5 '70			
RESERVE			
JE 3 '71			
GAYLORD			PRINTED IN U.S.A.